Together for a season:

All-age seasonal resources for Advent, Christmas and Epiphany

Gill Ambrose, Peter Craig-Wild,
Diane Craven, Mary Hawes

Edited by Gill Ambrose

CHURCH HOUSE
PUBLISHING

Church House Publishing
Church House
Great Smith Street
London SW1P 3NZ

ISBN-13 978-0-7151-4062-8
ISBN-10 0 7151 4062 0

Published 2006 by Church House Publishing.

The opinions expressed in this book are those of the individual authors and do not necessarily reflect the official policy of the General Synod or The Archbishops' Council of the Church of England.

Cover design by blue pig design ltd

Printed in England by Cromwell Press Ltd, Trowbridge, Wiltshire

Contents

Epiphany

Foreword

As Christmas gets nearer, worship in most churches takes on a new feel. In the past this might have been simply the lighting of an Advent ring or inclusion of a nativity play. But *Common Worship* and other new forms of worship – with adults and children all giving praise together – have brought about little less than a revolution. *Together for a Season* is an exciting series of books that will transform things still further. There is something for everyone here. This material takes all ages seriously and uses all the senses – movement, sound, space and light – to provide an enriching experience for children who worship together with the whole community.

This pattern of worship and celebration builds on the wealth of the Christian tradition. A brief visit to Assisi at St Francistide or to Santiago da Compostela at the Feast of St James dramatically shows the visitor how these places have been shaped by centuries of Christian life and worship, shared by adults and children alike. It is not only the worship, but the sense of carnival and celebration, which touches every part of life. All this makes clear how the story of Jesus, as focused in the saints and those who have been touched by them, has fashioned the life of the wider community. It was something similar that St Francis captured when he pioneered the making of cribs for Christmastide.

The Church of England, showing a characteristic reticence, once treated its 'red letter days' and great seasonal feasts with much modesty. The arrival of *Lent, Holy Week and Easter* and *The Promise of his Glory* transformed this. *Common Worship: Times and Seasons* brings together material from these two classic volumes and new resources for the Christian Year. The new series *Together for a Season* will complement these riches, allowing parishes and other local Christian congregations to take this material into both homes and communities. These volumes indicate that Christian worship and life, adults and children are all entirely 'of a piece'. They form part of the seamless garment of Christ himself, which is his Church.

The 'pathways' through the seasons and sample services included in these volumes offer an opportunity to make connections between worship and living the gospel within every aspect of our lives. This will not displace the quiet celebration of our great feasts; it will complement that. It may, however, allow our own communities to echo some of the carnival already celebrated in other parts of the world.

And it will be a carnival where all worship together and celebrate together – at home, in church and in the community.

✠ Stephen Wakefield

Acknowledgements

Extracts from the Christingle Service of the Church in Wales are copyright © The Church in Wales 2006.

The prayer 'Christ be our light' on p.18 is copyright © 1994, Bernadette Farrell. Published by OCP Publications, 5536 NE Hassalo, Portland, Oregon, OR97213. All rights reserved. Used with permission.

All prayers in this book that are not otherwise acknowledged were written by Diane Craven.

The writers would like to thank the people of St Mary, Mirfield and St Mary and St Michael, Trumpington, where some of the material used in this book was first tried out. We would like to thank the people of St Mary's Church, Grantchester, for their generosity in sharing the details of their village nativity for us to use in this book. We are grateful to Tom Ambrose, who wrote a good deal of the material for the crib pathway and provided material for the Jesse tree section, including, in particular, the Advent carol service based on the Jesse tree in St Mary's Church, Morpeth. We are grateful to the Rector of Morpeth for permission to photograph extensively the east window of the church, and for members of the congregation who provided valuable assistance in this task.

We owe our gratitude to Peter Moger, National Worship Development Officer, who read the entire text of the book and provided valuable feedback and advice. Tracey Messenger, Commissioning Editor at Church House Publishing, has cajoled us, reminded us of deadlines, all with infinite patience and good humour, but most of all she encouraged us. Without her the text would not be before you!

How to use this book

A companion to *Common Worship: Times and Seasons*

This book, the first of three volumes, has been created as a companion to *Common Worship: Times and Seasons* (T&S), the Church of England Liturgical Commission's directory of liturgical material for the seasons of the Christian Year. It provides ideas and suggestions for bringing to life the liturgical texts provided in T&S, both in formal worship and in groups for adults and children alike, as well as in the home and in outreach in the local community. The authors have taken as their starting point the assumption that worship and the Christian life are inclusive. There are times when it is appropriate for different groups of people to do things separately, and provision is made for this. There is material for groups of children and adults to use separately. But, basically, we belong together: we learn and teach one another, young and old, experienced and inexperienced, academic and practical alike. Each of the worked-out services provided ensures that there is something for everyone. Use is made of space, light and symbol as well as word and text. The rich tradition of Christian worship is drawn upon fully. Much of the material provided for use at home and in outreach is suitable for anyone to use and is specifically designed to work with mixed age groups.

Three seasons, one big idea

The present book covers the seasons of Advent, Christmas and Epiphany. It provides a number of worked out services for different significant occasions within these three seasons that hold together to prepare for and celebrate the Incarnation. Additionally, it provides the opportunity to follow a particular symbolic pathway through the three seasons to encourage a visual identity and an appreciation of how the seasons hold together, yet celebrate different aspects of a big idea.

Three pathways

The three pathways are based on three visual devices that have been used, through Christian time, to help us think about different aspects of the birth of Christ.

Wreath

The Advent wreath forms the first pathway. The Advent wreath almost certainly came to Britain from Germany, along with many other signs of Christmas, the best known of which is the Christmas tree. It is likely that German Christians transformed a pagan winter custom of using circles of evergreen to symbolize the hope of new life at the end of dark winter days, by the addition of four candles marking the four Sundays of Advent. This seems to have been in use in Lutheran households shortly after the Reformation. The tradition has been developed further with the addition of a central, white candle to be lit at Christmas, marking the birth of Christ.

Crib

The crib is probably the most familiar: very many churches will display a crib scene somewhere in or around the building over the Christmas period. The tradition is attributed to St Francis, who sought to make the Christmas Mass come alive for his followers in the Middle Ages.

Jesse tree

The Jesse tree, perhaps the least known of the three pathways, emerged as a way of depicting the family history of Jesus in medieval manuscripts. It was taken up by other artists, particularly stained glass makers, and is now found widely in medieval glass and later windows across Europe.

Choose your pathway

The suggestion in the pages that follow is that churches might choose one of these pathways (the Crib, the wreath or the Jesse tree) as a visual liturgical focus for a particular year, using it from Advent Sunday through to Candlemas as a centrepiece for visual aspects of the liturgy and exploring the word. This will require some imagination and a willingness to transform a familiar symbol and widen its use. The wreath, for example, has traditionally been used in Advent. A later tradition added the central, Christmas candle. We are now suggesting a further adaptation, to use it, transformed, as a focus through Epiphany until Candlemas. The crib and the Jesse tree are used in the same way.

The book therefore offers a choice of three pathways through Advent, Christmas and Epiphany. This is a choice: no one should try to follow all three at once! Each pathway provides material for worship, study, outreach and exploration at home from Advent Sunday until Candlemas.

Sample services

In addition, there are several services for significant occasions, using texts and suggestions from *Times and Seasons*. Each service uses the texts from the Church of England's book and is laid out in full in tabular form, to demonstrate the different strands to which we need to be sensitive in building a liturgy. The column headings, following the observations made in the introductory essay, 'Living liturgy', by Peter Craig-Wild, are these:

Structure, movement and flow	Words/ text	Multisensory aspects	Participation of the congregation

The services offered in this way for the period from Advent to Candlemas are:
- A Service of the Word for Advent Sunday
- A simple Christingle service
- A Christmas Eucharist
- A blue Christmas service
- A crib service for a small congregation
- A crib service for a large congregation
- A Eucharist for the Feast of the Epiphany: The arrival of the Magi
- An Epiphany procession
- A Eucharist for the Feast of the Presentation of Christ in the Temple (Candlemas).

The structure

Following the introductory sections, the book divides into material for each of the three seasons, Advent, Christmas and Epiphany. Each seasonal section is further subdivided into five:
1. **A seasonal introduction**, which describes for us the 'feel' of the season and provides some background to the way in which we celebrate.
2. **Stand-alone seasonal material**, which includes the fully laid out services, with their words and the suggestions for multisensory provision and participation by the congregation.
3. **The crib pathway**, with material to use in inclusive worship, material for use by groups of adults and groups for children, material to use at home and suggestions for outreach into the local community.
4. **The wreath pathway**, with material to use in inclusive worship, material for use by groups of adults and groups for children, material to use at home and suggestions for outreach into the local community.
5. **The Jesse tree pathway**, with material to use in inclusive worship, material for use by groups of adults and groups for children, material to use at home and suggestions for outreach into the local community.

How to use the material

The services

The worked out services provide a model for the way in which material from *Times and Seasons* might be used. However, they are also designed to be used as they are by readers of this book. A warning though! Don't pick up the book on Saturday night and expect to be able to present these services the following morning! Each service has been planned to be as interactive and multisensory as possible. All the ideas are provided, but you will need to determine how to make them fit your circumstances. All the services can be used with large and small congregations alike, and in any sort of building, but you will need to think about how you do this, and who will be involved. Once you have used one or two of them, you will get the feel of how they work and you will then be able to take the material from *Times and Seasons* and build more services yourself on this model.

New Patterns for Worship

In preparing to plan worship in this way, it would also be helpful to read (or reread) the beginning of the book *New Patterns for Worship*. The first 50 pages of that book provide much helpful background and advice about planning services in this way, and might be regarded as a companion to the material we offer here.[1]

The pathways

You will need to choose just one pathway for any particular year. The pathway you choose will then determine a route through the three seasons, with ideas for use of the main symbol of the pathway as a focus around which worship is built for much of the season. Material for worship is complemented by group study material, things to do at home, ideas for children's groups and for outreach.

The choice of one particular pathway does not mean that other symbols may not be used. If you choose to use the Advent wreath pathway one year, for example, it does not mean that the crib is banned! Few churches would contemplate Christmas worship without a crib scene. It does mean, however, that the focus through Advent would be particularly on ideas that the wreath facilitates particularly well, and that you would probably move the wreath to be near the crib for Christmas services, using it to 'illuminate' the crib. You might like to note here that the ideas for the Jesse tree work best in Years A and C of the *Common Worship* Lectionary, and there are no suggestions provided for the Jesse tree in Year B.

Music, hymns and songs

Music is important in worship, especially at Christmas time when people love to sing familiar carols. There are some thoughts about the use of music in worship in one of the introductory essays, 'Living Liturgy' (see page 1). Throughout the book, suggestions are made for appropriate hymns and songs for acts of worship, and sometimes to sing in groups. Except where they are difficult to find, or they are only in one particular book, the book does not provide an indication where they are to be found. There are now so many Christian hymn and song books that this would be an almost impossible task: it is certainly beyond the scope of this book. If you are familiar with your own collection of books,

you will probably know where to find most of them in any case. If you need help in locating them, then the RSCM publication, *Sunday by Sunday*,[2] which provides suggestions for music for worship for every Sunday and festival day of the year, might be helpful. It is published quarterly by RSCM, so it is very accurate. The address from which it can be ordered can be found in the Resources section at the back of the book. A publication that does the same kind of job, but in a single volume rather than being published each quarter is *Sing God's Glory: Hymns for Sundays and Holy Days, Years A, B and C*.[3]

In the sample services throughout the book, the title of a particular hymn or song is given only where that particular hymn contributes to the shape and flow of the service. Quite often the worship planner is simply advised that a hymn or song may be sung. It is assumed then that you will choose your own. Even the prepared services in the book therefore provide plenty of scope for music to reflect your own tradition. It also ought to go without saying that, where a hymn is suggested and you know it would be impossible to sing in your situation, then the sensible thing to do will be to change it. But do replace it with something appropriate! And don't just cut it out because you don't know it. Many new hymns and songs are not very difficult to learn, and it does us all good to learn something new from time to time.

A final musical thought. Advent hymns are for Advent and Christmas carols are for Christmas. Mixing them up tends to reduce the distinctiveness of each season – and this book is all about that distinctiveness (three seasons that hold together as one big idea). There may well be times, later in Advent, when community groups will come to the church for their own carol services and concerts, and it would be churlish in the extreme to refuse to let them sing carols! However, in your week by week regular worship during Advent, stick to Advent hymns and songs.

Collects

In the sample services throughout the book, where a collect for the day is used, it has been drawn from *Common Worship: Additional Collects*.[4] This is a new collection of contemporary collects written to provide modern prayers for worship in the Church of England. The new prayers offer an alternative to, and complement, the original collects in *Common*

Worship. If you wish to substitute what is suggested with one of the original *Common Worship* collects, then of course you should do so.

The material for groups

Material is provided for groups of adults and children. There is little group work provision for the Christmas season as it is rare for groups to meet over this short period. The material provided is intended to be enough for about an hour for children's groups, and slightly longer, perhaps approaching an hour and a half, for adult groups. However, the material is all designed to be used flexibly so you can add to or subtract from the given material if that is what your situation demands. The children's material is not banded by age and is almost all suitable to use in mixed age groups or by any age group.

Schools

There is a good deal of material in this book that is just as well suited to use in a school as in a church. Much of the material for use at home would be equally at home in the community that is a primary school classroom! Some of the worship resources would also be useful in school collective worship. The outreach section for Advent in the Jesse tree pathway provides an idea that is very suitable for school use and this way of using it is described.

Resources

There is a Resources section at the end of the book on page 174. This includes full details of all the books and other resources mentioned throughout the text.

Note on abbreviations

Material has been used from three main sources, which have been abbreviated as follows:

- CW: *Common Worship: Services and Prayers for the Church of England,* Church House Publishing, 2000;
- NP: *New Patterns for Worship,* Church House Publishing, 2002;
- T&S: *Common Worship: Times and Seasons,* Church House Publishing, 2006.

Icons used in the book

 The CD-ROM icon appears wherever text is also available to be downloaded from the CD-ROM.

CD-ROM contents

A Service of the Word for Advent

A simple Christingle service

Symbols for the Advent Antiphons

How to make an Advent wreath

Crib festival (Posada) dialogues and prayers

A crib blessing prayer

How to make a Jesse tree

Words of Jesse tree prophets

Advent carol service based on the Jesse tree

Christmas Eucharist

A blue Christmas

New Year celebration

Christmas wreath meditations

Crib service – for a smaller congregation

Crib service – for a larger congregation

Text for Jesse tree card

Eucharist for the Feast of the Epiphany: the Arrival of
the Magi

Epiphany procession

Candlemas service

How to make Candlemas lanterns

Templates of stained-glass window, prophet and
seated Madonna

Photographs

Living liturgy:
transforming the texts

A living liturgy

Just as a symphony is far more than a collection of notes on the stave, so liturgy is far more than texts. The conductor of the orchestra has to interpret the score and draw the best from the musicians in order to bring it to life. Worship planners, too, have to take the texts and, using whatever resources are available, construct a symphony of worship where the words jump off the page and resonate with our experience, bringing liturgy into life and life into liturgy.

In 2006, *Common Worship: Times and Seasons* was finally published. *Times and Seasons* does 'exactly what it says on the tin'. It is a book of texts to help the Church celebrate the seasons and festivals of the Christian year. The publication was like a marriage ceremony: it was a great occasion and cause for celebration but, for those at the heart of it, the real work lies ahead. The task now is to transform those texts into living acts of worship that engage everyone regardless of age or stage of Christian development. *Together for a Season* is designed to encourage and enable worship planners and crafters to engage with that creative process.

Changes in society, and the expectations that accompany them, place ever greater demands on those who craft worship. The past decade has seen a shift in emphasis in our expectations of worship. It is no longer enough to say the words and sing the songs, or even to present the liturgy with visual or dramatic excellence. Increasingly, the demand is for worshippers to engage actively with the God whom we worship. Awareness of this is essential in constructing worship today.

For this reason we present worship as having multiple strands, each needing care and consideration as they are woven together. Throughout this book we will try to make clear how we have moved from one strand to another until the process is complete and we have an engaging, multidimensional act of worship. We hope that, by presenting our work this way, we will be offering not just ideas, but also a process of producing worship that truly engages the people of God.

Preliminary questions

One difficulty with *Common Worship* is that the selection and use of the plethora of material demands a high degree of liturgical competence. With the *Times And Seasons* material alone one could be forgiven for banging one's head against the nearest brick wall and, like the wine buff at the wedding at Cana, screaming 'Just where do I start?'

Times and Seasons contains both fully worked out services for the major festivals throughout the year as well as banks of seasonal resource material. One issue that immediately confronts us is whether we use a set text as it stands, edit it to fit our own local circumstances, or even produce our own order of service. In many cases it is right to create our own services and we need to be exorcised of the attitude that says the 'real' thing is the service in the book. Local creations are *not* second best.

Times and Seasons focuses on those times of the year when the Lectionary readings are compulsory.[1] This should not be seen as stifling creativity but as a compass to guide us on the journey through each part of the liturgical year. If we are dealing with the principal service of the day, the readings are a 'given'. However, if we are dealing with other services, the choice of Bible readings needs to be made at this preliminary stage.

Throughout *Together for a Season*, we will assume the lectionary readings, particularly the relevant Gospel stories, as the principal readings of the day and as a starting point for all our thinking.

Questions to ask at this stage might be:
- Are we going to use the set text given in *Times and Seasons*, adapt it, or create our own service from scratch?
- Which passages from the Bible will be used?
- What are we trying to achieve in the service?
- How does it fit into the structure of the whole season?

The strand of theme and structure

When planning worship there is a great temptation to zoom in to the detail: what prayers will be used; what hymns might be sung; who might do what, etc. This often happens before any real thought has been given to the bigger picture.

First, we need to be clear in our minds what the theme or the direction of the service is going to be. Often this might appear to be a 'given', but even, for example, on Christmas Day, there are many ways we can celebrate the birth of Jesus. If the parish has recently experienced a trauma, the emphasis might be on the birth of the Saviour into a world of pain; or if homelessness is a current issue, 'no room at the inn' might be pertinent. Sometimes, maybe even most times, the telling of the story through the liturgy might be enough and we can give people space to find resonances with their own lives. On other occasions we might want to draw out a particular aspect of the story because it relates clearly to the life events of the community.

Having decided on a theme for the service, we can then ask what might be the most appropriate structure, or the elements we want to emphasize. Ought we to place more emphasis on the confession, or the intercessions, or the offertory?

Questions to ask at this stage might be:
- Is there anything in the story we might want to emphasize?
- What are the key elements of the service we need for our worship in St Dido's?
- What is the best order for those elements to follow?
- Are there elements that are non-negotiable? If you need more help with this, please see pages 8 to 18 of *New Patterns for Worship*.[2]
- What is the appropriate mood for each part of the service: joyful, exuberant, reflective, sad, and so on?
- Does that order make sense, and 'flow'?

Ask the question:
What would be the most effective structure to make the worship work?

We can now move on to the *next strand* of word and text, whether written, spoken or sung.

The strand of word and text

Times and Seasons offers resources or complete texts for every occasion through the Church's year. Words are important as they are one of the main ways in which we communicate with one another and with God. Attempts have been made to ensure that the texts of *Times and Seasons* are suitable for use across all ages and stages of the Christian life. However, there are still critical questions to be asked.

Each set service contains its own suggested texts but there are alternatives in the Resources sections that might relate better to the theme. There may be shorter or longer options we could use that enable us to highlight better certain sections of the liturgy.

Some texts are clearly mandatory but, like much of *Common Worship*, there are occasions when it is appropriate to compose our own local texts written specifically for that single celebration.

Questions to ask at this stage might be:
- Is the register and style of words best suited to the congregation concerned?
- If certain texts allow alternatives, are there more suitable ones?
- Are there points at which our own composition may be more appropriate?

Ask the question:
What are the best words for each element of the service we are planning?

Once we have settled on a textual format, we can begin to look at the *third strand*, which takes us beyond the words.

The strand of the visual, the symbolic and the multisensory

It has been said that Anglican worship assumes that a human body is made up of just two buttocks and two ears. It used to be the case that turning text into worship was simply a case of inserting appropriate hymns, readings and music. Since then, our society and its culture have changed beyond recognition, making the task far more complex.

With the advent of film and TV, we have been moving inexorably towards becoming a visual rather than a textual/auditory culture. Even newspapers are no longer 'black and white and pink all over', and now use pictures to grab the attention of their readers.

The advent of the computer has accelerated the trend. All this demands that the emphasis of worship change from being primarily textual to visual.

But the visual alone is not enough. Over the past few decades we have become aware of the need to engage *all* the senses in worship: touch, smell and taste as well as hearing and sight. By using a multisensory approach, we not only engage more of our congregation, we also engage more of our humanity. For example, by using sweet smelling oil (of chrism) in baptism, we reinforce that we really do become new, so much so that the candidate even smells different (sometimes quite necessary!) We know that the sense of smell provokes the most powerful memories and it is possible that the scent of baptism may remain with the candidate long after the other memories have faded.

Scripture readings often suggest ways into the multisensory. If the reading is about a land flowing with milk and honey, why not find an opportunity for people actually to taste milk and honey during the service? The multisensory strand of worship is no longer just a 'nice' added extra but a necessary dimension we ignore at our peril.

Music is the food of love and a highway into the heart of worship. Liturgical music is much more than hymns, songs, voluntaries or anthems that break up a service into bite-sized chunks – though that is one of its functions. Music is a powerful tool, enabling and effecting transitions from one part of a service to another, or from one mood to another. Music makes the heart more open to God and also serves to help make God known. This might happen when music underscores words: drawing out their meaning and lifting them from the purely cerebral or when, of itself, it helps move the worshipper to a more profound understanding of the presence of God. We need to break away from the voluntary/hymn/anthem model and ask instead how we might employ music *as* liturgy.

The Early Church had no hesitation, particularly in sacramental worship, in using every means at its disposal to enable worshippers to experience the meaning of a particular rite. They were unashamed of their dramatic use of light and incense and water and oil, even to the extent of making baptism candidates feel they really were drowning! The current emphasis on multisensory worship is therefore not new but a rediscovery of our liturgical inheritance. Professor John Harper has used the phrase 'thinking polyphonically' when we are planning worship. We have many instruments at our disposal and we need to learn to use them all.

Questions to ask at this stage might be:
- Can we present the meaning of the text visually?
- Does the reading itself suggest the use of something multisensory?
- How is it possible to use symbol and action?
- Could the Bible story be 'told' in another way?
- Are words necessary at all?

Ask the question:

Which elements of this service can be made more multisensory?

Once we have explored this layer, we may be ready to explore the *fourth layer*, making our worship engaging.

The strand of active participation and engagement

Gone are the days when we can assume that people will be passive spectators while the important people do all the action up front! For decades there has been the breakdown of trust in institutions, including the Church, to the point where authority is treated with cynicism. People have to 'try it for themselves'. This is demonstrated today by the way we use computers to engage with the world through virtual reality. In worship, though, we want people to engage not with virtual, but ultimate reality.

Worship needs to move from the presentation of the truth about God in worship to engaging people with the God whom they worship. Our society is one in which people want to judge by their own experience. If we are going to provide worship that resonates with our society, we need to move our mindset from presentation to engagement.

In practice this means asking how we can involve the congregation rather than doing it for them. It is, for example, no use simply lighting a candle for some reason. We need to find ways of enabling everyone to engage with it – maybe by getting people to light their own candles. It needs a fresh approach from the one we have adopted in the past.

Ask the question:

How can we find ways to enable worshippers not merely to be presented with God's truth, but to engage with the work of God contained in each part of the liturgy?

We now move on to the *strand* that explores the setting in which worship is to take place.

The strand of place and space

At this point I cannot help thinking of the story of the man who stopped his car and asked a passer-by the way to Dublin, only to be bemused by the reply, 'Well, if I was going to Dublin, I wouldn't start from here.' For many people the excitement of doing anything creative in their church is immediately crushed by thoughts of their building. There is a church version of Murphy's Law: the diocesan arsonist always strikes somewhere else. While many elements of place and space are immovable, that is not the same as unusable, and part of the art of liturgical creativity has to be that of working within all the limitations – of text, of personnel and of environment – imposed upon us. It might even be worth asking the question, 'What are the immovable items?' These are just as likely to be people as things but with a little thought even the immovable can be used in the praise of God.

One of the most simple, effective and inexpensive ways of transforming a worship space is with light. Most of the time we just switch the lights on (or at least those that work) and leave it at that. Why not explore what it is like with some lights switched off, or a few lights placed on the floor in strategic positions? I remember one Holy Week that produced more positive comments than any other. We cast a different light over the church by placing a coloured filter on two borrowed overhead projectors positioned so as to cast their light into the nave. On Maundy Thursday the colour was blue for water at the washing of feet; on Good Friday it was red for the blood of Christ; on Easter Day it was gold for the

glory of the resurrection. The impact was profound. We can use lighting in all sorts of simple ways – don't just have them on or off! Effective use of even simple lighting can have a dramatic impact.

It is the practice of many churches now to change the colours of the hangings to mark the change of liturgical seasons. We could change the lighting too, but why not drape appropriately coloured fabrics around the church; use coloured candles or even scented ones in Eastertide and Christmas (though where you buy stable scented candles I am not sure)? A good principle to adopt is that of making the seasons very different from Ordinary Time. Decorate the worship space to reflect the nature of the season and to be a complete contrast to ordinary time. And please, do not decorate a church in Lent in the same way as in Advent – one is about the coming of the King and hope while the other is about penitence and preparation. They are totally different and should look so – Advent purple is imperial; Lenten array should be more like sackcloth! If you can't use different hangings, why not remove them altogether in Lent?

Often the inner meanings of the different elements of the service can be brought out by conducting them from different places. Leading the intercessions from the crib during the Christmas season or by placing prayers on the cross during Passiontide can draw out the mood and meaning of the season. And why not move the whole congregation rather than just the leaders? *Times and Seasons* includes two new services that are intended to be processional services: the Way of the Cross and the Stations of the Resurrection. Moving the congregation from one place to another can also be adapted in many other of the liturgies of these seasons.

There are many other subjects we could explore here, but why not go into the worship space and note all the external factors that might have an effect on the worship you are planning?

Ask the question:
What might be the most effective way to create a setting for this particular act of worship?

A final word of caution: do not try to do everything in one service. Imagine a service where every prayer or hymn or acclamation was accompanied by visual images, processions, etc. It would be just too much!

Living the liturgy

We have offered a few hints about how to construct liturgy that engages, but we have a further purpose to our work that takes us beyond weekly worship. The title Living Liturgy has a glorious ambiguity. It contains not only the idea that liturgy might come alive, but also that the worshippers might be formed by their worship as they live liturgy in their daily lives.

Secularism has led to a divorce of faith and life. Public worship has become not so much an extension to life but an escape from it. Gone are the days of the Celtic Christians when there was a prayer or action for almost every situation from getting up in the morning to milking the cow; from kindling the fire to getting ready for bed at night …

I will raise the hearth fire as Mary would.
The encirclement of Bride and of Mary
on the fire and on the floor,
and on the household all.
From the *Carmina Gadelica*.[3]

Yet we are rediscovering the need to re-establish these deep connections between the routine of daily life and corporate worship. Something of this lies behind the increasing use of some form of daily office and the popularity of Celtic spirituality where the ordinary events of life are drawn into the worship of God and contribute to the spiritual formation of the worshippers. Such a connected person does not conceive of public worship as a special event on a Sunday but as part and parcel of the natural rhythms of life. Liturgy is meant to form the people of God, but it can happen only if liturgy is lived day by day.

Together for a Season makes suggestions that are intended to help us reconnect our daily life and prayer with the public celebrations of Sunday worship. With the demise of a weekly pattern of church attendance, a liturgy 'lived' at home becomes increasingly important as the place where we engage with God. So, we offer ways in which the spirituality of the home or the small group might connect with worship in church so that our liturgy might be lived not just on Sunday, but every day.

Peter Craig-Wild

Another way of knowing:
signs and symbols in worship

Symbols, symbols everywhere

In the weeks before Christmas the world around us is alive with symbols. This is not just in church buildings; it is evident practically everywhere we go. Long before the end of October, however much we may regret it, the shops are full of Hallowe'en goods. (Although this trend may be attributed to commercial inflation of what was formerly a relatively insignificant occasion, there is no doubt at all that it puts an affinity with symbol firmly on the supermarket shelves.) Poppies for Remembrance Sunday soon follow and then, for two months, Christmas decorations, alive with symbolic suggestion both religious and secular, surround us. We may regret this commercial exploitation of symbol, particularly where its manifestation is crass or manipulative. But it is also possible for those of us concerned both with Christian worship and Christian education to use this symbol-rich ambience and build on it to draw people (of all ages) closer to an awareness of God. We must remind ourselves, moreover, that it is not new. The idea of the Jesse tree, which seems to have emerged in the tenth century and which forms an important strand in this book, involves an encounter with very many signs and symbols, as well as providing an opportunity to hear words of Scripture. The Advent (or Great O) Antiphons, which were traditionally used as a refrain for the Magnificat at Vespers on the last seven evenings before Christmas Eve, can each, also, be illuminated by a visual symbol. It may be useful to consider briefly not only the potential of this approach for today, but also its roots in the tradition of the Church.

Jonny Baker, a well-known writer about alternative worship, suggests that 'God meets us in ritual … It opens up windows in the soul and the community through which the breeze of the Spirit can blow.' We live, in the contemporary West, in an age and place where consumption is centre stage and those who seek an encounter with God and wish to express this spiritually may well 'choose to do this by weaving meaningful religious experience and community into their lives in new ways'. This may not be through

traditional religious expression in the local community (worship in the village church) but nevertheless these 'pilgrims' (as Baker terms them) will be 'looking to make meaningful connections between rituals and their life story'.[1]

The Early Church

Church art historians Anne Dawtry and Christopher Irvine suggest that this may not be too far from the experience of those in the Christian communities that were emerging across the Mediterranean in the third century. They describe the decoration in a house adapted for worship in Dura Europas in modern day Syria, and in the catacombs in Rome, suggesting that 'the whole assembly of images and emblems functions in an anamnetic way, that is, making visible the invisible presence of Christ and mediating the truth of God's saving works'.[2]

From this period on, art developed a way of conveying narrative and expressing Christian belief symbolically. This expression and an ability to relate to it flourished in the West until the Reformation, when in many reformed traditions the move to impress upon people the need to read the Scriptures for themselves led to its eclipse. Dawtry and Irvine suggest, therefore, that 'Christians of the third century occupied a social and religious world that was more sensitive to symbolic meaning than our own'.[3] At one level this may be true: the tourist in a medieval cathedral today may often wish to rely on the guide for an interpretation of its symbolic meaning. But this is only part of the story and we must explore further to discover why this is.

An innate grasp

Observing children might provide us with a clue. This story, told by Gertrud Mueller Nelson at the opening of her book *To Dance with God*, is a good example:

Some years ago, I spent an afternoon caught up in a piece of sewing I was doing. The waste basket near my sewing machine was filled with scraps of fabric cut away from my project. This basket of discards was fascinating to my daughter Annika, who, at the time, was not yet four years old. She rooted through the scraps searching out long bright strips, collected them to herself and went off. When I took a moment to check on her, I tracked her whereabouts to the back garden where I found her sitting on the grass with a long pole. She was affixing the scraps to the top of the pole with great sticky wads of tape. 'I'm making a banner for a procession', she said. 'I need a procession so that God will come down and dance with us.' With that she solemnly lifted her banner to flutter in the wind and slowly she began to dance.[4]

This child had an innate grasp of the way in which a symbol mediates God.

Jerome Berryman, in the first volume of his *Complete Guide to Godly Play,* sheds light on this. Human beings developed a unique ability to use language. At the same time, and independently, a non-verbal communication system evolved in the brain developed, providing an interpretative framework for verbal communication. For example, you can say exactly the same words with a smile or a sneer and mean something completely different.[5]

Berryman goes on to emphasize the importance of non-verbal communication for religious growth and development, indeed for religious expression. Where there is discord between verbal and non-verbal communication, he argues, souls may wither and die.

Levels of meaning

Peter Craig-Wild describes how his experience of inviting people to pray has led him to the conclusion that 'people respond more freely and more deeply to a symbolic representation of the love of God than to a verbal presentation from a leader'.[6] He suggests that, like storytelling, symbolic action is open to meaning-making in a variety of ways and at a variety of levels. He calls this *polyvalence.*

Four layers of meaning within ritual action and symbolic worship, by Peter Craig-Wild:[7]
1. The Private Level – what the symbol means to the individual.
2. The Public Level – where there is some corporate or congregational consensus about what is happening.
3. The Official Level – what the authorities say the meaning is.

4. The Paradigmatic Level – where the meaning is given by its outcome, or how it moves us or affects us.

Although some would avoid symbolic action precisely because it cannot be held within the confines of official theological meanings, Craig-Wild suggests that the thought and action of worshippers cannot realistically be thus controlled and 'the use of symbols and symbolic action can liberate worshippers into encounters with God in new and personal ways'.[8] Annika, with her banner of cast-off fabric scraps, was seeking an encounter with God, as were the worshippers in the Dura Europas and the Roman catacombs. And the tourist in the medieval cathedral without a guide is not completely lost: much in the building still speaks to him or her.

Action first, explanation later

The eminent American liturgist Louis Weil reminds us that, in the early centuries of the Church, 'the mystery of God's action in Baptism and Eucharist was first experienced, and only then was education given'.[9] He goes on to suggest that 'When liturgy is apprehended first through experience, the appropriateness of the full participation is evident. Children experience much that they cannot verbally articulate. We do not delay the first bath until the child understands hygiene, nor do we require knowledge of nutrition prior to the first meal.' He considers the experience of ritual action and symbol at home as being fundamental to development as participation in the liturgy is fundamental to religious development. However, he identifies a problem.

The best family liturgy on a Sunday morning cannot alone convey to children the meaning of Christian life and prayer. It should be learned at home. But one would be naïve not to know … the embarrassment such a suggestion provokes … for the great majority even of practising Christians, both corporate and private prayer is seen as something apart from real life … The full incorporation of children into our corporate prayer will require an enormous change of mentality on the part of the Church at large. It will elicit a deeper sensitivity to the nonverbal dimensions of worship. It will require an end to stuffy formality. Best of all, it will help us to discover the naturalness of Christian prayer.[10]

Linking church and home

Many of the suggestions in this book seek to use symbol in this way to link home and church and to use verbal and non-verbal expression. They are in response to much of this thinking.

You will use them in a variety of ways. Use may evolve over time if you choose to use these ideas at this season over a number of years. In some places, usage may be very sophisticated, with symbols made by talented and experienced crafts people. In other places, what you create may be far more spontaneous and, indeed, unsophisticated. It would not be difficult to make the symbols yourselves using simple materials: they may even be the spontaneous drawings of children undertaken during an act of worship. You may want to download images from the Internet, use books of symbols for reference, or work freehand from your own experience. All these ways are valid and some will be appropriate at one time and in one place, others in another. And we shall need to remember that people will respond, too, in a variety of ways. As we have seen, symbol and ritual are multilayered and responses will depend on the experience of the responder and be appropriate to each.

At home, a family with children may want to use one of the published books of Advent activities: this kind of Advent activity would work well in parallel with what is happening week by week in church, but because there is an opportunity to explore an idea briefly each day, more and different ground might seem to be covered. It is clear, for example, that different traditions of creating the Jesse tree have evolved at different times and in different places, probably in response to different pastoral needs. None is 'the correct one'. This serves to underline, by way of encounter with the tradition, the importance and potential of the polyvalence that symbol affords. It should also be recognized that the opportunity to build and explore the crib or the wreath or the Jesse tree at home does not need to be limited to a family that consists of children with adults: the possibility for an adult or a group of adults to create their own, or develop their own Christmas decorations to reflect the names of the coming Messiah described in the O Antiphons, for example, is filled with attractions and possibilities for the creative, whether they work with paint, glass, fabric, wood, metal or any other medium.

Gill Ambrose

Advent, Christmas and Epiphany:
mapping the journey

Introduction

It is often said that the church year begins on Advent Sunday. The practical side of this is found in the fact that the Lectionary changes on Advent Sunday: we move from Year A to Year B or Year B to Year C, and a new calendar is published to help us in this. But this can seem to be a bit of a puzzle. When the secular calendar year changes just five weeks later, why is the Church different? There are several ways of addressing this problem, none of which is really an answer to the question, but which nevertheless shed light on it. Christianity evolved out of Judaism, and the cycle of Jewish festivals emerged in response to the life of the Jewish people, the cycle of nature and its impact on yearly agricultural practice and also the great festivals, when the people remembered momentous events in their history and gave thanks to God. In the same way, it became Christian practice to celebrate momentous events in the history of the faith, the foremost of which was the Resurrection, and as Jesus died and rose over the period of the Jewish Passover, Easter came more or less to coincide with Passover, celebrated in the spring. Other festivals emerged and a pattern developed. At the same time, Christian faith, grounded in its Jewish roots of profound thanksgiving to God for all his gifts, came in time to respond to the local seasons more closely and to reflect everyday life in its religious practice. We can find evidence of this, for example, in the very many carvings, in medieval churches all over Europe, of the calendar of the agricultural months.

The time chosen for the celebration of the Incarnation, the birth of Christ, emerged much later than the Easter celebration. There are those who would argue that the Christian Church simply imposed one of its major festivals on the midwinter festivals of the pagans whom they sought to convert. Another idea, based on Jewish beliefs about the dates of significant events and worked out by some of the Fathers of the Early Church, suggests that the dates of 25 December for Christmas and 6 January for Epiphany were quite deliberately chosen. An account of this is to be found in a book that might be thought of as a predecessor to *Times and Seasons*, that is, *The Promise of His Glory*.[1]

No matter how the date of Christmas was determined, there is no doubt that today, in north-west Europe where the Church of England finds its home, the way in which we keep Advent, Christmas and Epiphany, three seasons that hold together in one of the two big cycles of the Christian year, is powerfully influenced by the natural calendar. We keep Christmas in winter and winter determines how we keep it. Of course, the experiences of our brothers and sisters who live in other parts of the globe are different in this respect. We in the north will have much to learn from them, in their keeping of this season in another climate and in a different way. Most of what you will find here will work anywhere and little in the book depends on climate and location.

Let us find our way, then, onto the road that leads through these three great seasons, and see where it takes us.

Advent

Reflection in darkness …

Imagine, if you will, the velvety darkness of the night sky, shot through with a few stars; pale points of light against the blackness. There is frost in the air, bare branches of trees are etched in silhouette and the garden looks forlorn in the closing cold. As we move towards the darkest time of the year, we sense again the ancient stirrings of hope for the return of the light of the sun to warm the earth and bring with it the possibility of spring and new life. From ancient times, winter has been a time for rituals expressing the hope for new life and re-enacting the twin themes of light triumphing over darkness and the fragile but certain hope that light will return to banish the primal terror of the darkness. Evergreen was often used as a symbol of enduring life amidst the dead of winter, and fire as a reminder of light and warmth and as a kind of defence against a darkness that seemed all pervasive and never ending. No accident, then, that the Church sets Advent at this time of the year and that Advent marks the beginning of our church year. It is a time for reflection in darkness, for renewal of hope and for a movement towards a beginning born out of darkness and perhaps also made possible because of the darkness.

The colour purple

No accident, either, that purple is the colour commonly used at Advent – a rich and complex colour with multiple shades of meaning. Tyrian purple was used for Emperors' robes in ancient Rome, an incredibly expensive dye – each robe cost the life of around ten thousand of the molluscs from which the dye was extracted – it was an indicator of high rank and no ordinary person was allowed to wear it. Purple goods were highly prized and were used as offerings to kings and princes in ancient times. But there are other associations. Violet is the last colour in the rainbow spectrum and therefore came to represent the ending of the known and the beginning of the unknown, making it a suitable colour for mourning. The tent containing the Ark of the Covenant included purple curtains linking the colour with holiness, divinity and mystery.

A season of paradox

Just as the colour associations are complex, it would seem that one of the markers of this whole season is paradox. There is hope and expectation but tinged with a darker note of longing unfulfilled and some sadness, even anger, at the not yet of this world order. 'How long, O Lord, how long? Will you tarry for ever?' is the cry of God's people through time; a cry that God would bring about the promised kingdom, restore justice and judge with mercy and equity. Now and not yet … passionate longing … the cry of the heart … but the kingdom seems as far off as ever and we see it only in glimpses, not yet in fullness, and the longed-for saviour, when he appears, lies naked and vulnerable in a cattle trough – a most unroyal birthplace for a coming king.

A season of questions

In Advent we face again the questions about the kind of king we wish to serve; the kind of Jesus we hold in our hearts; and the kind of kingdom we seek to build. In Advent we consider again what it is that we most desire:

- What kind of world do we want to build?
- What choices will we have to make for this to be possible?
- And at the end of all things, how will we answer for the choices we have made?

These are questions most often asked in silence and solitude or possibly in the dark hours before dawn. Hence they find their rightful place in the stripped down, pared back Advent place. These are questions often articulated most challengingly by children and young people, so it is vital that we find ways of helping them to find a place to express their own hopes and dreams, for themselves and for the world. The challenge to the adults is perhaps to be called back to the responsibility of modelling committed choice in a world where it seems we can have it all.

A season of simplicity

Like God's people throughout history, we are also faced with questions about where our desire is truly located and what it is we spend our energy, time and money to obtain, and whether, in the final analysis, these things are truly worth our commitment and hope. In a culture of instant access and credit to obtain what we want when we want it, even when it is beyond our means, Advent calls the Church back to a core of simplicity. We are urged to align our lives again to the gospel disciplines of waiting, longing and hoping; the gospel voice that cries out on behalf of the have-nots and the dispossessed and the gospel imperative to live in the light of Christ today because time is short. There is, then, a powerful prophetic edge here as we rediscover our vision of the kingdom and the lost tradition of protest and lament for all that is not subject to the just and gentle rule of Christ.

Christmas

The meaning of Christmas

Tinsel, trees, fairy lights and trifle? Carol singers, cribs, cards, reindeer and mince pies? I wonder what our first associations are with the word 'Christmas' and whether any of them take us anywhere near the heart of its meaning, or if we are so taken up with the commercial and sentimental celebration of Christmas that we are likely to miss its countercultural heartbeat and its darker side.

There is amazement, wonder and joy here. There are hosts of angels filling the night sky with singing; a group of astounded shepherds on a hillside who find their lives and expectations turned upside down; there is a shining star and the birth of a child, which, like many other births before and since, brings hope and possibility. And then again … the stable is warm and cosy and filled with fondly gazing animals or so we imagine … Mary has had an easy labour – or so it would seem. There is a beatific baby who never seems to cry (if we think the carols have the last word) and there our thoughts seem to fix themselves, with an Incarnation separate from the messy realities of birth, and unconnected to the man Jesus and the costly salvation he came to bring. But look again … there is a lot of pain and blood in this season. The baby Jesus was born to an unmarried mother in a cave. Mary and Joseph were a long way from home and were almost without any kind of shelter. Mary was young and may have been afraid. Shepherds left everything behind – no easy thing to leave your entire livelihoods behind to visit a child. I wonder how they explained their moment of encounter with Jesus. Soon, Mary, Joseph and the newborn are forced to flee to Egypt to escape Herod's persecution, forced into an alien culture further than ever from their homeland and now under the threat of murder.

God with us

Incarnation here is realized in the muck of the stable floor, the agony of childbirth, the frightening vulnerability and dependence of a newborn baby and the flight of the dispossessed – a far cry from sentimentality and tinsel. The infant Christ comes into the world at the very darkest time of the year, picking up the resonance with the winter solstice and using imagery of the sun, rising to banish not only the darkness without, but also the darkness within. The God we see here is truly 'bone of our bone and flesh of our flesh'; not an unmoved mover, but intrinsically one with us in the mess and at home in the humanity that at its creation was called 'good' and whose original purpose was to be one with its creator.

I wonder where the emphasis lies in our marking of the Feast of the Incarnation in church and what image of God we take from it into our lives? And I wonder which Christmas story we think might be most suitable for children and why? And which story we would prefer to preach about?

St Stephen's Day and beyond: the cost of following Christ

The festival of St Stephen, the first martyr, following hard on the heels of Christmas, reminds us of the price Stephen paid for seeking to bear witness to Christ – it cost him his life and serves as a reminder to the Church of the cost of fleshing out the gospel in the world. The splash of red with its associations with both passion and blood is a stark reminder, in the midst of the Christmas white and gold, of the cost of living for the love of Christ. Remembering John, Apostle and Evangelist, again draws our attention to reflecting on the meaning of the Christmas story and how we can find ways of articulating its meaning in today's culture.

The Feast of the Holy Innocents then takes us where we would rather not go – into a place of ultimate horror where the innocent suffer and the perpetrators go unpunished; where the cries of children go unheard and no one can save them from death. Yet in today's world perhaps we need this stark reminder of the darker possibilities for humanity. And there are countless examples today of children who suffer the world over through wars and famines and who lose their innocence, their homelands, their parents, their lives because of actions, abuse or neglect of adults and we need to remember them and to pray for a world where there is no more weeping for the children who are no more and there shall be again hope for the future.

Epiphany

We three kings …

I wonder if our thoughts of Epiphany are inextricably linked to nativity play renderings of 'We three kings of Orient are'? The three mysterious strangers, their exotic gifts and the journey they undertook following the shining star have fuelled the imagination of painters and poets down the centuries and still hold meaning for us today. Lest we lose sight of the identity of the babe in the manger, the symbolism of the gifts the Magi offer to the child spell it out for us: gold, a precious, pure metal with links to kingship; frankincense for divinity and holiness; myrrh, with its bitter perfume, for suffering and mourning.

Who do you say that I am?

And it is the issue of identity that weaves through the Scriptures of the season – Christ's baptism; the voice from heaven confirming what our eyes and the witness of John have told us, that this is the Son of God; the picture language of the Lamb of God with its rich associations with sacrifice and sin offering; Nathaniel's confession of the Son of God; Jesus preaching, teaching and casting out demons; Jesus performing miracles and healings that act as signs of who Jesus is; and the water into wine giving us symbolic clues of the purpose of Christ's coming – to transform the old order.

And so we come to Candlemas, and Simeon's recognition that the child in his arms is the salvation of Israel and of the whole world. And it is at this point that the shadow of the cross falls retrospectively over our Advent hope and over the stable and the nativity as we turn our faces towards Lent. The cost of owning Christ in the fullness of who he is casts its shadow over our own sense of calling and vocation. This season is often a time for reflection on and recommitment to our baptismal calling and promises, just as (on the third Sunday of Epiphany in Year A) the account of the call of the disciples urges us again to hear the call to follow, leaving behind the old familiar ways in order to follow in The Way – just as the Magi left home in a risk-taking venture following the star that promised a new world order. There are powerful links to play with here between the Magi's journey; the journey we begin at baptism; and the journey deeper into the heart of the mystery of Christ and into the Christ story in which we engage year on year. We remember T. S. Eliot's words: '… were we led all that way for Birth or Death?'[2]

The road less travelled

In a culture of celebrity watching, Epiphany calls us to question the signs we follow and the path we tread. What light do we travel by and where are we heading? We are reminded that the call that comes to us from God is not only a one-off commitment but also an ongoing journey of discovery and discipleship and a constant recommitment to choose 'the road less travelled' – not for our own ease of comfort, but for the sake of the Word in the world. The Christ we worship is too great to be possessed by us. Nor is he to be contained inside the confines of church or human religious systems, for he is the Christ in and for the world.

Following in the way

For children and young people as well as for adults living in a postmodern era with its multiplicity of (seemingly equally valid) lifestyle options and a vast array of choices spread out like consumer goods on a shelf, how vital it becomes that, in the Church, we learn to model the cost of commitment and the joyful as well as the challenging consequences of choice. As Harry Potter's Professor Dumbledore remarks, it is our choices that determine who we are and what we become – and, in biblical terms, this means taking the idea of discipleship seriously, choosing life over easy imitations, and patterning the meaning of the Magi's gifts into our lives – recognizing the kingship of Christ, reflecting holiness and accepting the cost of following in the way.

Diane Craven

ADVENT

Seasonal introduction

The challenge of Advent

Advent has been in many respects a neglected season in the church calendar. We are surrounded by window displays full of Christmas goodies and we go in and out of shops that play Christmas carols from the end of November. On top of this, we are faced with magazines, advertisements and sales pitches that create an enormous pressure to rush around to find the best presents, to look perfect, to have the best dressed tree and to provide a feast to remember. With all this going on, it is not easy to find time and space to reflect or to be at all still.

And churches don't always help. They are often faced with crowded schedules of school concerts, end-of-term services, nativity plays and a whole host of events and commitments that turn the mind to Christmas before the last chords of 'Lo! He comes with clouds descending' fade away into the night air.

Absence

A sense of absence is vital to unlocking some of the importance of this season for us. The winter itself is a season of absence and the readings express the hope for a kingdom that is 'not yet'. Discovering this sense of absence might include taking seriously the idea of de-cluttering the church and our homes, setting apart space for meditation in our churches, or our homes, and using colour and symbols or pictures to provide a focus.

Creating such a set-apart physical space can sometimes assist us to make the necessary emotional space to centre our lives, to take time to draw breath and to attend to the longings of our hearts. It is only then that we can begin the work of true repentance and the task of realigning our desires. We glibly say 'absence makes the heart grow fonder', but it is interesting to consider that it is the seeming absence of God that calls out from his people both the hope and the cry for justice and redemption. It is the interplay of 'now you see him, now you don't' that creates a dance of intimacy between us and God; and between God and the world he brought to being in love and which he longs to gather again to himself.

Colour

The liturgical colour for Advent is purple and this should be used for frontals and vestments in this season. It might also be used in any spaces in which we gather more informally as church or in family groupings during this season. Flowers, if used, are in restrained style, emphasizing the mood of the season: perhaps a single bloom among simple greenery, or among a heap of stones, reminding us of the blooms in the desert.

Often we will not use flowers at all, creating the sense of space that emphasizes absence and concentrating the eye on the particular visual imagery and symbols of the season. Wreaths do not generally include flowers until Christmas, another small example of creating absence.

The Third Sunday of Advent, Gaudete Sunday

The season of Advent, as it first emerged in the Church in the fourth and fifth centuries, lasted, like Lent, for 40 days. Later tradition developed the observance we know today, of four Sundays before Christmas Day. Within this tradition the third Sunday emerged as rather distinctive (mirroring the fourth, middle, Sunday of Lent) and became known as Gaudete Sunday, from the words of its traditional introit, *Gaudete in Domino semper* (Rejoice in the Lord always) and the New Testament Reading (still used in Year C) from Philippians 4, 'Rejoice in the Lord always'. On this third Sunday, the rose or pink coloured candle is lit, and rose coloured vestments are sometimes worn. During the otherwise penitential season of Advent, the readings on the third Sunday emphasize the joyous anticipation of the Lord's coming.

Prayer

It might be good to offer some meditative prayer times for members of the congregation or to provide some simple meditation techniques, using Scriptures of the season, that can be practised in the midst of daily life. Meditation is another 'less is more' way of providing a sense of absence and space. This might also be an opportunity for more reflective styles of prayer in the intercessions and for making space within the liturgy.

A prayer space

Create a prayer space in the church or, if you have one already, you might like to consider how to give it a particularly Advent focus and flavour. Use purple drapes. Try not to use flowers, or create restrained arrangements in keeping with the season. Perhaps choose instead some twisted willow or dry branches and place these alongside texts taken from the reading about the wilderness and the dry land shall being glad (Isaiah 35.1). Another approach would be to use the colour purple and black, stars, silver cloth and cut-out symbols of the alpha and the omega (the beginning and the end). Black cloth spangled with stars might be used with verses from Scripture that describe the majesty of God and the glory of the heavens (Job 38.4-7; Psalms 8.3-4, 147.4-5), as described so memorably in the Advent hymn 'Creator of the stars of night'.

Some churches use very simple purple banners with the alpha and omega letters on them, one hung from a pillar at each side of the church as a visual focus. Another idea for visual focus for banners would be to use symbols from the O Antiphons.

If you are in a place where light pollution does not prevent you from seeing the stars in the night sky, you might like to take time literally to 'consider the heavens', using a telescope if you can.

Advent carols

Advent carols focus on the themes of longing for the promised Messiah, linked to the second coming. The themes of death, judgement, heaven and hell (sometimes known as the Four Last Things) are also common. Advent music often features minor keys and the use of plainsong also picks up the moods of restraint, longing and reflection that are important in this season.

The well-loved carol, 'O come, O come, Emmanuel' picks up the words and images of the Great O Antiphons, which were originally sung from 17 December (for an introduction to the O Antiphons, see page 29). This carol could provide the basis for reflection and meditation during the Advent season.

Advent:
Stand-alone seasonal material

A Service of the Word for Advent (Sunday)

Preparatory notes

Crib, Jesse tree or wreath: which pathway?

If you are planning to use material throughout the Advent, Christmas and Epiphany seasons from one of the three pathways suggested in this book, you will need to decide, in planning this service, how you include the ideas provided in each pathway for Advent Sunday. If you are planning to follow the wreath pathway, for example, you will include the Prayers around the Wreath, suggested in the Practical Inclusive Ideas section at the point of lighting the wreath, and the Intercessions in this service. If you are going to follow the crib pathway, use the ideas suggested in the crib pathway section at the point in this service that is called Alternative Intercessions. The Jesse tree pathway material is most appropriately used during the Liturgy of the Word with the Old Testament reading or during the sermon.

On the other three Sundays of Advent, and during Christmas and Epiphany, the Inclusive Worship ideas for each pathway may be used at a similar point in the main service of the Sunday or feast day.

What needs to be prepared leading up to the service?

Think about the way the worship space might be decorated to highlight the season of Advent. The traditional colour is purple but we can do far more than simply change altar and pulpit hangings. Why not use purple candles on the holy table, put a purple filter on an overhead projector, project purple light across the church generally or at a specific point, or drape purple fabric at strategic places around the worship area?

If there is to be an empty crib, this could be prepared in the days leading up to the service.

CRIB

WREATH

JESSE TREE

What needs to happen before the service?

If different voices from the congregation are to be used, the people concerned need to be invited and prepared. Service sheets could be annotated and highlighted for each participant.

What needs to be made ready immediately before the service?

The bowl with charcoal and incense should be ready as near as possible to the start of the service. Charcoal generates a lot of heat and care should be taken to ensure that the person carrying it does not find it too hot to hold or even get burnt. It is helpful to carry the bowl on a thick block of wood. If incense is to be used in this way, first crush some aluminium foil into the bottom of the bowl, making sure that air can circulate underneath it. Then place self-igniting charcoal on top of the foil.

Questions

As you read through the text of the service it might be helpful to jot down any questions that arise for you as you begin to plan. They may be questions about why this particular suggestion is made, or they may be about how you would execute a particular suggestion in your situation, and whether it needs to be adapted. You are reminded to ask these questions as you work your way through this table.

Structure, movement and flow	Words/Text	Multisensory	Participation
The ministers enter quietly and are in place before the service begins.			
THE GATHERING			
Acclamation	Our Lord says, 'I am coming soon.' **Amen. Come, Lord Jesus.** [T&S 41]		This could be led by someone who is in the congregation and could be repeated at different points through the service, led by the same or different people but always from the congregation.
Hymn or song		During which something that might represent the presence of God (such as a large bowl of charcoal with incense already burning) is brought into the middle of the congregation. The group carrying it stays there for the Confession.	
Greeting	*Silence* The Lord is here. **His Spirit is with us.**		Once the hymn/song has finished, there is a silence so that people can watch, smell and feel the incense and so become aware of the presence of God.
	If necessary, the leader introduces the service.		
The Confession which is a key element of the service and so should be given some time.	*The leader introduces the confession, saying* A voice cries out in the wilderness, 'Make straight the way of the Lord.' So let us listen, and turn to the Lord in penitence and faith. *Silence for reflection.* God, through Jesus Christ, will judge the secret thoughts of all: Lord, have mercy. **Lord, have mercy.**		The introduction to Confession could be spoken by one or two voices from the congregation as also could each of the sentences before the Lord have mercy *(or)* The introduction and the three sentences could be done by four people, each in a corner of the church.

	Not everyone who says to me, 'Lord, Lord,' will enter the kingdom of heaven: Christ, have mercy. **Christ, have mercy.** Let anyone who has an ear listen to what the Spirit is saying to the churches: Lord, have mercy. **Lord, have mercy.** [T&S 35] *We sing* **Longing for light, we wait in darkness.** **Longing for truth, we turn to you.** **Make us your own, your holy people,** **light for the world to see.** *Christ, be our light! Shine in our hearts.* *Shine through the darkness.* *Christ, be our light! Shine in your Church gathered today.* *The Absolution is given.*	More incense is put into the bowl.	
Lighting the Advent wreath	*We sing* **Longing for peace, our world is troubled.** **Longing for hope, many despair.** **Your word alone has power to save us.** **Make us your living voice.** *Christ, be our light! Shine in our hearts.* *Shine through the darkness.* *Christ, be our light! Shine in your Church Gathered today.* *This prayer is said* People of God: awake! The day is coming soon when you shall see God face to face. Remember the ways and the works of God. God calls you out of darkness to walk in the light of his coming. You are God's children. **Lord, make us one as we walk with Christ today and for ever.** **Amen.** [T&S 51] *We sing* *Christ, be our light! Shine in our hearts.* *Shine through the darkness.* *Christ, be our light! Shine in your Church gathered today.* [© Bernadette Farrell, 1993]	The person carrying the incense places it in a suitable place near the front of the church. The first Advent candle is lit. (If this service takes place on one of the other Sundays in Advent, the prayer before the lighting of the candle should be that of the appropriate Sunday and the appropriate number of candles should be lit.)	

The Collect	The Collect of the day is said by the leader		
Questions	*What are your questions about the Gathering section of the service?*		
THE LITURGY OF THE WORD			
Readings	One or more of the readings for Advent Sunday found in the *Common Worship* lectionary should be used.		
Acclamation You may use this between the readings or as a Gospel acclamation.	Our Lord says, 'I am coming soon.' **Amen. Come, Lord Jesus.** [T&S 41]		
Sermon			The sermon might raise a question about to whom Jesus might be coming when he comes again. Answers could be offered from the congregation such as 'the poor', ' the sick', 'the lonely', which could then be picked up later in the Intercessions.
Affirmation of Faith	We say together in faith **Holy, holy, holy is the Lord God almighty, who was, and is, and is to come.** We believe in God the Father, who created all things: **for by his will they were created and have their being.** We believe in God the Son, who was slain: **for with his blood, he purchased us for God, from every tribe and language, from every people and nation.** We believe in God the Holy Spirit: **the Spirit and the Bride say, 'Come!' Even so come, Lord Jesus! Amen.** *cf Revelation 4.8,11; 5.9; 22.17,20* [CW 148]	If the charcoal is still hot enough, more incense may be placed in the large bowl.	

Questions	What are your questions about the Liturgy of the Word?		
Prayers			
Acclamation	Our Lord says, 'I am coming soon'. **Amen. Come, Lord Jesus!** [T&S 41]		
Intercessions	These could take the form of a short Litany with the response **Come, Lord Jesus** at the end of each bidding. For example: To a world in turmoil, **Come, Lord Jesus.** To hungry nations, **Come, Lord Jesus.** To the persecuted and exploited, **Come, Lord Jesus.** To the sick and suffering, **Come, Lord Jesus.** It is often more effective to have a short series of biddings followed by a pause. The leader could conclude with a more traditional collect style prayer. The prayers end with **The Lord's Prayer**.	After each short series of biddings, if the charcoal is still hot enough, more incense could be placed in the bowl as a sign of our prayers rising like incense to heaven.	These prayers could be scripted at the beginning and then further biddings could be encouraged from the congregation. Alternatively, these prayers might pick up some of the themes of the sermon. If this is to be the case, the prayers must be prepared as the sermon takes place.
(or) **Alternative Intercessions**	The empty crib could be set up with no animals or people in it.		People are encouraged to write the name of a situation or a person on a piece of paper. Once people have done that, all *process* from their places to the empty crib and place their 'prayer papers' on the floor of the crib or wherever might be appropriate. As they do so, they are encouraged to pray either aloud or silently 'Lord Jesus come to . . . (whatever is written on the paper)'. Singing continues throughout. When all have placed their prayer papers in the crib, the prayers end with **The Lord's Prayer**.

Praise	Blessed be the Lord, the God of Israel, **who has come to his people and set them free.** Hosanna to the Son of David. Blessed is he who comes in the name of the Lord. **Hosanna in the highest.** Blessed is the coming kingdom of our father David. **Hosanna in the highest.** Blessed be the name of the Lord, **now and for ever. Amen.** [T&S 48]		
The Peace	Blessed is the King who comes in the name of the Lord. Peace in heaven and glory in the highest. The peace of the Lord be always with you **and also with you.**		All share the peace and return to their seats.
Questions	*What are your questions about the Prayers?*		
CONCLUSION			
Hymn/song			During which people gather around the door.
Acclamation	With love and compassion, **come, Lord Jesus.** With judgement and mercy, **come, Lord Jesus.** In power and glory, **come, Lord Jesus.** In wisdom and truth, **come, Lord Jesus.** [T&S 42]		Each of these acclamations could come from the body of the congregation.
The Dismissal Gospel	Hear the Gospel of our Lord Jesus Christ according to Mark. **Glory to you, O Lord.** Mark 1.14,15 *At the end the reader says:* This is the Gospel of the Lord. **Praise to you, O Christ.**		

Blessing	*This or another blessing may be used* May God the Father, judge all-merciful, make us worthy of a place in his kingdom. **Amen.** May God the Son, coming among us in power, reveal in our midst the promise of his glory. **Amen.** May God the Holy Spirit make us steadfast in faith, joyful in hope and constant in love. **Amen.** And the blessing of God almighty, the Father, the Son, and the Holy Spirit, be among you and remain with you always. **Amen.** [T&S 41]		
Dismissal	As we await our coming Saviour, go in peace to love and serve the Lord. **In the name of Christ. Amen.** *(or)* … go in the peace of Christ. **Thanks be to God.** [T&S 43]		
Questions	*What are your questions about the Conclusion?*		

A simple Christingle service

Preparatory notes

Prepare the Christingles

You will need to prepare sufficient Christingles for at least every child who attends the service. If you do not know roughly how many children to expect, be sure to over-provide. If you find that you have Christingles left when every child has received one, they can always be given to adults.

Details of how to make a Christingle are provided below. Put the prepared Christingles on trays so that they can be carried easily either to the distribution points, or directly to people in their places.

How to make a Christingle

You will need:

- sweets from market stalls
  – dolly mixture, small fruit gums;
- cherries (look festive);
- sultanas or raisins;
- red sticky tape (suitable tape can be ordered *free* from the Children's Society – don't pin the tape on);
- small candles;
- oranges;
- cocktail sticks – four for each orange;
- tinfoil cut into 75 mm/3 inch in squares.

METHOD

1. Make sure the orange will stand without rocking. If necessary, trim the base with a knife.
2. Fasten a piece of red sticky tape around the middle of the orange.
3. Lay a square of silver foil on the top of each orange. The foil will help prevent hot wax running onto a child's hand.
4. Cut a small cross through the foil into the top of each orange (place it on a tray to catch the juice).
5. Place a candle on top and wedge it firmly into the orange.
6. Load four cocktail sticks with raisins, sultanas, cherries or soft sweets. (Avoid nuts – they are difficult to spear and some people may be allergic to them.)

7. Insert cocktail sticks into the orange around the base of the candle.

Store the Christingles upright in trays in a cool place. Greengrocers' fruit trays are ideal if you can get them.

NOTE

When handing out Christingles during your service, don't light them first.

Give out unlit Christingles, and then pass the light from one person to the next.

Collections

The Christingle Service developed in the Moravian Church and was introduced into the Church of England by the Children's Society. The idea was to bring people together for a special Christmas service and for the collection at the service to be given to the charity. Many churches and organizations still continue this. You may like to decide to give the collection from your service to the Society.

Fire precautions

Extreme care needs to be taken to ensure that sufficient precautions against the possibility of fire are provided. Ensure that all the church doors are unlocked (even doors that you would not normally use) so that you can evacuate the building instantly should this become necessary. Point out the exits before the service begins. There should be fire extinguishers in the church. Make sure that stewards know where they are and how to use them. For this service, it is useful also to have a fire blanket. All this might sound rather alarming. However, it is better to be safe than sorry. Accidents are accidents and can happen at any time, but they are much more likely to happen when people have not planned properly and are ill prepared.

Distributing the Christingles

You will need to decide how you are going to distribute the Christingles. If there is plenty of room to circulate in the church, then people might come to a particular point and collect their own while a hymn or song is sung. If the church building is crowded, it would be better to take the Christingles to people where they are sitting. Light the Christingles when they have been distributed, as it is rather difficult for small children to carry them lit. It is also less likely that they will drip hot wax on hands, (which hurts) and clothes, (which is tedious to remove).

- Label them if that would help.
- Make sure that you have the relevant number of large candles.

What needs to happen before the service?
- Ensure that you have the Christingles on trays ready for distribution.
- Make sure that you have the means to light the Christingles when the time comes.
- Appoint someone to turn the lights on and off at the required points in the service. Make sure this person knows which are the relevant switches.

What needs to be made ready immediately before the service?
- Ensure that there are enough stewards to guide the congregation, particularly when the Christingle candles are lit.
- Unlock the doors. Point out the exits to people before the service begins.
- Make sure that you have a fire blanket available.

Structure, movement and flow	Words/text	Multisensory	Participation
THE GATHERING			
Response	Christ has brought us out of darkness: **to live in his marvellous light.**		
Hymn, carol or song		During this hymn a large candle is carried in and is placed in its stand. The bearer stays by the candle.	
	Christ has brought us out of darkness: **to live in his marvellous light.** *This or another introduction may be used* In the name of Christ, welcome to [name of your church or community] today. We have come together in the presence of God our Father to rejoice in the gift of Jesus to us as the light of the world. In this service we hear and receive the story and message of the coming of Christ, and to offer to God our thanksgiving in prayer and song. [From the Church in Wales Christingle Service][1]		

| Thanksgiving | Lord Jesus,
thank you for Mary,
who was visited by an angel
and became your mother.

Jesus, light of the world,
we worship and adore you.

Thank you for being born as one of us,
not rich and in a palace,
but poor and in a stable.

Jesus, light of the world,
we worship and adore you.

Thank you for the shepherds,
who listened to the song of the angels,
left sheep and fields
and hurried to worship you.

Jesus, light of the world,
we worship and adore you.

Thank you for the wise men,
who brought three wonderful gifts:
gold, frankincense and myrrh.

Jesus, light of the world,
we worship and adore you.

Thank you for Simeon and Anna,
who waited a lifetime to see you,
praised God in the Temple,
and welcomed you as the light of the world.

Jesus, light of the world,
we worship and adore you.
[From the Church in Wales Christingle Service]

(or)

Glory to Christ, Son of Mary;
born a child, you share our life.
Glory to God in the highest.

Glory to Christ, Son of David;
born to be King,
you receive gifts from the wise.
Glory to God in the highest.

Glory to Christ, Son of man;
born our Saviour,
you are the light of the world.
Glory to God in the highest.

Each thanksgiving ends with this prayer
Lord Jesus,
with Mary and the shepherds,
with the wise men, with Simeon and Anna,
we worship and adore you,
light of the world,
now and for ever. **Amen.**

[From the Church in Wales Christingle Service] | | This thanksgiving could be led from the crib by a number of different people while the response is led by the person who brought in the light.

(Some of the sections could be omitted, depending on when the service takes place.) |

Lighting the Advent wreath	*The Advent wreath is lit in the customary way for the church.*		
Hymn, carol or song			
Questions	*What are your questions about the Gathering?*		
THE LITURGY OF THE WORD			
Reading	*The reading may be preceded by this acclamation* Christ has brought us out of darkness: **to live in his marvellous light.**		
Address			
Hymn, carol or song	*As the gifts are received, this prayer is used* **Blessed are you, Lord our God, king of the universe!** **All we have comes from you.** **Help us to use these gifts for your glory.** **Blessed be God for ever!** [From the Church in Wales Christingle Service]		During this hymn the Collection is offered.
The Prayers	The Christingle reminds us of our world and so let us pray: for all people in their daily life and work: for our families, friends and neighbours, and for all those who are alone; for all Christians, that we may shine in the dark places of the world; Jesus, light of the world, **hear our prayer.** for help to care for your world: for those who do not share the good things we take for granted; for those who do not know the light of Jesus in their lives; Jesus, light of the world, **hear our prayer.** for the peace of the world: for our own needs and for the needs of others; for those who lead us, teach us, and help us to live together; Jesus, light of the world, **hear our prayer.**	The person(s) leading the prayers stand beside the large candle that was lit at the beginning of the service. For each section of the prayers a different coloured large candle may be brought in and placed at a central visible point around the large candle used at the beginning. The candle bearer may lead the response of 'Jesus, light of the world …'	

	for everyone who is sad, in danger, or in trouble: for all children and young people who have no food, home, or clothes; for those who need God's help, especially the sick and anxious, the lonely and the afraid; and for those who look after them. Jesus, light of the world, **hear our prayer.** [From the Church in Wales Christingle Service] We bring all our prayers before God, saying together, as Jesus taught us **Our Father, who art in heaven,** **hallowed be thy name;** **thy kingdom come;** **thy will be done;** **on earth as it is in heaven.** **Give us this day our daily bread.** **And forgive us our trespasses,** **as we forgive those who trespass against us.** **And lead us not into temptation;** **but deliver us from evil.** **For thine is the kingdom,** **the power and the glory,** **for ever and ever.** **Amen.**		
Hymn, carol or song			During which people come to collect Christingles. If numbers are small enough, form a circle around the church. If there are too many people to do this, encourage people to return to their places. You may prefer to take the Christingles to people in their places, particularly if the congregation is large. When all have received one, light the Christingles.

Prayer with Christingles		Lights are switched off and the church is made as dark as possible.	
	The leader says this prayer: Father of lights, from whom comes every good and perfect gift; keep us in the light of Christ, to shine in your world, that all may believe in you through Jesus Christ our Lord. **Amen.** *Silence is kept*		
Carol	Christ has brought us out of darkness: **to live in his marvellous light.**	The lights are switched on.	A reflective carol is sung, such as 'Away in a manger'. If possible, it should be one that can be sung from memory.
			People return to their places.
Hymn, carol or song			
CONCLUSION			
Blessing	Christ the Sun of Righteousness shine upon you, scatter the darkness from before your path, and make you ready to meet him when he comes in glory; and the blessing of God almighty, the Father, the Son, and the Holy Spirit, be among you and remain with you always. **Amen.** [T&S 41]		
Dismissal	Christ has brought us out of darkness: **to live in his marvellous light.** Go, and share the light of Christ. **Amen.**		
Questions	*What are your questions about the Prayers section of the service?*		

The Advent Antiphons

History of the Advent Antiphons

The Advent Antiphons are refrains, short verses, all beginning with the word 'O ...', that were sung before and after the Magnificat (The Song of Mary: Luke 1.46-55) at the evening service in monastic communities on the seven days preceding Christmas Eve, i.e. 17–23 December. They are calls to God, asking for him to come as teacher and deliverer, with a tapestry of scriptural titles and pictures that describe his saving work in Christ. They are best known to us today in the well-known Advent hymn 'O come, O come, Emmanuel'. Each of the antiphons ends with a plea for the Messiah to come and, as Christmas draws close, the cry becomes ever more urgent. The compiler of the antiphons is unknown but they seem to have been composed in the seventh or eighth century and are based on Old Testament texts looking forward to the coming of salvation. They reflect a rich mosaic of images.

There is a more curious, and perhaps mysterious, feature about them. The first letter of each Latin name invoked forms an acrostic in reverse. Sapientia, Adonai, Radix, Clavis, Oriens, Rex, and Emmanuel form the Latin words *ERO CRAS* (Tomorrow I will be there).

This mixture of word and image still provides us today with powerful ideas to think about as we await the arrival of Jesus. We could put it this way: 'I wonder what Jesus will be like when he comes?' The Bible uses all sorts of names for God and there is a wonderful children's book that helps us to think about this. *In God's Name* by Sandy Eisenberg Sasso [2] explores the way in which people in ancient times sought to find a name for God and you might like to read it before you begin to work with the Advent Antiphons.

Below are the words of the antiphons, translated into English, with their Latin titles, the date on which they are used and the references to the Old Testament verses from which they are drawn, followed by some ideas for using and exploring the Advent Antiphons at home, and in worship together.

17 December – O Sapientia
O Wisdom, coming forth from the mouth of the
　Most High,
reaching from one end to the other mightily,
and sweetly ordering all things:
Come and teach us the way of prudence.
cf Ecclesiasticus 24.3; Wisdom 8.1

18 December – O Adonai
O Adonai, and leader of the House of Israel,
who appeared to Moses in the fire of the burning bush
and gave him the law on Sinai:
Come and redeem us with an outstretched arm.
cf Exodus 3.2; 24.12

19 December – O Radix Jesse
O Root of Jesse, standing as a sign among the peoples;
before you kings will shut their mouths,
　to you the nations will make their prayer:
Come and deliver us, and delay no longer.
cf Isaiah 11.10; 45.14; 52.15; Romans 15.12

20 December – O Clavis David
O Key of David and sceptre of the House of Israel;
you open and no one can shut;
you shut and no one can open:
Come and lead the prisoners from the prison house,
those who dwell in darkness and the shadow of death.
cf Isaiah 22.22; 42.7

21 December – O Oriens
O Morning Star,
splendour of light eternal and sun of righteousness:
Come and enlighten those who dwell in darkness
　and the shadow of death.
cf Malachi 4.2

22 December – O Rex Gentium
O King of the nations, and their desire,
the cornerstone making both one:
Come and save the human race,
which you fashioned from clay.
cf Isaiah 28.16; Ephesians 2.14

23 December – O Emmanuel
O Emmanuel, our King and our lawgiver,
the hope of the nations and their Saviour:
Come and save us, O Lord our God.
cf Isaiah 7.14

[T&S 51–2]

Using the Advent Antiphons today

The Antiphons were intended to be used at the beginning and end of the Magnificat from 17 to 23 December and, for those who say an evening office on a daily basis, this is the way they should be used.

However, people using other forms of prayer, either in a church building or elsewhere, might use them also. The practice of recalling other names of God, other attributes of the Saviour, might serve to remind us in the rush of the late Advent/Christmas season, with many carol services and much shopping, that the coming baby Jesus is also the longed-for Messiah, who comes to deliver us. Here are some ideas for using them.

 Suggested visual symbols for the antiphons

Date	Latin title	English title	Visual symbol	
17 December	O Sapientia	O Wisdom	an eye within a triangle – an ancient symbol for the wisdom of God	
18 December	O Adonai	O Lord	tablets of the Law	
19 December	O Radix Jesse	O Root of Jesse	a growing plant with its roots visible	
20 December	O Clavis David	O Key of David	a key	
21 December	O Oriens	O Morning Star	a star	
22 December	O Rex Gentium	O King of the nations	a crown	
23 December	O Emmanuel	O Emmanuel (God with us)	the crib	

Making the visual symbols for the antiphons

The symbols listed above are available as templates on the CD-ROM. If you don't wish to use those, try the following:

COLLECTING THE IMAGES

If you start well before Advent and keep in mind the images you are looking for, then you may find them in the course of everyday life. Some will be easier than others. For example, there are all sorts of places in which you might find the image of a crown, a star or a key. Once Christmas decorations are in the shops, a crib will be easy to find. The plant should not be too difficult, though the visible roots might prove a problem: an air plant or a bonsai tree might be a possibility. The eye within the triangle and the tablets of the Law will prove the greatest challenge and will require real dedication!

SOME WAYS TO MAKE THE IMAGES YOURSELF:

- You will find helpful images as a basis for your own designs at www.domestic-church.com: click on Fridge Art; then Advent and Christmas; then and The O Antiphons.

- A very simple way to do this would be to create them out of gold card. Use your own imagination, or find templates to draw around.

- If you would like to do something a bit more refined, you could make circles out of gold coloured wire or ribbon (representing the 'O' of each antiphon) and then create a shape to go inside each one. These would look good hanging up.

- You might make a rigid frame out of wire, metal or wood and then fill this with the images made of coloured thread, or tissue paper or cellophane.

- You could make the shapes out of clay or some other modelling medium. You may then like to paint them. Making the shapes out of coloured air-drying modelling clay would be fun.

- An embroiderer might make them on fabric. Such a project might vary in complexity from simple cross stitch on basic canvas to complex ecclesiastical embroidery by a practised expert.

- This idea is from Germany, where, in Advent, florist shops sell bells and stars and so on cut out of plywood, painted and mounted on thin pieces of dowelling. These are then stuck into Christmas flower arrangements and Advent wreaths. It would be quite easy to adapt this idea to the symbols of the Antiphons.

- You could make simple little paper shapes on paper of different strong colours.

Very simple prayers to reflect each of the antiphons

These prayers might be used in the home or with a small group during the days of 17 to 23 December:

Come, O Wisdom, word of the Most High God,
Come, Wisdom, and teach us the ways of the Lord. Amen.

Come, O Adonai, who appeared to Moses in the burning bush, and gave him the Law on Mount Sinai,
Come Adonai, and save us. Amen.

Come, O Root of Jesse, be a sign among the people,
Come, Root of Jesse and deliver us now [show us the way]. Amen.

Come, O Key of David, free the captives and those in darkness,
Come Key of David, lead us into light. Amen.

Come, O Morning Star, Everlasting Light.
Come, Morning Star and shine on us. Amen.

Come, O King of the nations, save us your creatures.
Come, King of the nations, save us now. Amen.

Come, O Emmanuel, God with us,
Come, Emmanuel, and save us. Amen.

Using the antiphons in a church setting

You might move, for the conclusion of your time of prayer together on each of these days, to a particular place, perhaps to the awaiting crib, perhaps to a stained-glass window showing Jesus, perhaps to a statue. Another possibility would be to move to a different place on each of the days, reflecting each particular antiphon, for example:

17 December: Wisdom – the holy table;

18 December: Adonai – the lectern or reading desk;

19 December: Root of Jesse – the church Christmas tree;

20 December: Key of David – the door;

21 December: Morning Star – move outside and look at the stars if it is dark, or watch the sun if it is daylight;

22 December: King of the nations and cornerstone – if your church has a foundation stone, you might move there, or under an arch, remembering that it is the keystone that ensures that the arch stands;

23 December: Emmanuel – the crib.

At each station you might light a candle, say together the words of the antiphon and then, perhaps, the short responsive prayer above.

The antiphons in groups

This fairly simple activity could be undertaken on one of the earlier Sundays in Advent. It might be a useful activity to occupy those not currently involved while a nativity play rehearsal is taking place. Or it might be an activity for a pre-Christmas workshop. You could even undertake this activity in an adult group to create a set of presents for adults to give to their children, grandchildren or neighbours.

A fairly simple version of the activity is provided here but, according to usage, it could be made more detailed and complicated.

You will need:
- seven small envelopes for each person (the kind sometimes called 'wages envelopes' measuring about 10 cm by 7 cm would be ideal);
- templates for the antiphon symbols;
- gold or silver card;
- scissors and pencils;
- hole punch;
- gold or silver thread;
- the words of each antiphon on slips of paper to fit into the envelopes easily (9 cm by 6 cm), either already cut out or typed onto an A4 sheet of paper or card and framed by a border so they are easy to cut out;
- the titles of each antiphon printed either on sticky labels or on strips of paper that could be stuck onto the envelopes.

For the activity

Talk about the antiphons and read them in whatever way is appropriate for your group. You might like to have a ready-made set of cards to use for this. You could look at the symbols and see if anyone can associate any of them with some of the names that we sometimes give to God, before you actually read them.

Draw around the templates onto the gold or silver card and cut out the symbols.

Punch the top of each and thread through some gold or silver thread so that the symbols may be hung up.

Cut out the words of each antiphon from the sheet of words and cut out the names. Match them all together and lay each set on one of the envelopes. Stick the name label on the outside of each envelope and then put the symbols and their matching words into the relevant envelope. You might like to provide a larger envelope or a plastic bag in which to keep each set together. People can then take them home. A way to use these might be that one is opened each night on the relevant date, or they could be set as tiny table presents for a family meal, with individuals opening their envelope and reading out the antiphon before hanging them up or placing them in a Christmas flower arrangement or decoration.

The antiphons at home

You might use the antiphons instead of meal prayers around the dining table, or as a short night-time prayer each evening at bedtime.

You could use seven votive candles in glass jars or a candelabrum with seven candlesticks (or eight, and use the final one on Christmas Eve to welcome the Christ-child). You could decorate each glass jar with the symbol of each antiphon or hang a picture on each candlestick of the candelabrum. Perhaps you could use a different coloured candle for each antiphon: you could have fun deciding together which colour is appropriate for each one. Each day you would light the candle of the antiphons already used, then perhaps read the antiphon together, or in a home where there are very young children, simply use the responsive prayer.

Or you could, perhaps, put up your Christmas tree on 17 December and add the Wisdom picture as the first decoration, using the antiphon or the simple prayer as it is hung on the tree. On each successive day you could add the next picture and say the next antiphon or prayer until all have been hung on the Christmas tree.

If you are a family that sings, you could also sing the hymn 'O come, O come, Emmanuel': even small children will learn the refrain after a few days, so this does not need to exclude small people!

Advent:
The wreath pathway

Introduction

The history of the Advent wreath

North European customs

In the Christian Church, the Advent wreath has been in liturgical use since the nineteenth century, though it had become a well-established Lutheran family custom in the home by the seventeenth century.

However, the roots of the Advent wreath as we know it possibly lie in the ancient pagan practices of bringing evergreens into the home in winter as a symbol of life. The use of evergreens during the winter by pre-Christian Germanic and Scandinavian peoples seems to have been well established. The use of evergreen symbolizing life in the winter darkness is a tangible reminder of hope in the midst of death, and evergreen plants had powerful associations in pagan rituals during the winter months. The church year picks up on these ritual links, which are deeply embedded in the psyche of northern Europeans and reflect justifiable, primitive fears of winter, the dead season. Evergreen provides a symbol of hope that life will continue and, in the end, triumph over decay and death. Light is another symbol closely bound up with these rituals, a reminder of the hope that darkness and death will one day be banished from the earth as the spring returns.

The Christian layer

For Christians there is a link to be made between the idea of life struggling to triumph through the winter darkness, and Christ, the eternal Word, whose coming into this dark world forms the substance of our Advent longings. The candles, rooted in the evergreen wreath, strengthen this image of hope and, as the light grows week by week, reflect the growing expectation as the coming of Christ draws nearer.

Holly used in an Advent wreath has obvious links to the story of salvation, reflected in the ancient carol 'The holly and the ivy'. The circular shape of the wreath might remind us, too, that the seasons we mark are cyclical and dynamic and that God is both beginning and end, whose love and mercy are everlasting.

The increasing light of the wreath, as the candles are added week by week, reflects the penitential aspect of this season: the growing light illuminates the darkness in our hearts and minds (2 Corinthians 4.6), which, if we are to live as lights in the world, we must bring before Christ for his forgiveness and healing.

The beginning of Advent

Some churches bring greenery into the church in a formal way at the beginning of Advent, using it as a symbol of the hope of new life that will come to us in Christ. This may involve a short service, with appropriate Advent Scriptures and prayers as the wreath and other Advent symbols are placed in the worship space.

At home

In the home, the Advent wreath can be an important marker of the beginning of the church year and the movement into the season. If it is made at home, its construction will help to mark the beginning of the season. The wreath can provide a helpful focus for prayer and for the reading of short passages of Scripture when the candles are lit.

Making an Advent wreath

The Advent wreath is usually a circle of greenery with four candles rising from it and a single white candle in the middle. There should be three purple candles, and a pink one for the third Sunday of Advent. The central candle should be white. The candles are lit in the same order each week so, by the fourth week, the candles have burnt down by different amounts, creating a stepped effect. Alternatively, you could use four red candles and a white one.

You can make your own wreath by following the steps below.

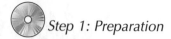 *Step 1: Preparation*

Greenery: Collect a range of suitable greenery. Use strong scissors or some secateurs to help with this. Try to find greenery that is evergreen such as spruce, blue pine, or fir for the base layers. Pine cones or seed pods might be added if desired but there should not be bright berries or flowers, in keeping with the Advent mood of restraint.

Cut the greenery into small branches of an appropriate length. You will need to remove any leaves or spines from the bottom part of the branches so that you can insert them into the wreath. If the wreath is on a tall stand, you may wish to trail greenery such as ivy around the stem of the stand, to the floor.

Candle holders: You can buy plastic candle holders from a craft shop, garden centre or florist. You can also make holders for the candles using strong wire twisted around the base of the candles. You need to be particularly careful that this kind of fitting holds the candles securely because of the fire risk and you will need to make sure that there is no movement of the candles. If you are using a wreath made of wire, wickerwork, sphagnum moss or straw (see below), you can insert nails through the wreath, from the underside up, that are long enough to protrude so as to hold a candle on them. Place the candle holders into the ring at four points spaced at equal distances round it.

Step 2: Choose a base for the wreath

You will need to read through the possible ways to make a wreath described below and, having decided which method is for you, obtain or make a suitable base.

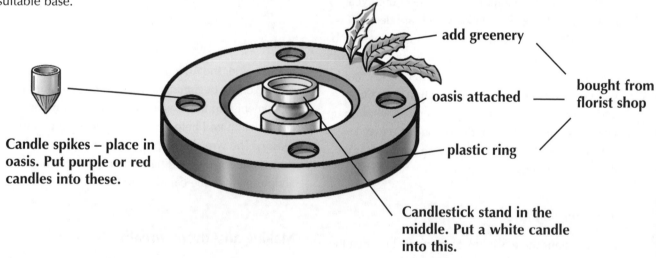

add greenery

bought from florist shop

oasis attached

plastic ring

Candle spikes – place in oasis. Put purple or red candles into these.

Candlestick stand in the middle. Put a white candle into this.

Step 3: Methods

Using a ring of florists' foam

One way to make an Advent wreath is to use florists' foam that has been placed in a plastic ring. You can buy these from florist shops.

Insert four plastic candle spikes into the florists' foam rather than pushing the candles themselves in.

Arrange your greenery so that it entirely covers the foam and its plastic casing. Place the candles in their spikes. Stand the wreath on a flat surface and add the white candle in a suitable candlestick in the centre.

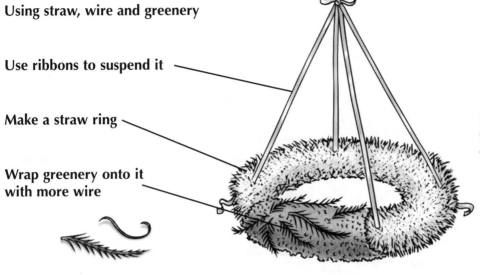

Using straw, wire and greenery

Use ribbons to suspend it

Make a straw ring

Wrap greenery onto it with more wire

Buy candle spikes to hold the candles. Fix these on with some more wire.

USING A WROUGHT IRON ADVENT WREATH CANDLE HOLDER

There are also purpose-made wrought iron Advent candle rings available from church suppliers. If you use one of these, you will need to find a way to add the greenery. You could perhaps stand it on a tray or a flower pedestal with a large tray fixed to the top and surround it with pieces of florist's foam. Then add your greenery to the foam, arranging it so that it follows the circular shape of the candle stand. Holly, ivy and other broadleaved evergreens work well for this sort of ring.

Start with a wicker ring. Then either weave the greenery into this, or bind soaked sphagnum moss onto it with wire.

Then wrap some greenery (cypress, pine or yew) onto this with more wire.

USING A WIRE, WICKER OR SPHAGNUM MOSS RING

It may also be possible to buy a ring framework from a florist shop: these are made of wire or basket reeds and form a good framework on which to fix your greenery. The very adventurous or talented could make their own base ring. Straw might also be used, wrapped in wire. It forms a good shape but don't forget that it could catch light very easily. Another possibility is to soak sphagnum moss and then wrap it in plastic bound with wire. This tends to drip quite a lot at first. Conversely, you will need frequently to spray a wreath that has a wire or wicker base with a good deal of water to keep in looking fresh.

Greenery can be bound to the ring using fine florists' wire or natural green string. Pine, yew, eucalyptus or cypresses work particularly well for this sort of ring, producing a smooth finish. This is the best way to make a ring that is to be suspended and you can make something really large in this manner. With a really large ring you can add candles that are larger in diameter and so burn more slowly. You will need to find a way to bind candle saucers on to the resulting ring and this can be done with wire or string.

ADVENT

Using a bought wreath

Some florists sell ready-made wreaths that come complete with greenery, but this takes away from some of the ritual activity surrounding the making and placing of the wreath in the home. You could also use a simple arrangement of five candles in suitable holders, perhaps interlaced with some suitable greenery.

A suspended wreath

Some church suppliers make hanging versions of the wrought iron wreath for use in church buildings. You can also suspend a wreath made of straw or wire using strong ribbons. You might want to consider the use of purple ribbons wound around the chain or rope for hanging the wreath. These ribbons could be changed for other seasonally appropriate coloured ribbons at Christmas and Epiphany.

Practical inclusive ideas

Location of the wreath

Ensure that the wreath is visible to most of the worshippers in the church. It needs to be big enough to be seen and set in a space where it can be a focus. During Advent the wreath will be a particular focus. You may want to move it at Christmas to stand beside a crib in a way that draws attention to the holy family but, for Advent, the wreath, with its candles marking the passing of the weeks, demands attention for itself.

A suspended wreath

If there is a facility for suspending a huge wreath overhead, then this could make a dramatic focal point, a kind of Advent crown. If this is done then, for health and safety reasons, the candles would not necessarily be included on the wreath itself. You might consider using four floor-standing candlesticks instead or a simple set of candle holders could be placed in front of the lectern from which the Advent wreath prayers would then be said. If you have a large crossing space, you might wish to place four floor-standing candle holders at the 'corners' of the crossing space and the prayers could then be said from these points.

 There are photographs of the making of an Advent wreath on the CD-ROM.

In using the wreath liturgically in church, several things are important to remember. The wreath needs to be large enough, placed high enough and be positioned in such a way as to make visual appeal and to create liturgical significance. All too often the Advent wreath is a kind of 'extra' in the service and its place never firmly established within the liturgical space. As with all symbolic aspects of liturgy, if something is significant, then its positioning and the connected actions are as important as the words or prayers being said.

Space and absence

It is also important to take seriously the idea of Advent being a stripped back season and to think through how this might translate into spatial arrangements and the environment for worship. Remove clutter and refrain from the use of flowers. Remove banners – if these are part of your tradition. Keep the liturgy, and the space in which it is enacted, unencumbered and sparse. All these things can help to add to the feeling of restraint that is suitable for the season and can help to provide a contrast to the celebration to come at Christmas. If you have a Christmas tree and it arrives well before Christmas, think about where this is placed so that it does not acquire quasi-sacramental status within the liturgical space.

Lighting

If you have spotlights in the church, you might want to arrange these in such a way as to direct attention to the Advent wreath, or use floor-standing spots. In terms of the main lighting of the church, you might wish to use a mauve/purple filter to give a hint of the seasonal colour. (You would then change this coloured filter as you move into the seasons of Christmas and Epiphany.)

How to light the candles

Practical matters need consideration also.
- Who will light the candle?
- Where will the light be taken from? (This says a great deal about how the congregation will receive the significance of the symbolism here.)
- Who says the prayer? Can this person be seen and will there be adequate amplification? At

what point during the liturgy will the candle be lit? Liturgically, there are choices to be made about this and the choices made have an effect on the style and type of prayer that may then be most appropriate.

For example, suitable places might be:

- Immediately after the words of greeting as part of the gathering, providing focus and creating a scene- and mood-setting function linked to the readings.
- Before the Peace, which would require a scriptural sentence and focus as a lead in to the Peace and would suggest an emphasis on the peace Christ comes to bring.

Using the wreath liturgically – suggested prayers around the wreath in Advent

The first and second prayers provided for each of the Sundays in Advent may be used if the wreath candles are lit after the Greeting. The third prayer provided for each of the Sundays in Advent may be used before the Peace.

The First Sunday of Advent

We light this light in the name of the everlasting Word –
stilling chaos, forming the earth and calling forth light
*   from darkness.*
Alpha and Omega, author and ending of all that is made,
now yearning for the birth of a new creation,
fill us with longing for all things to be restored
and speak the hope of the kingdom deep in our hearts;
that as we wait for your purpose to be revealed
we may live each day in the light of your coming;
so your glory may be seen in all the earth.
O God, who in Christ makes all things new by the
*   Spirit's power,*
our hope is in you for ever.
Amen.

We give thanks today for the world that we know,
and offer our need for fresh hope and new life.
God who is beginning and ending,
creator of known and unimagined worlds;
give us hope to believe that you make all things new
and courage to live in the light of this promise.
Amen.

People of God: awake!
The day is coming soon
when you shall see God face to face.
Remember the ways and the works of God.

God calls you out of darkness
to walk in the light of his coming.
You are God's children.
Lord, make us one as we walk with Christ
**   today and for ever.**
Amen.

[T&S 51]

RESPONSIVE PRAYER FOR ADVENT SUNDAY

(This prayer might be used before the Prayer of Preparation.)

Save us, O God, when we call upon you.
Let your mercy fall like rain!

Lord of all, king of Glory,
hear the cry of your people!
Save us, O God, when we call upon you.
Let your mercy fall like rain!

Cover our sinfulness
and humble our pride.
Save us, O God, when we call upon you.
Let your mercy fall like rain!

Sweep over the nations
and pour out your justice.
Save us, O God, when we call upon you.
Let your mercy fall like rain!

Enter into our loneliness
and breathe comfort in our despair.
Save us, O God, when we call upon you.
Let your mercy fall like rain!

Rekindle our longing for you
and awaken our hope in your kingdom.
Save us, O God, when we call upon you.
Let your mercy fall like rain!

Turn to us and let your face shine upon us;
restore us to your favour and bless us.
Save us, O God, when we call upon you.
Let your mercy fall like rain!
Amen.

The Second Sunday of Advent

We light this light in the name of the Word of truth,
a voice that cries in the desert wind and the
*   wilderness,*
calling us to return to you with all our hearts.
Open up a straight path into our lives
and judge us with justice and mercy, O God,

that knowing ourselves welcomed in love by you,
we may reach out to the least and the lost
as a sign to the world that you are our God.
O God, who in Christ calls us and brings us home,
in the Spirit's freedom,
our hope is in you for ever!
Amen.

We give thanks today for truth spoken and lived,
for the lone voice in the wilderness, which calls us
    back to you;
for the story of God's people and all who speak of
    peace –
crying out for justice and standing for the right.
O God, make plain the road that leads to you;
guide our feet into your ways whatever the cost
and turn us from darkness to walk in your light.
Amen.

People of God: return!
You are called to be God's own.
From the mountains announce the good news.
God comes in justice and peace,
to all who follow his ways.
You are God's children.
Lord, make us one in the peace of Christ
today and for ever.
Amen.

[T&S 53]

The Third Sunday of Advent

We light this light in the name of the word of grace;
burning with fire in the mouth of the prophets
to renew our lives in the love of God.
Take away judgement, O God our Redeemer.
Give us joy instead of mourning
and restore your image in us;
that we may shine with your glory and know you as
    the one who saves
and, bearing the fruits of true repentance,
may speak the good news of your coming with great
    rejoicing.
O God, who in Christ comes to save,
in the strength of the Spirit,
our hope is in you for ever!
Amen.

We give thanks today for the love of our God,
for love which knows us, forgives us and heals;
for love which delights in us and brings us back home;
which knows the world's sorrow and stands with us
    there.

Give us courage and grace to live lives of love;
bearing witness to God who makes all things whole.
Amen.

People of God: be glad!
Your God delights in you,
giving you joy for sadness
and turning the dark to light.
Be strong in hope therefore;
for your God comes to save.
You are God's children.
Lord, make us one in the love of Christ
today and for ever.
Amen.

[T&S 52]

RESPONSIVE PRAYER FOR THE THIRD SUNDAY OF ADVENT:
GAUDETE SUNDAY

Rejoice in the Lord always
He has done great things for us!

The Lord has taken away judgement:
He has done great things for us!

The Lord will bring comfort to those who mourn:
He has done great things for us!

Our hope is in the Lord:
He has done great things for us!

The Lord gives freedom to those held captive:
He has done great things for us!

The Lord gives justice to the oppressed:
He has done great things for us!

Rejoice in the Lord always:
He has done great things for us!
Amen.

The Fourth Sunday of Advent

We light a light in the name of the word of life;
the everlasting God, who called worlds into being
    and stars beyond all number.
He it is who loves us, counts the hairs of our head
    and calls us each by name
and will bring us home, gathering us in his arms as a
    mother gathers her children.
O Emmanuel, whose coming was announced in the
    message of the angel;
make us alive to your presence and ready to receive
    you;
that as we hear your voice we may, like Mary, say
    'yes' to you

and be bearers of the word to a world in waiting.
O God, who in Christ will exult over us with singing,
in the joy of the Spirit, our hope is in you for ever!
Amen.

O Emmanuel: come to your world;
and come to your people who wait for you!
Teach us to see and to believe
the signs of your life already here.
Teach us to work, teach us to hope;
living in the light of the kingdom today.
Amen.

People of God: prepare!
God, above all, maker of all,
is one with us in Christ.
Maranatha!
Come, Lord Jesus!

God, the mighty God,
bends down in love to earth.
Maranatha!
Come, Lord Jesus!

God with us, God beside us,
comes soon to the world he has made.
Maranatha!
Come, Lord Jesus!

We are God's children,
we seek the coming Christ.
Maranatha!
Come, Lord Jesus!

[T&S 54]

The wreath in groups

Children

It can be difficult to introduce children to the idea of Advent as a season in its own right. So much of contemporary culture and the run-up to Christmas militates against an understanding of Advent as a waiting time and a time for reflecting on our deepest hopes and dreams. It is a good idea then to spend some time and energy in preparing a space – both physical and emotional – in which the work of this season can take place and which feels distinctive from the tinsel-clad anticipation of Christmas.

The ideas below provide the basis for a session lasting about an hour for each of the weeks of Advent. Each session concludes with a response time in which the children should be provided with a variety of art and craft materials and invited to use them to respond in

any way they wish to the teaching and worship session they have just experienced.

Week 1: Space, symbol, image and silence

PREPARATION

A good deal of this session will be preparing the space where you normally meet so that Advent may be kept there. Resist the temptation to prepare the space before the children arrive, as the work of the week is to get ready.

Nevertheless, you will need to prepare carefully, otherwise chaos will ensue! Be sure you know what you want moved to where and make yourself a list of instructions so you know exactly what you are asking people to do. Do not worry if this is all you do in this session. This is your work today.

YOU WILL NEED

- a table to become a focal table;
- at least one purple cloth – if you get hold of more, use them;
- an Advent wreath, or the materials to make one: a framework, three purple and one pink candle and a white one, or four red and one white;
- a single big, white, candle;
- a hanging wreath, if you prefer this (details of how to make an Advent wreath are on page 33–5);
- some little silver or gold stars or a tube of glitter.

CLEAR THE SPACE

Preparing the space may become an activity in its own right. During the session you will clear the room where the children meet of as much clutter as possible and re-order the space to make a clear focal point. The focal point itself is of particular interest during this season. Just as the season itself is marked by absence and longing for what is not yet, so too should the spatial adornments, symbols and images be used to reflect a sense of absence, and even of emptiness, rather than of presence. You will need to create a plan for clearing the space so that each child knows what his or her task is.

THE FOCAL TABLE

The principal colour in your cleared space should be purple. A purple cloth can be used to cover a focal table. Place your wreath either on the table or a large

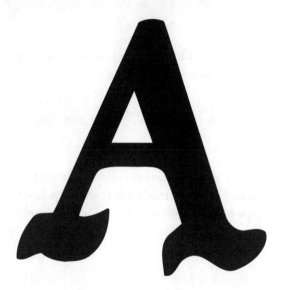

stand. If your wreath is on a stand, then purple drapes could be added week on week.

Add also:

- An open Bible, placed on a cushion or stand, suggesting the story of God's people recorded for us in the pages of Scripture and the story of salvation, of which we are a part;
- A candle representing the light of Christ;
- Alpha and Omega symbols to remind the group of God who is beginning and ending (see illustration);
- Pictures: for the first three weeks of Advent you may wish to select a different picture each week to reflect either the Old Testament reading or the Gospel reading. Alternatively, you could use a picture that reflects and illuminates the idea you are exploring on each occasion. You might be able to use an icon: for example, the icon of the Holy Trinity by Andrei Rublev is a richly evocative focus suggesting something of the mystery of God who is relationship and the opening out of that relationship to include us and all of creation as suggested by the open space at the front of the icon. On the fourth Sunday of Advent, use a picture of Mary. A wide and diverse range of images can be found at www.biblia.com/mary.
- If you can find a way to hang a wreath (no candles) suspended by purple ribbons over the focal table, that would also add to the significance of the table. Week by week, instead of lighting candles, a star could be hung over the wreath ring to represent one of the hopes of the Advent season. The stars could be made simply by cutting out star shapes from stiff card and covering them with foil or similar. You should be able to buy silver card from art shops. Punch a small hole in the top of the star. Use a piece of wire 45 cm long to make an attachment. Put one end of the wire through the hole and twist round itself to make it secure. Shape the other end into a hook to hang over your

wreath. It may be possible to devise a temporary 'washing line' between two points in the room (above a door or window, for example), from which to hang the wreath and the star.

TALK TOGETHER

Once your space is prepared, sit down in a circle around the focal table and discuss the space. What do people like best? Does anyone feel that there is anything missing? What might be added? Can anything be taken away? Decide together if you would like to make any adjustments.

KEEP SILENCE TOGETHER

Try to allow more opportunity for silence in the group since this is in keeping with the overall mood of the season. If it is not your usual practice to include silence, perhaps this is an opportunity to try it. Sit in a circle around the focal table. Before you begin, make sure your children know the prayer response 'Lord, in your mercy, hear our prayer'. If this is not familiar to them, either practise it once or twice or use some words that are more familiar. Light the first candle on the wreath and also the large candle representing the light of Christ. If you have a hanging wreath, hang on the first star.

Ask the children to cup their hands then, very deliberately, move around the circle and give each child a few little shiny stars or a pinch of glitter. Turn off the electric lights in the room. Ask the children to hold stars or glitter very carefully in their cupped hands and to imagine that these represent their prayers or their deepest longings for the world. Ask them to think for a moment what these might be and to keep silence, holding these prayers gently and carefully in their hands.

After a few moments (you will need to judge yourself how long is appropriate) say 'Lord in your mercy' and encourage the children to reply 'Hear our prayer'. Invite the children then, one at a time, to place the stars or glitter on the purple cloth around the Alpha and Omega.

The response time

If there is still time, you might want to think about ways of allowing children time to respond to God in a variety of ways. Provide a variety of materials and give the children time to use these in whatever way they choose, to respond to the space they have created and the prayers they have offered.

Week 2: A world made new and the hope of a saviour

Preparation

This session focuses on the penitential aspects of Advent and seeks to wonder at the gifts of God in creation while recognizing the kinds of temptation we all face in our everyday lives, and particularly in the challenges posed to us by the materialism that surrounds Christmas. Don't be afraid of challenging and unresolved discussion: this is the stuff of which theology is made. We are teaching our children not to be afraid to face hard questions.

You will need

- The focal table that you created last week.
- A picture of the earth from space or another picture of the globe or the world. A search on the Internet will supply this if you do not have anything to hand.
- A pile of advertisements – collect the junk mail you receive for a few weeks or cut advertisements out of newspapers and magazines.
- The poster that was to have been used by the Churches' Advertising Network for their
- Christmas campaign in 2001. It can be found at www.churchads.org.uk/Christmas2001.html.
- Sufficient large pebbles for everyone to have one.

The Gathering

Sit down in a circle around the focal table. Talk about the week you have each had, and perhaps sing together. Then light two lights on your Advent wreath and the candle representing the light of Christ and hang a second star on your hanging wreath if you have one.

Talk together

Tell the creation story or read a version from a children's Bible or a picture book. There are suggestions for suitable books in the Resources section.

Place a picture of the earth from space, or a simple picture of the world, in front of the focal table, where all can see it.

Ask the children:

> What do they like best about the picture?
> What did they like best about the story?
> How has the earth been spoilt?

Give the children a large pebble each, to hold in their cupped hands and ask them to imagine that what they are cradling in their hands is the whole world. What would they each like to do to help make it a better place now? Keep silence for a few moments and, this time, share your ideas together.

Discuss why this might be difficult. Now place over the pictures of the earth a pile of advertisements: you can use junk mail that has come during the week, pages torn from colour supplements and so on.

Try to use advertising targeted at a variety of age groups. Then place beside this the picture of two children surrounded by presents from the Churches' Advertising Network web site. Talk together about why it so hard to resist always wanting more things. Talk about the slogan on the advert 'What would love do now?' This is a hard question and there is no right answer. Many adults were frightened of this picture when it was first published. But just have a discussion about it – you don't have to reach any conclusion, and disagreement is fine.

Saying sorry – prayer of penitence

Then use the following prayers from the Advent confession section in *Times and Seasons*.

A voice cries out in the wilderness, 'Make straight the way of the Lord.' So let us listen, and turn to the Lord in penitence and faith.

John 1.23

Lord Jesus, you came to gather the nations into the peace of your kingdom:
Lord, have mercy.
Lord, have mercy.

You come in word and sacrament to strengthen us in holiness:

Christ, have mercy.
Christ, have mercy.

You will come in glory
with salvation for your people:
Lord, have mercy.
Lord, have mercy.

[T&S 35]

THE RESPONSE TIME

Share the Peace with one another before you leave. If there is time available, invite the children to use the creative materials in whatever way they like to respond to the ideas they have explored, as they did last week.

Week 3: Come, Emmanuel

PREPARATION

This session explores the idea that we are each precious to God, who says, 'Do not fear, for I have redeemed you. I have called you by name, you are mine.' (Isaiah 43.1) It then goes on to explore some of the names attributed to God and celebrated in the coming of the Messiah, which are celebrated in the Advent antiphons identifying the symbols associated with these.

YOU WILL NEED
- Pieces of card which have on them the names of the children who will be present. Take some spare pieces in case you get any newcomers or visitors. On the reverse of each card, write the meaning of the name. Many Internet sites provide the meaning of names, and there are names from many cultures and traditions. If you have children whose names you cannot find, it might be worth contacting their parents to see if they can help. If there is a language problem, parents may be able to undertake the required search for you.
- Tiny model figures: they could be pieces out of a game, Godly Play 'People of God' figures or toy people from children's construction sets – it really doesn't matter
- Symbols of the Advent Antiphons and the meaning of these (see the Advent Antiphons section on page 29).

THE GATHERING

Sit down in a circle around the focal table. Talk about the week you have each had, and perhaps sing together. Then light three lights on your Advent wreath and the candle representing the light of Christ and hang a third star on your hanging wreath if you have one.

Talk together and explore names: set down in front of the focal table some small cards on which you have written the names of the children present.

On the back of the card, have the meaning of their name written. Invite the children to select their card and turn it over. Work out together, if necessary, that what is on the back of the card is the meaning of their name. Little ones may need help with reading. Discuss whether there are any surprises: some children will be aware of the meaning of their name but many probably won't be. Discuss how people feel about the meaning of their name: glad, surprised, not very pleased and so on. Do any know how their family came to choose their name? Again, some children may know and some may not. Some may be called after an ancestor, some after a hero, some because their family liked the name.

Give everyone a little model person. Ask all the children to cup their hands and hold the little figure in their cupped hands. Keep a moment of silence and ask people to look at their little figure and care for him or her during the silence. Suggest that they use the silence to choose a name for their figure. When you end the silence, go round the group and ask each person to name his or her figure, saying 'This is N'. Talk about how easy or difficult it was to choose the name. Choosing names is a big responsibility.

WE ARE EACH PRECIOUS

Ask people to hold their little person carefully in their hands once more and read to them these words from the prophet Isaiah: God says, 'Do not fear, for I have redeemed you. I have called you by name, you are mine.'

THE ADVENT ANTIPHONS
- Wisdom
- Adonai
- Root of Jesse
- Key of David
- Morning Star
- King of the nations
- Emmanuel (which means God with us)

Read out the list slowly and suggest that people look at the symbols as you read them. Then ask people if they can match any of the names to the symbols. Some are easy and will be done immediately. Others are more difficult and some help may be needed. You may all have to work together with clues to solve the last ones. When you have matched up the symbols with the names you could hang the hanging symbols on the hanging wreath, or lay them around the wreath on the table, together with the Alpha and Omega symbols. You might like to sing the well-known Advent hymn 'O come, O come, Emmanuel'. Even if you cannot sing all of it, children will enjoy the chorus. Maybe older children could sing a verse or two.

THE RESPONSE TIME

Share the Peace with one another before you leave. If there is time available, invite the children to use the creative materials in whatever way they like to respond to the ideas they have explored, as they did last week.

Week 4: The promise God made to us

PREPARATION

This session explores the traditional subject of the fourth Sunday of Advent, the Annunciation to Mary.

YOU WILL NEED

One big picture of Mary and a sufficient number of small ones for each child to have one (though in the end they may share if more than one child chooses the same picture). If you don't have pictures available, find them on the Internet, using a search engine and then print them off. If you don't have a colour printer, persuade a friend to help.

THE GATHERING

Sit down in a circle around the focal table. Talk about the week you have each had, and perhaps sing together. Then light four lights on your Advent wreath and the candle representing the light of Christ and hang a fourth star on your hanging wreath if you have one.

TALK TOGETHER

Place a picture of Mary in front of the focal table. You may like to use an icon if you are able to obtain one. Talk about the picture before you. What do people like about it? Is there anything that is puzzling? Is there anything they don't like about it?

Put down some more pictures of Mary and invite the

children to spend a bit of time looking at them, then ask them to choose the one they like best. If more than one person selects the same picture, invite them to sit together and share the picture.

Read the story of the Annunciation to Mary from Luke's Gospel (Luke 1.26-38). You may prefer to read the story from a children's Bible or picture book.

REFLECT TOGETHER

Ask the children to think about the story for a moment or two in silence while they look at the picture they have chosen. Then discuss the question 'I wonder what it would be like to be really close to an angel?'

PRAY TOGETHER

Say this prayer:
Lord Jesus, light of the world,
blessed is Gabriel, who brought good news;
blessed is Mary, your mother and ours.
Bless your Church preparing for Christmas;
and bless us your children, who long for your
**   coming.**
Amen.

[T&S 54]

THE RESPONSE TIME

Share the Peace with one another before you leave. If there is time available, invite the children to use the creative materials in whatever way they like to respond to the ideas they have explored, as they did last week.

Adults

The material below is provided for a group session lasting between an hour and an hour and a half.

Session 1: Things hoped for …

Scripture references:

> Hebrews 11.1-3
> Isaiah 2.1-5 (set for the First Sunday of Advent, Year A)
> Isaiah 64.1-9 (set for the First Sunday of Advent, Year B)

PREPARATION

- Gather together a selection of advertisements and news stories.

- Create a focal table in the room where the group meets. Use the colour purple and perhaps some black cloth with silver thread in it. Place the wreath on this.
- For the worship you will need either sticky notes or cut-out star shapes in two different colours, and pens, crayons and/or pencils.
- Matches.

FOR DISCUSSION

Look at the advertisements. Consider together what the subliminal messages of these advertisements are. What are the longings and cravings of the human heart that the products say they can satisfy? What do the advertisements reveal about human nature, about us?

How easy is it to long for God in a culture so used to easy access and swift results?

Look at some of the news stories of the week. How do God's desires and human impulses and motivations differ?

FOR GROUP MEMBERS TO THINK ABOUT

Where do we long to see:

the peace of God?

the hope of God's kingdom?

the joy of God?

the judgement of God?

STUDY THE BIBLE

Read aloud two of the passages suggested for this week.

How do they make us question contemporary assumptions and address the longing we have for the kingdom of God?

WORSHIP

Give each person two sticky notes or two stars. On one of the sticky notes or stars, invite group members to write or to draw a hope for themselves or those close to them. On the other, invite them to write or draw a hope for the world in which we live.

Then light the first candle on the wreath, and say the following:

Leader: We hold before God our own hopes and dreams and we commit them tonight/today into his care and keeping.

Members of the group lay notes or stars around the wreath.
Keep silence.

Leader: We hold before God our hopes and dreams for the world of his making and ask for his saving hand to bless all that speaks of his kingdom and his ways.

Members of the group lay second notes or stars around the wreath.
Keep silence.

Leader: Let us bless the Lord.

All: Thanks be to God.

Session 2: With righteousness he shall judge the poor; every valley shall be lifted up

Scripture references

Luke 1.46-55, The Magnificat;

Matthew 5.1-12, The Beatitudes.

PREPARATION

You will need:
- pieces of card that are about postcard size and pens or pencils for everyone;
- the Advent wreath;
- purple material and a piece of sackcloth or hessian;
- matches.

FOR DISCUSSION

Give people cards and ask them to write on them in letters large enough for everyone to read:
- words or phrases describing situations that involve injustice;
- slogans they remember from groups or organizations campaigning for justice both today and in the past.

When everyone is ready, put the cards down where all can see them and discuss together what you see.

STUDY THE BIBLE

Read the Bible passages aloud.

The teachings of Jesus presented to us in these challenging statements are about our values and the values of the kingdom of God. What Jesus says is important in our behaviour and attitudes is not what society may be saying: for example, God's kingdom is in the hands of the powerless and the poor. Each Beatitude invites us to turn our usual values upside down.

Where does this sit with the Advent Scriptures about the justice of God?

Who is God's justice for?

WORSHIP

Use a piece of sackcloth with the purple cloth for today's worship. Light two candles on the wreath.

Read Matthew 5.3-10 out loud, slowly.

Say a prayer for those whom the group has identified as the poor in spirit, those who mourn today. You might like to use the following words:

Leader: We pray for all those who feel that they are not wanted in the kingdom of God, and for all who feel rejected.
All: God says that the kingdom is for you.

Leader: We pray for all those who are alone or bereaved and for those who cannot love themselves.
All: God says that the kingdom is for you.

Leader: We pray for those who search for God and who don't give up the search.
All: God says that the kingdom is for you.

Leader: We pray for those who put themselves at risk to make peace.
All: God says that the kingdom is for you.

Leader: We pray that we would work to build your kingdom and that we would welcome all those who seek you just as we have been welcomed by you. This we ask in the name of Christ, who came in search of us to bring us home and who will one day gather all creation to himself.
All: Amen.

Session 3: The voice crying in the wilderness

Scripture references:
- Luke 1.67-79: Zechariah's prophecy concerning John the Baptist and Jesus;
- Matthew 3.1-12: John the Baptist.

PREPARATION

You will need:
- the Advent wreath;
- a small collection of pebbles;
- pens and writing paper;
- matches.

FOR DISCUSSION

Whom do we admire and why?

What is a prophet?

What things do you think are wrong with the world today?

What part can we as individuals and as church do to live out the values of the kingdom of God?

Who do you think are the prophets of our day and what are the things they stand for?

STUDY THE BIBLE

John the Baptist was known as the forerunner – the one who told people that Jesus would come and that they should make themselves ready for his coming. He preached a hard message of God's judgement, telling people to repent. Later, John's no-compromise stand against sin got him into trouble. He was put into prison for criticizing the lifestyle of the ruler and he was later beheaded.

Read today's passages out loud.

FOR DISCUSSION
- What things do you think we should speak out against and when do you think it is best to keep quiet?
- How far should we go in standing up for what we believe?
- How can living in community in the Church be an important witness in the world today?
- What kind of prophetic voice should or could the Church have today?

WORSHIP
- Surround the wreath today with stones to symbolize the wilderness, and pens and letter-writing paper as a symbol of protest.
- Light three candles on the Advent wreath.
- Pray for each other that you might be faithful in preparing the way of Christ and living in the light of the kingdom.

You may like to say:

We light this light in the name of the word of grace; burning with fire in the mouth of the prophets to renew our lives in the love of God. Take away judgement, O God our Redeemer. Give us joy instead of mourning and restore your image in us; that we may shine with your glory and know you as

the one who saves
and, bearing the fruits of true repentance,
may speak the good news of your coming with great rejoicing.
O God, who in Christ comes to save,
in the strength of the Spirit,
our hope is in you for ever!
Amen.

End by saying the Lord's Prayer together.

Session 4: Come, Lord, come!

SCRIPTURE REFERENCE

Luke 1.26-38; 2.1-20.

PREPARATION

You will need:
- the Advent wreath;
- pictures of angels (see below);
- straw;
- matches.

For this session, you will need to identify and obtain some pictures of angels.

You can find the paintings listed below at www.nationalgallery.co.uk:

Fra Filippo Lippi: *The Annunciation;*

Carlo Crivelli: *The Annunciation with St Emidius;*

Duccio: *The Annunciation;*

Geertgen tot Sint Jans: *Nativity at Night;*

Rembrandt: *The Adoration of the Shepherds;*

Le Nain Brothers: *The Adoration of the Shepherds.*

Or you could use Christmas cards that have already arrived featuring the Annunciation and Nativity.

You might also use images from the CMS resource packs: *The Christ We Share* and *Born Among Us* (see Resources for more details).

An image search on any search engine should also yield results.

FOR DISCUSSION

Spread a variety of images of angels out on the floor. Ask members of the group to choose an image they feel interested in or drawn to and then ask them to reflect on this image in pairs or in the whole group.

Some questions for consideration:

1. What aspect of God do these images of angels represent?
2. What is surprising in any of these images?
3. What do you notice about the figures depicted in the picture, their arrangement and posture? Is there anything particularly noticeable about them?
4. Which image are you drawn to and why? Which image do you have questions about?
5. Is there any image that makes you feel uncomfortable?

STUDY THE BIBLE

Read aloud the passages from Luke and then, in the light of hearing the Scriptures afresh, reconsider the pictures you have been looking at. Is there anything that surprises you?

WORSHIP

Surround the wreath today with angels and straw. Light four candles on the Advent wreath.

Give thanks for messengers and messages:
- for the letters and cards we have received, with news of friends near and far away, as Christmas approaches;
- for those who first told us of the birth of Christ.

Pray for those who share the good news now:
- for all those who will be involved in religious broadcasting at Christmas;
- for those who will write newspaper and magazine articles published in the coming week;
- for all who will participate in Christmas worship.

You may like to say:
We light a light in the name of the word of life;
the everlasting God, who called worlds into being
* and stars beyond all number.*
He it is who loves us, counts the hairs of our head
* and calls us each by name*
and will bring us home, gathering us in his arms as a
* mother gathers her children.*
O Emmanuel, whose coming was announced in the
* message of the angel;*
make us alive to your presence and ready to receive
* you;*
that as we hear your voice we may, like Mary, say
* 'yes' to you*
and be bearers of the word to a world in waiting.

O God, who in Christ will exult over us with singing, in the joy of the Spirit, our hope is in you for ever!

Amen.

Conclude by saying the Grace together.

The wreath at home

Make a focal point in the home on which to place the Advent wreath or the symbols of the season that you have chosen to use. Use a piece of purple cloth on which to place the wreath. If you are living with other people, decide together where the wreath should be placed.

You can buy wreaths ready made in many florists but you might want to make your own. (For instructions, see pages 33–5.)

Use one of the prayers to say as the candles are lit each week – the third prayer in the sets is probably the most appropriate. Try to find a regular time to light the candle and say the prayer.

You might also want to make a prayer space in your home for the Advent period and try to make a time for quiet reflection and prayer each day or at least once each week.

Later in Advent the names of God feature in the O Antiphons and in the well-known Advent hymn 'O come, O come, Emmanuel'. You might like to write these names of God on silver card and place them around the wreath as the prayer is said on the Sunday following 17 December. See page 29.

The wreath in outreach

The cry for justice echoes through the Scriptures of the season. How might we respond and take up the cry: 'How long, O Lord, how long?'

Some ideas

- In small groups or as a whole church, you might like to consider taking up one of the places or peoples who are in need of demonstrable justice today.
- You might want to consider the plight of oppressed peoples in the world and make it a task to discover more about the organizations that are working to make the world a more just and equitable place.

- People sometimes say, 'Christmas is for children'. Make this a reality by focusing on the children who are most vulnerable, for example those who spend their lives as runaways on the streets. This is a concern in the UK as well as in countries of the developing world. The Children's Society has worked for some years on the issue of runaways in the UK.
- You may wish to find out about children orphaned by AIDS, children sold into slavery by parents living in massive poverty, children who run away to escape brutality at home. Your local Mothers' Union branch may work to support a women's refuge and, particularly at Christmas, to provide presents for children staying there. The Children's Society, Christian Aid, Oxfam, Save the Children and UNICEF all have projects that will provide information and which need support. (See www.childrenssociety.org.uk, www.christianaid.org.uk, www.oxfam.org, www.savethechildren.org.uk, www.unicef.org.).
- Some organizations have separate sites for children and young people so this thinking and reflection can be an all-age concern.
- Make it an Advent project to find a way, as a community, to support one of these projects financially so that you are 'buying presents' for children at Christmas.
- You might want to focus on fairly traded goods. Both Oxfam and Traidcraft have a wide range of Christmas goods. Organize a shopping trip to Oxfam, invite a Traidcraft representative to bring Christmas goods, both food and gifts, to sell after an Advent service or get some catalogues to circulate and organize the purchase of fair trade Christmas shopping. Most of the materials needed to make an Advent wreath would be available in an Oxfam shop, so maybe you could use a wreath made from Oxfam materials as an advertisement for what you can buy. You would need to do this before Advent begins, of course.
- You might wish to practise simple hospitality during this season – rather than a full-blown two or three course meal, maybe a simple lunch could be offered instead after one of the Sunday services.

Advent:
The crib pathway

Introduction

How the crib came to be

On Christmas Eve 1223 in the Italian town of Greccio, St Francis instituted the tradition of creating a crib as the focus for worship on the Feast of the Nativity. As the parishioners gathered, they found themselves facing a cave in which there were living animals, just as there might have been in the stable at Bethlehem. And in a manger, a carving of an infant was laid. As St Francis retold it, the Christmas story was brought to life before the eyes of those who were gathered to celebrate the birth of the Saviour.

Since that time, cribs have gradually become part of the Christmas celebrations in most Christian traditions. The presence of a crib is a visual reminder of the Incarnation and Christ's presence with us. Building up the crib during Advent gives a visual focus to the sense of preparation for which this season calls. Placing the Christ-child in the manger on Christmas Day celebrates the Incarnation. At Epiphany, the Magi arrive at the stable (though they may have been making their way across the room or church throughout Advent) and replace the shepherds. Retaining the crib scene until Candlemas reminds us that Christmas is not just for a day but a whole season.

Choosing and setting up a crib

Choosing a crib needs careful consideration.

In a church setting you might want to consider:
- How faithfully do the figures reflect the Holy Family and how will they communicate to and reflect the community for whom they are to be a focus?
- Is the Christ-child a separate figure that can be placed in the manger on Christmas Day?
- Can the figures be easily seen? Are they an appropriate size for the setting?
- Where will the crib scene be located? Will all ages be able to see it, or will small children have to be lifted up?

- Might it be possible and appropriate to create a life-size scene using papier mâché models or tailors' dummies?
- Whether people will be allowed to handle the figures. If they will, then they need to be sturdy enough to withstand this.
- Would it be helpful to provide prayers that people can use as they contemplate the crib scene?

At home you might want to consider:
- Making your own crib scene rather than buying one.
- Where your crib will be placed – perhaps next to an Advent candle or calendar, or in a well-lit window where it can be seen by people outside as well as those in the house.
- Placing the crib against a purple background (cloth or cardboard) during Advent and changing the background to gold or white for Christmas.
- The sturdiness of the figures – will they withstand being handled by children in the household and those who might visit?
- Placing a basket of prayer cards near the crib to be used when figures are added to the scene throughout the season.
- Creating additional figures to add to the crib, representing family and friends.
- Allowing the three wise men (the Magi) to journey through the various rooms of the house during Advent until they reach the crib at Epiphany.

A suggested order for building up the crib scene at church or home

The First Sunday of Advent: Stable and innkeeper.

The Second Sunday of Advent: Shepherds and animals.

The Third Sunday of Advent: Angels.

The Fourth Sunday of Advent: Mary and Joseph.

Christmas Day: The Christ-child.

Epiphany: Remove the shepherds. Add the Magi (the three wise men) and the star.

Candlemas: Remove the Magi. Change the stable into the Temple. To do this you will need to remove the stable building, the manger and the animals. In church you could move the figures of the Holy Family to another place in the building, which will 'become' the Temple for the act of worship, and add Simeon and Anna. Add some symbols that remind people of the Temple – a Hebrew Bible or Old Testament, and some burning incense. Try to choose a place that can be a focal point for the liturgy and which is spacious enough to give an impression of size while still making it possible to see the figures. At home you may like to use bricks or even cardboard boxes to build high walls on either side of the figures, giving an impression of their smallness in the vast building.

Creating a crib scene: Location, location, location

'We always have the crib set up there.' If that's the usual cry in your church, maybe now is the time to do something different. Gather a small group of people, of varying ages, and explore your building. Working together, decide on the best place for the crib at the beginning of Advent each year.

Might any of the following be suitable locations for the crib?

IN FRONT OF THE COMMUNION TABLE

This would allow the crib to be the focus as people come into the worshipping space. If space is restricted and construction of the table allows, remove the frontal and construct the crib under the table.

IN A SIDE CHAPEL/SIDE ROOM

Maybe the whole chapel could become the stable and the setting for life-size crib figures. This would allow people to enter the stable for themselves and experience being part of the Nativity. If there is enough space, it could also become a place for worship, prayer or guided meditation.

IN THE NARTHEX/ENTRANCE AREA

If you have glass doors to your building, a crib located near them would allow people to see it even when the building is closed. Make sure it is illuminated during the long hours of winter evenings so people will see it through the glass.

BY A VOTIVE CANDLE STAND

A small crib set near a candle stand or prayer board, with a couple of chairs or prayer stools, would give a quiet focus for people's prayers.

OUTSIDE THE BUILDING

Although it could become a target for vandalism, an outside crib scene is a good reminder that Christ came into the world, not into the Church. If you have a photograph of the crib with the people who built the scene, the local paper would be sure to print the picture if the crib were vandalized!

Choosing your crib figures

SIZE MATTERS

Once you have decided where your crib scene is to be located, consider the size that the figures need to be. Life-size figures can be made from tailors' dummies, or papier mâché over a chicken wire construction. If the crib is to be a main focus, the figures will need to be large enough to be seen from a distance.

HANDLE WITH CARE

Not all crib sets are designed to withstand small hands. If you want to encourage people to touch or move the figures, make sure that they are sturdy enough to withstand handling.

ETHNICITY

Crib sets remind us of the Incarnation. Do the figures in your set allow people the opportunity to identify with the Holy Family, or to see themselves within the stable scene? Traditionally, the wise men represent people of different ages: one young and beardless, one middle-aged with a dark beard, one older still with a bald head and grey beard. They can also represent people of different continents, perhaps Asia, Africa and Europe.

THE CHRIST-CHILD

Christ was born on Christmas Day – but not all crib sets have a Christ-child separate from the manger. If you want to be able to have the manger empty until Christmas Eve or midnight or Christmas morning, make sure your crib set has a separate manger and child.

OTHER VISITORS

There is a Spanish tradition of placing extra characters in the crib scene – representations of local people who come to see the Christ-child. Maybe members of the congregation could fashion figures of themselves out of modelling clay to be added to the crib during the Christmas season.

Practical inclusive ideas

The lectionary and the crib

Create a space for prayer and meditation beside your crib scene.

Place a shallow bowl beside the crib.

Each week select phrases or sentences from the Scripture readings to be written on slips of paper. Roll these up and place them in the bowl beside the crib and tie with tiny bows of purple ribbon. Invite people to take a sentence and use it as an aid for prayer, thought or meditation during the week.

Here are some suggestions for these Scripture sentences:

Year A

From the readings for the First Sunday of Advent:

Let us walk in the light of the Lord.

Let us then lay aside the works of darkness and put on the armour of light.

Keep awake therefore, for you do not know on what day your Lord is coming.

From the readings for the Second Sunday of Advent:

A little child shall lead them.

Welcome one another, therefore, just as Christ has welcomed you.

Bear fruit worthy of repentance.

From the readings for the Third Sunday of Advent:

Be strong, do not fear! Here is your God.

Strengthen your hearts, for the coming of the Lord is near.

Are you the one who is to come, or are we to wait for another?

From the readings for the Fourth Sunday of Advent:

The young woman is with child and shall bear a son, and shall name him Immanuel.

Grace to you and peace from God our Father and the Lord Jesus Christ.

You are to name him Jesus, for he will save his people from their sins.

Year B

From the readings for the First Sunday of Advent:

We are the clay, and you are our potter.

God is faithful.

Keep awake – for you do not know when the master of the house will come.

From the readings for the Second Sunday of Advent:

He will feed his flock like a shepherd; he will carry the lambs in his arms.

With the Lord one day is like a thousand years, and a thousand years are like one day.

Prepare the way of the Lord, make his paths straight.

From the readings for the Third Sunday of Advent:

I the Lord love justice.

Rejoice always, pray without ceasing, give thanks in all circumstances.

[John] came as a witness to testify to the light.

From the readings for the Fourth Sunday of Advent:

[David], your house and your kingdom shall be made sure for ever before me; your throne shall be established for ever.

To God be the glory for ever!

Let it be with me according to your word.

Year C

From the readings for the First Sunday of Advent:

The Lord is our righteousness.

May the Lord make you increase and abound in love for one another.

Heaven and earth will pass away, but my words will not pass away.

From the readings for the Second Sunday of Advent:

Take off the garment of your sorrow and affliction, O Jerusalem, and put on forever the beauty of the glory from God.

I am confident of this, that the one who began a good work in you will bring it to completion by the day of Jesus Christ.

All flesh shall see the salvation of God.

From the readings for the Third Sunday of Advent:

The king of Israel, the Lord, is in your midst.

The Lord is near.

He will baptize you with the Holy Spirit and fire.

From the readings for the Fourth Sunday of Advent:

He shall stand and feed his flock in the strength of the Lord.

I have come to do your will.

The Mighty One has done great things for me, and holy is his name.

Intercessions at the crib

During the four Sundays of Advent, build up the crib scene adding extra figures each week. As the figures are added, the following prayers could be used as a focus for intercession:

The First Sunday of Advent: The stable

When the Christ-child was born, there was no room for him except in a stable.

We pray for people without room in our world:
- *the homeless forced to wander the streets, seeking shelter in doorways and hostels;*
- *refugees seeking asylum but meeting with hostility;*
- *people whose way of life causes them to be shunned by society.*

Lord God, as we journey towards Christmas, help us to make room in our lives and in our church for those who need a place of shelter and rest.

Lord in your mercy:

Hear our prayer.

(or)

People of God, as we journey towards Christmas, will you strive to make room in our church and in your lives for those who need a place of shelter and rest?

With the help of God, we will.

The Second Sunday of Advent: The innkeeper

When the Christ-child was born, the innkeeper offered the Holy Family welcome and shelter.

We give thanks for people who have welcomed us into their homes and lives:
- *family and friends;*
- *carers and teachers;*
- *and strangers who have opened their doors to us.*

Lord God, as we journey towards Christmas, help us to offer welcome to friend and stranger so that they may receive your love through us.

Lord in your mercy:

Hear our prayer.

(or)

People of God, as we journey towards Christmas, will you strive to offer welcome to friend and stranger so that they may receive God's love through us?

With the help of God, we will.

The Third Sunday of Advent: Joseph and Mary

When the Christ-child was born, Mary and Joseph heard and obeyed God's call.

We pray for ourselves, that we may be attentive to God's voice and willing to obey his commands.

Lord God, as we journey towards Christmas, open our eyes and ears to your word so that we may be ready to listen and do your will.

Lord in your mercy:

Hear our prayer.

(or)

People of God, will you strive to open your eyes and ears to God's word, so that you are ready to listen and do his will?

With the help of God, we will.

The Fourth Sunday of Advent: The shepherds

When the Christ-child was born, angels brought the good news to the shepherds and, leaving everything, they hurried to worship the Christ-child.

We give thanks for the people who have shared with us the good news of Jesus through their words and their lives.

Lord God, as we journey towards Christmas, we pray that we may hear afresh the good news of Jesus, and, putting aside the busyness of our lives, we may come to worship him.

Lord in your mercy:

Hear our prayer.

(or)

People of God, as we journey towards Christmas, will you strive to put aside the busyness of your lives, hear afresh the good news of Jesus, and come to worship him?

With the help of God, we will.

The crib in groups

Children

Spend the weeks of Advent helping children to make their own Christmas crib. There is good precedent for this and a trawl of the Internet (type 'Christmas crib' into a search engine) will provide some good examples. Even if the children do not make the actual figures of Mary, Joseph, the child and the shepherds and so on, they could make a scene into which the figures are placed. In Spain, and probably elsewhere too, there are shops selling models, which include not only the Holy Family, but people working around the inn, other travellers arriving and departing and so on. In Krakow, Poland, there is a Christmas crib competition each year, and the cribs are carried to the Market Square and placed outside the town museum for judging. There is therefore a good precedent for homemade cribs and for developments on this theme.

Possible modelling techniques

Older and more dextrous children may like to make tiny figures out of coloured modelling clay or polymer modelling medium. The little Peruvian cribs that are sold in some charity shops might prove a useful inspiration for this.

Crib figures could be made out of clay or air-drying clay. To do this in a way that produces durable models will take time, so it should be a project that lasts several weeks if children are to make a complete set of figures for themselves. Alternatively, you could make a set for your club, with each child making one figure. If there are lots of members, you can make infinite numbers of sheep and quite few shepherds.

Clothes pegs (the dolly peg push-on type) make a good basis for figures. Use pipe cleaners for arms and then dress the figures in scraps of material. They can be made to stand independently with a plasticine or clay base.

There are various traditions among native American people of making cribs from natural materials, for example, the Mexican fruit crib. If you started in the autumn, you could collect all sorts of seeds and sticks to use in this way. Young children might particularly enjoy an activity like this. For example, half a walnut shell with a hazelnut head for Jesus and a little piece of felt for a blanket makes a wonderful manger. A pasta crib would be another possibility in this style if you would rather not collect natural materials.

If you want to use the crib figures you already have, but place them in a more extensive Bethlehem scene, consider doing this by building stone walls out of pebbles. You could build a yard round the inn and the stable, and create a fire to burn outside. You might have carts and market stalls round about and a few trees. You may like to build your own stable. Visitors to the church over the Christmas period will enjoy looking at this and delight in the extra parts of the scene, if their attention is drawn to them.

Telling the story

If you decide to have some fairly creative sessions making cribs in this way during Advent, you may like to start by reminding children of the Christmas story. There are many wonderfully illustrated tellings of the Christmas story now available in bookshops and you may like to use one of these to stimulate the imagination and creativity of the children.

Another alternative would be to run the creative sessions during the weeks of Advent, following the Godly Play Advent presentation each week. If you wish to do this, you can find them in *The Complete Guide to Godly Play Volume 3:20 Presentations for Winter.*[3]

Imagination

Do not be afraid to let children develop their own ideas in an exercise like this. Imagining the story and the characters in it is really valuable work for children. This imaginative encounter with the story falls within the tradition of Ignatian spirituality, which has been valued by the Church for over four centuries. Even if the product is not perfect, the process will have been hugely valuable. And often, given enough time, the product *will* be very impressive, for once children become engaged in such an exercise, they really want to produce something worthwhile!

Adults

A knitted crib set

A group of people who enjoy knitting might consider working together to make a knitted crib set. This might be used in a crèche or group for small children. It could become part of a church children's area or, if you can make several, they could become presents for families with children. Knitting patterns for crib figures are available. Finding all the different colours of wool required is best done as a shared activity. The resulting figures have enormous appeal.

Your local Mothers' Union may be able to find suitable patterns, or type 'nativity knitting patterns' into an Internet search engine.

Whilst the figures are the right size for a home, you may want double-sized ones if they are going to be used in a church, particularly if figures are to be carried to different places during services.

One other idea

In the outreach section of the Christmas section of the crib pathway (see page 54) is an idea for creating a community nativity play, acted outside in the local environment. A group focusing on the crib during Advent might work to bring this into being. Work would need to start before Advent of course, but the work entailed in the final production would be a challenging and prayerful task for a group during Advent.

The crib at home

Using crib figures

Think about the best place for a crib in your home. There may be a suitable focal corner where you could say a prayer together. Choosing the place and building the stable are the initial tasks. Then decide where the figures will go during this season of looking forward.

The ox and the ass live in the stable, so put them in the middle. They will need to move aside later, but for Advent, this is their home.

Shepherds and sheep can be somewhere else – 'out in the fields, keeping watch over their flocks'. They can be in a different room, but perhaps not too far from the stable in your 'Bethlehem'.

Mary and Joseph can also be in a place representing Nazareth, rather than Bethlehem. Remembering how insignificant a place Nazareth was (Nathaniel saying 'Can any good come out of Nazareth?'), you might choose a fairly obscure corner, the place where no one would naturally look. At some point they need to start their journey to Bethlehem. The hymn 'O come, O come, Emmanuel' provides seven verses, which are traditionally used, one on each of the days from 17 December until Christmas Eve, and the hymn expresses our longing in a very appealing way. One verse can be sung each day as Joseph and Mary make their way to Bethlehem. If you have small children, let them take it in turns to determine the route. Any number of deviations are to be permitted, for this was a difficult journey, but they do need to arrive on Christmas Eve!

Add the Christ-child at some time late on Christmas Eve or between Christmas Eve and Christmas Day.

The wise men need their own place representing the East. Until Jesus is born they don't know anything about him, so they don't need to move – yet!

Stained-glass window

If you have a prominent front window, consider placing the crib so that it can be seen from the street.

If your window is large, but at some distance from the street, you might consider decorating it to make it look like a stained-glass window. This might be just Mary and Joseph beside Jesus in the manger, or it could be larger with a stable and a dark centre that becomes populated over the first weeks of Advent. If you want to make the finished scene all at once, put a piece of black paper over the figure of Jesus in the crib until Christmas Eve.

Shepherds out in the fields with their sheep might be a subject for another window, with the angels covered until Christmas Eve.

If you need to create a design to work on before you start, you could use the template provided here (also available on the CD-ROM) or do this using a computer drawing programme and then scale up your picture.

What to do

Stick shaped strips of black thick paper on the glass for the 'lead' outlines of figures, and assemble this first. Then use coloured tissue paper for the stained glass.

Because it is translucent, it will give the impression of being evenly lit. Detail can be added either by adding smaller pieces of tissue paper of contrasting colours behind the initial sheet, or by drawing on the tissue paper with felt tipped pen. A larger version can be found at the end of the book on page 179.

Extra lighting may be added, and keep the scene lit throughout the hours of darkness.

If you do not have double glazing, condensation on the glass can be a problem. If you have an open fire, the circulation of air that this promotes can relieve the condensation problem.

The crib in outreach

Crib set festival

During the summer and autumn, flower festivals have long been used as a way of inviting people into church buildings. Often they have been undertaken in partnership with local flower clubs and have had a

fund-raising function. Over more recent years, Christmas tree festivals have sometimes fulfilled the same role in the weeks before Christmas. Christmas trees, decorated in a variety of ways and by different groups or families, fill the church. The festival might be complemented by a carol service or a Christmas concert.

A further development of this idea would be a crib set festival.

Invite people to lend their crib sets for the day or even a weekend. Try to find people who have crib sets from other countries and cultures. You could also ask the mission organizations to help out. Ask those who provide the cribs to share also any details they have about the origin and significance of their crib. Point out cultural distinctions. Print these all onto cards so that people can read about the cribs, but it would also be good to have present those who have supplied the cribs so that they can talk about them with people at first hand.

Set up the cribs on tables draped with cloth. If you have cribs for many parts of the world, you may like to mark their origin on a world map. You could even have available food to taste from that place.

It might also be good to have available a place where people could learn about simple ways in which they could make a crib set of their own. You would need to have available people who are competent in producing instant art with some simple craft materials. You could also have available on a sale or return basis some simple cribs from a fair trade retailer.

It will also be important to have a place for small children to explore the idea of the crib. Have some soft crib figures available to play with or some nativity dressing up clothes so that children can role play or play with the soft figures while adults and older children spend more time looking at the cribs on display. You might even have someone available to tell the Christmas story to small children using puppets. Examples of board books that tell the Christmas story would also be useful You will find suggestions given in the Resources section.

If you have a church bookstall, you could also sell Christmas storybooks. Perhaps you might like to have someone who reads a Christmas storybook at, say, hourly periods throughout the day.

You need not, of course, have the crib set festival in a church. It might be better to have it in a school, a local library or a shopping arcade.

Publicize the festival through the local press, notice boards and newsletters. Offer seasonal refreshments to visitors and publicize Christmas services.

Offer people copies of the following prayer to place beside their crib set at home. Print it in clear but beautiful lettering on robust computer card.

God our Father,
at the first Christmas
your Son Jesus Christ was born of the Virgin Mary
for us and for our salvation:
bless this crib,
which we have prepared to celebrate that holy birth;
may all who see it be strengthened in faith
and receive the fullness of life Jesus came to bring,
who lives and reigns for ever.
Amen.

[T&S 102 – adapted]

Posada

How it began

Nine days before Christmas, Mexicans begin to celebrate Las Posadas. Now a joyous festival involving the whole community, Las Posadas has its roots in sixteenth-century Spain with St Ignatius of Loyola. Working on the assumption that Mary and Joseph's journey from Nazareth to Bethlehem would have taken nine days, he suggested special prayers to be said during those days preceding Christmas. In 1580, St John of the Cross added a religious pageant to the prayers and in 1587 Spanish missionaries took this to Mexico as a way of teaching the nativity story.

What happens

Posada means inn or lodging and, each evening of Las Posadas, a small group of pilgrims re-enacts Mary and Joseph's journey. Dressed as the biblical characters, they visit three 'inns' each evening. By prearrangement, they are turned away from the first two, but find shelter in the third and usually celebrate there in some way. On Christmas Eve, the final lodging for the Holy Family is found in the local church, where Midnight Mass is celebrated and the Christ-child is placed in the crib.

Christ's Incarnation is for the world, not just for those in church! This adaptation of Las Posadas takes the crib figures from the church into homes in the area, giving people an opportunity to meet together outside the church walls to share the anticipation of Christmas.

Preparation

You will need:

- Mary and Joseph from a set of crib figures sturdy enough to survive being taken from home to home throughout Advent;
- a rota to start on the first Sunday in Advent – invite people to sign up in order to become innkeepers, hosting the crib figures for one night, and then pilgrims taking the crib figures to their next place of lodging. Don't limit this to families with children– the crib figures welcome hospitality in a variety of homes!
- to make any travel arrangements for people who are housebound or without a car who might like to be innkeepers and pilgrims;
- to copy the words and prayers so that they can accompany the crib figures on their journey;
- to encourage innkeepers to prepare a special place for Mary and Joseph, perhaps with an Advent candle placed next to it.

Print this dialogue onto card so that both pilgrims and innkeepers can have a copy.

When the door is opened

Pilgrims: We are travellers from Nazareth, weary and hungry from our journey. Will you give us shelter?

Innkeepers: Who is it asking for room in my house?

Pilgrims: We are Mary and Joseph, travelling to Bethlehem. We need a place to rest, for Mary is tired. She is expecting a baby who will be known as the Son of God.

Innkeepers: Come in, Holy Family. Though my house may be small, you are welcome to shelter here this night.

Prayer (said by the pilgrims):
Lord God, we ask your blessing on this home and on all who live here. Just as our crib figures have found a welcome here this night, may all who enter find a welcome that speaks of your love. **Amen.**

Prayer (said by the innkeepers):
Heavenly Father, we welcome these crib figures into our home. May they remind us that you are always with us. Bless this home and all who live here, as we prepare to celebrate the birth of your Son, our Saviour Jesus Christ. **Amen.**

On Christmas Eve

On Christmas Eve, the pilgrims bring the Holy Family to the church to be placed in the crib. This could take place at an early evening Crib Service or at the Midnight service. (If you do not have a service on Christmas Eve, have the pilgrims bring the Holy Family on Christmas Day.) The final innkeeper who receives the figures could be the service leader, or another member of the congregation. The pilgrims and innkeeper could be dressed in biblical costume.

During a carol at the start of the service, the pilgrims bring the Holy Family figures to the innkeeper at the front of the church.

Pilgrims: We are travellers from Nazareth, weary and hungry from our journey. Will you give us shelter?

Innkeeper: Who is it asking for room in my house?

Pilgrims: We are Mary and Joseph. We have travelled here to the place of Joseph's birth so that we may be counted in the census. We need a place to stay, for Mary is tired. She is expecting a baby who will be known as the Son of God.

Innkeeper: I have no room in my inn. It is full with travellers like yourselves. You will have to find somewhere else to stay.

Pilgrims: But it is almost night and close to the time that Mary's baby will be born.

Innkeeper: The only room I have is a stable. If you wish to sleep there you may.

Pilgrims: Thank you. We will rest in your stable this night.

The pilgrims hand the Holy Family figures to the innkeeper, who places them in the crib scene.

PRAYERS

In this holy night [day] there was no room for Mary and Joseph in the inn.
Protect with your love those who have no home and all who live in poverty.
Holy God
hear our prayer.

In this holy night Mary, in the pain of labour, brought your Son to birth.

Hold in your hand all who are in pain and distress.
Holy God
hear our prayer.

In this holy night your Christ came as a light shining in the darkness.
Bring comfort to all who suffer in the sadness of our world.
Holy God
hear our prayer.

In this holy night strangers found the Holy Family, and saw the Christ-child lying in the manger.
Bless our homes and all whom we love.
Holy God
hear our prayer.

In this holy night receive the worship we offer as we celebrate the birth of Christ our Saviour.
Holy God
hear our prayer.

Amen.

[T&S 68–9, adapted]

Further adaptations

The Holy Family might travel further afield than just to congregational homes. Links with the wider community could be made by arranging lodging for them:

- round the classrooms of a local school;
- in the reception areas of local surgeries, police stations, and so on;
- in local shop windows;
- round the wards of a local hospital.

The crib outside the church

This is a time when churches often want to draw attention to the needs of the homeless, and the child born in a stable because there was no room in the inn is known to all. Find a suitable prominent place with plenty of passers-by. If the busiest place is the local supermarket, ask if you can set up in the car park. A place with all-night shopping will be perfect. Make a stable in which a group of people will spend 24 hours, dressed as the figures from the nativity story. Publicize the fact that this is going to happen and that you are going to be in this rough shelter overnight.

Advent:
The Jesse tree pathway

Introduction

What is a Jesse tree?

The Jesse tree is a kind of picture of the family tree of Jesus, showing King David, from whom Jesus was said to be descended; Jesse, David's father; Solomon, David's son; then the Virgin Mary and the Christ-child. The rest of the picture is filled either with pictures of prophets, or with Old Testament scenes that foreshadow his coming. You often find Jesse tree pictures in stained-glass windows, sometimes in church carvings and sometimes in medieval manuscripts. There have been several Jesse tree activity books for children published in recent years. You will find details of some of these in the Resources section.

The origin of the Jesse tree

The image of the tree of Jesse has its origins in Isaiah 11.1-2:
A shoot shall come out from the stump of Jesse,
and a branch shall grow out of his roots.
The spirit of the Lord shall rest on him,
the spirit of wisdom and understanding,
the spirit of counsel and might,
the spirit of knowledge and the fear of the Lord.

The earliest known example of a Jesse tree is to be found in a Bohemian manuscript of the late eleventh century. It depicts Isaiah holding a scroll bearing the words of the passage, which wraps around a picture of Jesse who faces him. As it moves upwards, the scroll forms a tree with seven branches above the two figures, each with a haloed dove, representing a gift of the Holy Spirit, perched upon it. Across the top of the image is a Latin inscription that, translated, reads: 'A little rod from Jesse gives rise to a splendid flower.' In this manuscript (the Vysehrad Codex), the tree is found at the end of an Old Testament section and just before the opening text of Matthew's Gospel with its list of the ancestors of Christ. Within 60 years, this representation of the tree of Jesse had developed and become a widespread theme in Christian iconography and it can

be found today in stained-glass windows and sculptures in stone and wood on churches throughout Europe. Two early examples of the forms that became more typical were the one to be found in the Lambeth Palace Bible produced between 1140 and 1150 and that in a stained-glass window dating from between 1145 and 1150 in the west front of Chartres Cathedral in France. In the Lambeth version, Jesse is now lying down and the tree emerges from his groin. Numerous figures of prophets are wrapped in its curling branches while the Virgin Mary dominates the trunk and from her head sprouts the apex branch bearing the head of Christ with the seven doves of the Spirit.

The Chartres version is a tall lancet window. Again, Jesse reclines with the tree springing from his groin. Immediately above him in the trunk is King David and, above him, his son Solomon and two other unidentified kings, then Mary, leading to Christ at the apex, surrounded by the seven doves of the Spirit. Well-developed standing figures of Isaiah and other Old Testament prophets flank the tree on either side.

As the popularity of the Jesse tree grew, the theme was developed in a variety of ways. Many are like the Chartres window, with a simple family tree of Christ in the centre and images of the prophets, often with the words of their prophecy about the Messiah on a scroll, in window lights at either side. Some emphasize the lineage of Jesus, rather than the Messianic prophecies, showing the line of descent from Adam or Abraham to Jesus of Nazareth and they may show the significance of the relationship.

Others emphasize major Old Testament themes, events, or covenants, rather than simply pointing to the specific prophecies about the Messiah. They focus on interpretations, theological points of view and doctrines relating to Messianic prophecies. It is this latter form that has been the focus of several children's story or activity books in recent years.

This renewed interest in the Jesse tree has drawn our attention once again to the rich medieval iconography and varied scriptural imagery it offers to our exploration of the promise of the Messiah and the coming of Christ. Its study is thus particularly appropriate during Advent. It can fit well with the reading sets for Years A and C of the *Common Worship* Lectionary and offers the basis for Advent carol services as well as for exploration at home and in groups.

We offer here a set of ideas for its use in travelling through Advent, Christmas and Epiphany in worship at church and at home.

Liturgical use of the Jesse tree

The Jesse tree might be a focus in the church during the four weeks of Advent, through Christmas and beyond into Epiphany, in the same way that the Advent wreath and the crib have often been used. However, do not try to focus each year on all three! If you decide to focus on the Jesse tree, then locate it highly visibly in the church, in a place where it can be seen by most of the congregation. When you use the Jesse tree as a focus during Advent, it might be advisable to use the crib only at Christmas, rather than building it up through Advent. The Jesse tree might also replace the Advent wreath altogether. You may also wish to ensure that the Jesse tree and the Christmas tree do not vie with one another for attention. You could turn the Christmas tree into a Jesse tree and erect it on the first Sunday in Advent, adding the Jesse tree symbols as Advent proceeds. If you don't do this, and have both a Christmas tree and the Jesse tree in the church, consider locating them well apart from each other, perhaps putting the Christmas tree at the back of the church or in an aisle.

You may wish to build up your Jesse tree on the first Sunday in Advent, and one possibility for doing this is at an Advent carol service. A model service is provided on page 64, together also with patterns of readings provided in *Times and Seasons* for carol services with the theme of 'The King and his kingdom' or 'The Forerunner'.

Another possibility is to build up the Jesse tree throughout the weeks of Advent and you might do this by using it to help focus on the readings from the Lectionary for the main service. In this case the different figures might be added before, during or after the readings. This may be done with a short explanation or exposition relating the figures and symbols added to the tree to the readings.

Practical inclusive ideas

 How to make a Jesse tree

A tree made from natural materials

Contorted willow makes an excellent frame on which to hang symbols, as does the pruned branch of a fruit tree with its many nodes. Choose the size of your branch according to the size of the space in which it will stand. You might even buy a potted tree from a nursery so that your Jesse Tree can grow from year to year, but you would need to ensure that someone is available to water and nurture it through the rest of the year. Branches can be made to stand up in sand or gravel in a large pot. The advantage of using a real tree or a branch is that you do not have to predetermine a pattern for hanging the symbols and the pattern can be reordered to create different emphases as the seasons progress from Advent through Christmas to Epiphany and even beyond.

A wooden Jesse tree

A framework might be constructed from varying sizes of dowelling, with a sturdy piece of wood for the trunk of the tree inserted into a wooden base of sufficient size to support the whole structure, standing on the floor or a table, depending on the size of the space you wish to fill. Cup hooks or small brass eyelets might be used to hang the symbols on the frame. The advantage of this method is that the whole construction can be disassembled for easy storage from one year to the next.

The symbols

The symbols to hang on the Jesse tree could be made in any number of ways. A new way could be found each year or you could aim to produce a permanent set of figures that could be put away each year like Christmas tree ornaments.

Simple figures could be made from card using illustrations downloaded from the Internet, or copied from books. A template for a generic standing prophet figure and a seated virgin and child figure is provided here and at the end of the book on page 178 and on the CD-ROM. Longer-term projects might include figures made from fabric using embroidery or fabric painting, figures made using clay or wood, or figures painted onto glass. Some craft shops will cut glass to shape for you and edge it. Glass painted figures could be lit by Christmas tree lights, which are now available very cheaply, with lights held in place using

florists' wire. Another method might be to use simple biblical style figures to hang on the tree, distinguishing each with a scroll with biblical words that identify the character. To do this, you could make figures from pegs, with simple clothes made from squares of fabric tied at the waist with wool and with pipe cleaners for arms.

Yet another method, particularly good if you are following the major Old Testament themes and covenants pattern, could be to send people with a list of suitable symbols to find from the world around them: from their own homes, gift shops, Christmas decoration fairs and so on. This would make a particularly good community activity and would not require any particular artistic expertise.

All these methods have the potential to involve people from a church community of varying ages, capabilities and interests and, having found or created the figures, the opportunity to explore their biblical significance through the construction project and then through the liturgy.

How to find material from the Internet

Type the words 'Jesse tree' into a search engine and then follow up the entries. It may be worth following the links also to get even more material.

Choosing your prophets and the patterns in which you hang them

BASE YOUR PATTERN ON ONE OF THE WELL-KNOWN WINDOWS

One way to create a Jesse tree is simply to copy the arrangement of one of the well-known windows, for example that in Chartres Cathedral or the Abbey of St Denis in Paris. Thus Jesse will be at the bottom, with the Virgin and Christ at the top and David and Solomon in between, and various prophets and their prophecies hanging on other branches.

A pattern based on the fourteenth-century window in St Mary's, Morpeth, Northumberland is provided here and on page 180. There is a photograph of the window on the CD-ROM.

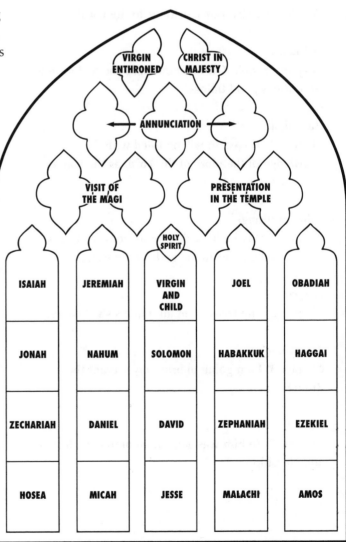

Isaiah

Chapter 11: **A shoot shall come out from the stock of Jesse.**

The words of the prophets from the tree

The full Bible references for these texts can be found in the Advent carol service, on pages 65–8.

Jeremiah

Chapter 23: **I will raise up for David a righteous Branch.**

Joel

Chapter 2: **For in Mount Zion and in Jerusalem there shall be those who escape.**

Obadiah

Verses17-end: **The kingdom shall be the Lord's.**

Jonah

Chapter 2: **Deliverance belongs to the Lord!**

Nahum

Chapter 1: **Look! On the mountains the feet of one who brings good tidings.**

Habakkuk

Chapter 2: **The earth will be filled with the knowledge of the glory of the Lord, as the waters cover the sea.**

Solomon (King)

Psalm 72: **May he have dominion from sea to sea, and from the River to the ends of the earth.**

Haggai

Chapter 2: **The treasure of all nations shall come.**

Zechariah

Chapter 3: **I am going to bring my servant the Branch.**

Daniel

Chapter 7: **To him was given dominion and glory and kingship.**

Zephaniah

Chapter 3: **The Lord, your God, is in your midst.**

Ezekiel

Chapter 44: **This gate shall remain shut; it shall not be opened, and no one shall enter by it; for the Lord, the God of Israel, has entered by it.**

Hosea

Chapter 11: **Out of Egypt I called my son.**

Micah

Chapter 1: **For lo, the Lord is coming out of his place.**

Malachi

Chapter 3: **The Lord whom you seek will suddenly come to his temple.**

Amos

Chapter 7: **How can Jacob stand? He is so small.**

THE OLD TESTAMENT THEME AND COVENANT PATTERN

Another possibility is to use symbols that denote Old Testament characters and events as a simple countdown to the coming of the Saviour through the writings of the Hebrew people until the coming of Jesus.

Character	Symbol
God	Dove
Adam and Eve	Fruit or apple
Noah	Rainbow or ark
Abraham	Field of stars
Isaac	Ram
Jacob	Ladder
Joseph	Sack of grain or coat
Moses	Burning bush
	Tablets of the Torah
Joshua	Ram's horn
Gideon	Clay water jar
Samuel	Crown
David	Harp
Elijah	Stone altar
Hezekiah	Empty tent
Isaiah	Fire tongs with hot coal
Jeremiah	Tears
Habakkuk	Watchtower
Nehemiah	City wall
John the Baptist	Scallop shell
Mary	White lily
Elizabeth	Mother and child
Zechariah	Pencil and tablet
Joseph	Carpenter's square or hammer
Magi	Star and/or three crowns
Jesus	Manger

Using the Jesse tree with the Main Service Lectionary

If you are intending to build your tree during a morning service using the Main Service (First Service) Lectionary in the Common Worship or Revised Common Lectionary, here are some suggestions of how you might do that. Years A and C are particularly suitable.

Note

In using a scheme like this, which uses the Jesse tree to focus particularly on the important Old Testament readings used in Advent, you may wish to add to the tree the prophets not featured in the readings as Advent progresses. They might be added as part of the sermon during the weeks of Advent, or they could be added as part of the dismissal or conclusion of the service. In a formal liturgical setting, the procession of ministers could move to the Jesse tree and the dismissal rite could be conducted from that place. Use the words of the prophets in conjunction with a blessing and dismissal from the Advent options on page 71 in *Times and Seasons*.

Here are some examples of how this might be done:

The prophet Habakkuk proclaimed that 'the earth will be filled with the knowledge of the glory of the Lord, as the waters cover the sea.'

And so

May God himself, the God of peace,
make you perfect and holy,
and keep you safe and blameless, in spirit, soul and
    body,
for the coming of our Lord Jesus Christ;
and the blessing …

[T&S 41]

(or)

The prophet Zephaniah proclaimed that 'the Lord,
    your God, is in your midst'.
May God the Father, judge all-merciful,
make us worthy of a place in his kingdom.

Amen.

May God the Son, coming among us in power,
reveal in our midst the promise of his glory.

Amen.

May God the Holy Spirit make us steadfast in faith,
joyful in hope and constant in love.

Amen.

And the blessing of God almighty,
the Father, the Son, and the Holy Spirit,
be among you and remain with you always.

Amen.

[T&S 41]

(or)

The prophet Nahum says 'Behold, on the mountains
the feet of him who brings good tidings.'
Our Lord says, 'I am coming soon.'
Amen. Come, Lord Jesus.

May the Lord, when he comes,
find us watching and waiting.
Amen.

[T&S 41]

In other, less formal, settings the congregation might gather around the tree while the other pictures or symbols are added and their proclamations are made, then the congregation might move to the door for the Dismissal.

Here are some suggestions for building the tree using the Old Testament and Gospel readings provided by the Common Worship Lectionary.

Year A

FIRST SUNDAY OF ADVENT: ISAIAH 2.1-5

> Establish on strong card a simple mountain scene, which will stand in front of the pot in which the tree will stand. One mountain should stand above the others.

> Beside it lay down a pruning hook (sickle), and a single ploughshare, and light a large candle.

> Add some of the words from the Old Testament reading as a flag to 'fly' on the mountains.

SECOND SUNDAY OF ADVENT: ISAIAH 11.1-10

This is the most significant reading of the Year A cycle for the Jesse tree.

> Plant your tree with Jesse at its foot. Add Isaiah the prophet and pictures of the wolf and the lamb, the calf and the lion, the cow and the bear.

> Put the mountain scene in front of the pot, with Jesse

above it. Add the pruning hook and the ploughshare from last week and light the large candle beside the tree.

Add last week's flag and a new one with some words from this week's reading.

You may like to add some of the other prophets and their words also, taken from the list on page 60.

THIRD SUNDAY OF ADVENT: ISAIAH 35.1-10

Add David and Solomon on the trunk of the tree ascending from Jesse towards where Christ will be at the top. You may like to add some blossoming flowers – possibly weave some winter jasmine stalks around the tree, or a branch from some other winter flowering shrub, or you could make tiny paper flowers. The lame person leaping and the dumb person singing would also be good symbols to add, as would something to represent the streams in the desert.

Add a new flag with some words from this week's reading.

You may like to add some of the other prophets and their words also, taken from the list on page 60.

FOURTH SUNDAY OF ADVENT: ISAIAH 7.10-16

This week add the Virgin towards the top of the tree. You may like to show her with the child on her knee and then add the child Jesus above her on Christmas Day or you may prefer to leave her without the child so that he is not shown at all until Christmas.

Add a new flag with some words from this week's reading.

You may like to add some of the other prophets and their words also, taken from the list on page 60.

Year B

The Jesse tree does not work at all well with the readings in Year B and it would probably not be fruitful to try to use it in this way.

Year C

However, it does work extremely well with the Old Testament readings during Year C. The Old Testament reading each week is taken from the writings of a different prophet and this would enable you to build the tree very naturally, referring to the writings of the different prophets.

Set up your tree before Advent Sunday, with Jesse at

the bottom, and use the welcome words of introduction at the beginning of the service to draw attention to the tree and to Jesse and provide some words of explanation. Even if you write the explanation on the service sheet, it is still worth introducing the idea aloud at the beginning of worship.

FIRST SUNDAY OF ADVENT: JEREMIAH 33.14-16

You could place a Christ in Majesty figure at the top of the tree before the Collect is said ('when he shall come again in his glorious majesty to judge the living and the dead').

Then, in association with the reading from Jeremiah, you could add Jeremiah and David.

In association with the Gospel reading, you may like to decorate the tree also with sun, moon and stars. You could also add clouds at the feet of the Son of Man who was placed there when the Collect was said. The creation and addition of the sun, moon and stars might be a task for children while the sermon is being given, in congregations where there is no special liturgy of the word for children.

SECOND SUNDAY OF ADVENT

The lectionary for the second Sunday of Advent provides alternatives for the Old Testament reading: Baruch or Malachi. In the service of the Jesse tree you could use both and omit the Canticle and the New Testament reading. The Malachi reading includes the words that form one of the great recitatives and arias from Handel's *Messiah*, so rather than having two passages of Scripture simply read one after the other, you could use the musical version instead of reading the Malachi. If you don't have an oratorio soloist in your congregation – which is very likely – use a recording. Handel's musical setting colours the words magnificently.

THIRD SUNDAY OF ADVENT

In the third week of Advent, the lectionary provides an Old Testament reading from the prophet Zephaniah (some of the words are again used by Handel), and a Canticle from Isaiah, facilitating the addition of two more prophets to your window during Scripture readings.

FOURTH SUNDAY OF ADVENT

The fourth Sunday of Advent provides for the addition of the prophet Micah during the Old Testament reading and the Virgin during the Collect or the Canticle, the Magnificat. The stage is now all set for the coming of the Messiah as the baby born in Bethlehem.

Notes

Suggestions are given at the beginning of this section on using the Jesse tree with the lectionary about how to add the other prophets at the end of the service, either formally, or informally, as part of a Dismissal rite.

For a continuation of these sequences during the seasons of Christmas and Epiphany, please turn to pages 115 and 168 respectively.

Advent carol service pattern

You may like to build a tree based on one of the patterns of readings for an Advent Carol Service given in *Times and Seasons*. The first and second sequences are those that would work best.

Sequence 1: The King and his kingdom

1.	Zechariah 9.9,10	Rejoice greatly, your king comes to you
2.	Jeremiah 23.5,6	I will raise up for David a righteous branch
3.	Psalm 118.19-29	Open me the gates of righteousness
4.	Isaiah 9.2,6,7	The people that walked in darkness have seen a great light
5.	Isaiah 7.10-15	Behold, a virgin shall conceive and bear a son
6.	Romans 12.1,2; 13.(8)11-14	Salvation is nearer to us now than when we first believed
Canticle	Te Deum	A Song of the Church
Gospel	Matthew 25.1-13	In Advent
Reading	Matthew 1.18-25	At Christmas

Sequence 2: The forerunner

1.	Exodus 3.1-6	The burning bush
2.	Isaiah 40.1-11	A voice cries in the wilderness: Prepare the way of the Lord
3.	Isaiah 52.7-10	How beautiful on the mountains
4.	Malachi 3.1-5	Behold, I send my messenger to prepare the way before me
5.	Isaiah 61.1-3,11	The Spirit of the Lord is upon me
6.	Philippians 4.4-7	The Lord is at hand.
Canticle	Benedictus	The Song of Zechariah
Gospel	Luke 1.5-25	The birth of John the Baptist is foretold
Reading		

[T&S 46]

An Advent carol service based on the Jesse tree

The Bible readings are based on the texts in a medieval Jesse tree window in St Mary's Church, Morpeth, Northumberland, dating from around 1320.

As each of the readings is read, an illustration of the prophet quoted should be hung on the tree. You may like to accompany each figure with a banner on which are written the quotation printed in bold in each of the readings from the service. A very simple way to make such a banner would be to use wide gold ribbon and stick on it a strip of paper on which the words have been printed, so the gold forms a margin around the words. Cut the end into a point or V shape and hang the resulting banner from your tree using gold thread.

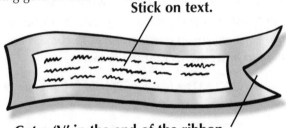

Stick on text.

Cut a 'V' in the end of the ribbon.

Suggested hymn: 'Creator of the stars of night'.

An introduction to the symbolism of the Jesse tree is provided for the congregation. This might be based on the background and introduction section to this pathway on page 57.

Suggested hymn: 'Come thou long-expected Jesus'.

Isaiah 11.1-3 (The figure of Jesse is placed at the base of the tree)

A shoot shall come out from the stock of Jesse, and a branch shall grow out of his roots.

The spirit of the Lord shall rest upon him, the spirit of wisdom and understanding, the spirit of counsel and might, the spirit of knowledge and the fear of the Lord.

His delight shall be in the fear of the Lord.

Suggested hymn: 'Hark, a thrilling voice is sounding'.

The words of the prophets from the tree

Jeremiah 23.5-6 (The figure of Jeremiah is hung on the tree)

The days are surely coming, says the Lord, when

I will raise up for David a righteous Branch, and he shall reign as king and deal wisely, and shall execute justice and righteousness in the land. In his days Judah will be saved and Israel will live in safety. And this is the name by which he will be called: 'The Lord is our righteousness.'

Joel 2.28-29,32 (The figure of Joel is hung on the tree)

Then afterwards I will pour out my spirit on all flesh;

your sons and your daughters shall prophesy, your old men shall dream dreams, and your young men shall see visions.

Even upon the male and female slaves, in those days, I will pour out my spirit.

*Then everyone who calls on the name of the Lord shall be saved; **for in Mount Zion and in Jerusalem there shall be those who escape**, as the Lord has said, and among the survivors shall be those whom the Lord calls.*

Suggested Carol: 'Adam lay y bounden'.

Obadiah 17-18,21 (The figure of Obadiah is hung on the tree)

But on Mount Zion there shall be those that escape, and it shall be holy;

and the house of Jacob shall take possession of those who dispossessed them.

The house of Jacob shall be a fire, and the house of Joseph a flame, and the house of Esau stubble;

they shall burn them and consume them, and there shall be no survivor of the house of Esau; for the Lord has spoken.

*Those who have been saved shall go up to Mount Zion to rule Mount Esau; and **the kingdom shall be the Lord's.***

Jonah 2.8-10 (The figure of Jonah is hung on the tree)

Those who worship vain idols forsake their true loyalty.

But I with the voice of thanksgiving will sacrifice to you;

*what I have vowed I will pay. **Deliverance belongs to the Lord!***

Then the Lord spoke to the fish, and it spewed Jonah out upon the dry land.

Suggested hymn: 'O come, O come, Emmanuel'.

Nahum 1.12,15 (The figure of Nahum is hung on the tree)

Thus says the Lord,

'Though they are at full strength and many, they will be cut off and pass away.

Though I have afflicted you, I will afflict you no more.

Look! On the mountains the feet of one who brings good tidings, *who proclaims peace!*

Celebrate your festivals, O Judah, fulfil your vows,

for never again shall the wicked invade you; they are utterly cut off.'

Habakkuk 2.2-4,14 (The figure of Habakkuk is hung on the tree)

Then the Lord answered me and said:

Write the vision; make it plain on tablets, so that a runner may read it.

For there is still a vision for the appointed time; it speaks of the end, and does not lie.

If it seems to tarry, wait for it; it will surely come, it will not delay.

Look at the proud! Their spirit is not right in them, but the righteous live by their faith.

But the earth will be filled with the knowledge of the glory of the Lord, as the waters cover the sea.

Suggested Carol: 'Es ist ein Ros'entsprungen' ('Lo, how a rose e'er blooming')

Psalm 72.1,2,8 (Attributed to Solomon) (The figure of Solomon is hung on the tree)

Give the king your justice, O God, and your righteousness to a king's son.

May he judge your people with righteousness, and your poor with justice.

***May he have dominion from sea to sea,
and from the River to the ends of the earth***.

Haggai 2.4b-9 (The figure of Haggai is hung on the tree)

Yet now take courage, O Zerubbabel, says the Lord; take courage, O Joshua, son of Jehozadak, the high priest; take courage, all you people of the land, says the Lord; work, for I am with you, says the Lord of hosts, according to the promise that I made you when you came out of Egypt. My spirit abides among

*you; do not fear. For thus says the Lord of hosts: Once again, in a little while, I will shake the heavens and the earth and the sea and the dry land; and I will shake all the nations, so that the **treasure of all nations shall come**, and I will fill this house with splendour, says the Lord of hosts. The silver is mine, and the gold is mine, says the Lord of hosts. The latter splendour of this house shall be greater than the former, says the Lord of hosts; and in this place I will give prosperity, says the Lord of hosts.*

Suggested hymn: 'Sleepers wake'

Zechariah 3.4,8 (The figure of Zechariah is hung on the tree)

*The angel said to those who were standing before him, 'Take off his filthy clothes.' And to him he said 'See, I have taken your guilt away from you, and I will clothe you in festal apparel. Now listen, Joshua, high priest, you and your colleagues who sit before you! For they are an omen of things to come: **I am going to bring my servant the Branch**.'*

Daniel 7.13,14 (The figure of Daniel is hung on the tree)

As I watched in the night visions,

I saw one like a human being coming with the clouds of heaven.

And he came to the Ancient One and was presented before him.

To him was given dominion and glory and kingship,

that all peoples, nations, and languages should serve him.

His dominion is an everlasting dominion that shall not pass away,

and his kingship is one that shall never be destroyed.

Suggested hymn: 'Hark, the glad sound'

Zephaniah 3.14-18a (The figure of Zephaniah is hung on the tree)

Sing aloud, O daughter of Zion; shout, O Israel!

Rejoice and exult with all your heart, O daughter of Jerusalem!

The Lord has taken away the judgements against you, he has turned away your enemies.

The King of Israel, the Lord, is in your midst; you shall fear disaster no more.

On that day it shall be said to Jerusalem:

Do not fear, O Zion; do not let your hands grow weak.

The Lord, your God, is in your midst, a warrior who gives victory;
he will rejoice over you with gladness, he will renew you in his love; he will exult over you with loud singing as on a day of festival.

Ezekiel 44.1-5 (The figure of Ezekiel is hung on the tree)

Then he brought me back to the outer gate of the sanctuary, which faces east; and it was shut. The Lord said to me: **This gate shall remain shut; it shall not be opened, and no one shall enter by it; for the Lord, the God of Israel, has entered by it**; therefore it shall remain shut. Only the prince … may sit in it to eat food before the Lord; he shall enter by way of the vestibule of the gate, and shall go out by the same way.

Then he brought me by way of the north gate to the front of the temple; and I looked, and lo! the glory of the Lord filled the temple of the Lord; and I fell upon my face. The Lord said to me: Mortal, mark well, look closely, and listen attentively to all that I shall tell you concerning all the ordinances of the temple of the Lord and all its laws; and mark well those who may be admitted to the temple and all those who are to be excluded from the sanctuary.

Suggested Carol: Jesus Christ the apple tree

Hosea 11.1-4 (The figure of Hosea is hung on the tree)

When Israel was a child, I loved him,
and **out of Egypt I called my son.**

The more I called them, the more they went from me;

they kept sacrificing to the Baals, and offering incense to idols.

Yet it was I who taught Ephraim to walk, I took them up in my arms; but they did not know that I healed them.

I led them with cords of human kindness, with the bands of love.

I was to them like those who lift infants to their cheeks. I bent down to them and fed them.

Micah 1.2-4; 4.6,7 (The figure of Micah is hung on the tree)

Hear, you peoples, all of you; listen, O earth, and all that is in it;

and let the Lord God be a witness against you, the Lord from his holy temple.

For lo, the Lord is coming out of his place, and will come down and tread upon the high places of the earth.

Then the mountains will melt under him and the valleys will burst open,

like wax near the fire, like waters poured down a steep place.

On that day, says the Lord, I will assemble the lame

and gather those who have been driven away, and those whom I have afflicted.

The lame I will make the remnant and those who were cast off, a strong nation;

and the Lord will reign over them in Mount Zion now and for evermore.

Suggested hymn: 'Long ago, prophets knew Christ would come'

Malachi 3.1-3 (The figure of Malachi is hung on the tree)

See, I am sending my messenger to prepare the way before me, and **the Lord whom you seek will suddenly come to his temple**. The messenger of the covenant in whom you delight – indeed, he is coming, says the Lord of hosts. But who can endure the day of his coming, and who can stand when he appears?

For he is like a refiner's fire and like fullers' soap; he will sit as a refiner and purifier of silver, and he will purify the descendants of Levi and refine them like gold and silver, until they present offerings to the Lord in righteousness.

Amos 7.1-9 (The figure of Amos is hung on the tree)

This is what the Lord God showed me: behold, he was forming locusts at the time the latter growth began to sprout (it was the latter growth after the king's mowings). When they had finished eating the grass of the land, I said,

'O Lord God, forgive, I beg you! How can Jacob stand? He is so small!'

The Lord relented concerning this; 'It shall not be,' said the Lord.

This is what the Lord God showed me: the Lord God was calling for a shower of fire, and it devoured the great deep and was eating up the land. Then I said,

'O Lord God, cease, I beg you! **How can Jacob stand? He is so small!'**

The Lord relented concerning this; 'This also shall not be,' said the Lord God.

This is what he showed me: the Lord was standing beside a wall built with a plumb-line, with a plumb-line in his hand. And the Lord said to me, 'Amos, what do you see?' And I said, 'A plumb-line.' Then the Lord said,

'See, I am setting a plumb-line in the midst of my people Israel; I will never again pass them by;

the high places of Isaac shall be made desolate, and the sanctuaries of Israel shall be laid waste, and I will rise against the house of Jeroboam with the sword.'

Suggested hymn: 'Lo, he comes with clouds descending'

The Blessing

The tree now stands throughout Advent as a reminder of the Messiah who is coming and what he will be like.

The figure of the Virgin could be added to the tree on the Fourth Sunday of Advent and the Christ-child is added at Christmas.

The Jesse tree in groups

Children

An Advent graffiti board based on the Jesse tree

This material is not suitable for use with tiny children and those under about seven (i.e. preschool and children in Key Stage 1 at school). For these children, it is best to concentrate in Advent on the key characters and events of the Christmas story. They may encounter the Jesse tree in worship, as a display and in art and this is fine, for they become familiar with the idea, but this more detailed working with the ideas of the prophets is better kept until later.

You will need:
- A Jesse tree. You could
  - use a PowerPoint presentation on a computer with a digital projector, using the images on the CD-ROM that accompanies this book;
  - or you could use images hung on a tree or branch;
  - or you could build up the tree using cards made from the pictures on the CD-ROM. (Build up the tree along with the words of the presentation.)

- A graffitti board: Use a board, covered in purple paper for Advent. You might want to give it a silver or gold border.

PRESENTATION

This is the family tree of Jesus.

Today most family trees are shown with the ancestors at the top and they work downwards, but this family tree works the other way round.

Here is the ancestor, Jesse, at the bottom. He often seems to be asleep. And the tree seems to be growing from him.

Here is Jesse's son, King David. (You can tell who it is because of the symbols: a crown for a king, and a harp to remind us of his music and his psalms.)

Here is David's son, King Solomon. (He, too, has a crown.)

And here is Mary, the mother of Jesus. (It was actually Joseph whose ancestors were Jesse, David and Solomon, but the old painters showed Mary instead. This is a kind of puzzle and you might want to think about it.)

We don't know much else about the ancestry of Jesus so the tree is not very tall. (Matthew gives us a written family history of Jesus at the beginning of his Gospel. You might like to look at it for yourself. It is fun to look at if you like puzzling over how to say names you have never seen before!)

But the tree is also broad.

The people of God were waiting for the Messiah, one who would come to save them.

The prophets reminded the people over and over again that they were God's people, that God loved them and that they should walk in God's ways. And sometimes they warned people. They warned them that they should not forget God, the creator and sustainer, and that they must keep God's laws. The prophets were writers, and poets, and teachers and dreamers, and mystics.

Let us add the prophets to the tree and hear what they have to say:

Isaiah tells us of Jesse and the image of the tree: *A shoot shall come forth from the stock of Jesse.*

And Jeremiah tells us of David and the tree's branches: *I will raise up for David a righteous Branch.*

Joel tells of escape from danger:
For in Mount Zion and in Jerusalem there shall be those who escape.

Obadiah tells us that:
The kingdom shall be the Lord's.

Jonah, the prophet in the story who spent three days inside the fish, told the people that:
Deliverance belongs to the Lord!

Nahum suggests that the people look out:
Look! On the mountains the feet of one who brings good tidings.

And Habakkuk dreams:
The earth will be filled with the knowledge of the glory of the Lord, as the waters cover the sea.

King Solomon was a prophet as well as a king. In Psalm 72 he reminded the people that:
His dominion shall stretch from sea to sea, and from the River to the ends of the earth.

Haggai wrote:
The treasure of all nations shall come.

Zechariah used the tree image too:
I am going to bring my servant the Branch.

Daniel knew that the Messiah, the one who was to come, would be a king.
To him was given dominion and glory and kingship.

Zephaniah reminded the people that God is ever present:
The Lord, your God, is in your midst.

Ezekiel said that God came to his people:
This gate shall remain shut; it shall not be opened, and no one shall enter by it; for the Lord, the God of Israel, has entered by it.

Hosea remembered that the people were slaves in Egypt. When Christ was born, Mary and Joseph would flee to Egypt with him to escape the threats of Herod.
Out of Egypt I called my son.

Micah said that the Lord would come to the people:
For lo, the Lord is coming out of his place.

And Malachi warned that the coming would be unexpected:
The Lord whom you seek will suddenly come to his temple.

While Amos thinks of the vulnerable and fragile:
How can Jacob stand? He is so small.

Add Christ in Majesty to the top of the tree.

The Messiah did come. He was called Jesus. He was born as a baby in Bethlehem and he came to save the people from their sins. He rode into Jerusalem on a donkey and people called him a king. He died on the cross and rose again. In the words of the great Te Deum:

You overcame the sting of death
and opened the kingdom of heaven to all believers.
You are seated at God's right hand in glory.
We believe that you will come and be our judge.
Come then, Lord, and help your people,
bought with the price of your own blood,
and bring us with your saints
to glory everlasting.

[CW 802]

ACTIVITIES

Give people a choice of activities over the time you have available. This might be the four weeks of Advent. It might be time in a day workshop. The activity is flexible and, with more or less direction, can be made to fit the time available.

1. Use green paper or paint to add a tree to the centre of the graffiti board. Make sure there is room for Jesse at the bottom and Christ in Majesty at the top. Make places for the prophets at the sides.
2. Create a figure to add to the Jesse tree. Will you add Jesse or Jesus, Solomon or Mary or David? Or will you create a prophet? What would a prophet look like?
3. Find the words of the prophets. You may like to write out the words of the prophets and add them to the tree. Will your prophets' words be in old illuminated script, or as a speech balloon? The choice is entirely yours.
4. Find the list of the ancestors of Jesus in St Matthew's Gospel and try to read the names. You might enjoy trying to say them aloud to one another.
5. If you were a prophet, waiting for Jesus to come to God's people today, what would you say to them? Write or create a prophetic message for today. You can write, paint, draw or use modelling material. The choice is entirely yours. Add your message or prophecy to the tree when it is ready.

Adults

The Jesse tree might provide a useful stimulus for exploring the books of the Old Testament prophets. During Advent, these Old Testament readings really come to the fore in the liturgy and this would be a good time to explore some of their background. The group may not meet for the four weeks of Advent as the last weeks before Christmas are often very busy. You should therefore plan your sessions to fit the number of weeks you have available and provide material accordingly. Material is not provided here for four weeks, but rather the outline of a project that can be adapted according to the amount of time available.

What to do

Divide up all the Old Testament prophets between members of the group. A list of the prophets is given on page 60. Give people the task of finding out about the prophets they have been given. If people are going to find out about more than one prophet (Isaiah, Jeremiah, Lamentations, Ezekiel and Daniel) each, it might be good if they could research a major and one or more minor prophets (the rest).

How to find out about the prophets

If you have a lot of time, use a Bible commentary to find out about the prophet you are researching. These books often have an introductory section before they launch into an analysis of the text. A minister in your church could probably lend one of these. However, for people who don't have much time, there are plenty of alternatives. Many Bibles have an introduction at the beginning of each book: the *Good News Bible*[4] does this particularly well in lucid but concise language.

Another possibility is to use the Internet. Use a search engine to find references to 'Old Testament Prophets'. Be sure to type in the 'Old Testament' bit or you will get far too many irrelevant references. The value of this approach is that you can read material from Jewish and Christian sites alongside one another, which provides several perspectives.

When you meet

Simply share your learning. Spend a bit of time listening to each member of the group talk about what they have found out.

Worship

Open the session with one of the Kyrie Confessions from the Advent section of *Times and Seasons* (pages 26–7).

After your discussion, use one of the Intercessions from Advent section of *Times and Seasons* (pages 28–9) and then use this conclusion from page 34:

Our Lord says, 'I am coming soon.'
Amen. Come, Lord Jesus.

May the Lord, when he comes,
find us watching and waiting.
Amen.

The Jesse tree at home

There are all sorts of ways in which the Jesse tree might be used at home by a family with children or without children. What you do will be determined by your own circumstances and so a variety of suggestions is given here for you to choose from.

Using a published Jesse tree book

Published books usually provide a short story or thought for each day from 1 December through to Christmas Eve with an accompanying activity. If Advent starts before 1 December, you can afford to miss some days; if it starts after 1 December, you may want to leave out one or two activities.

Making a Jesse tree for your own home

You can use the same kinds of technique as you would for making a Jesse tree for a church building, except that you might want to make it smaller! It would provide a purposeful winter task for someone with a creative hobby: almost any craft could be used to create the prophets to put on the tree and, as it grew, it would be an attractive talking point for visitors.

If you are not into intricate craft work, here are some other ideas:

Internet

Create the symbols or pictures by downloading them from the Internet. Make them into small squares that can be stuck on to card and cut out to be put on to your tree, one by one each day.

With chocolate!

If you really cannot get through Advent without chocolate, you might stick your little prophet or symbol squares onto individually wrapped chocolate rectangles or squares. Use fairly traded chocolate if you can. You could then have them in a basket by the tree and lift off the picture to hang on the tree after you have opened the chocolate. Or, if you wish to observe the Advent tradition of waiting (rather than just counting down), you could hang or stick the decorated chocolates on your tree and share them out on Christmas day.

Make your own Jesse tree window

You could make your own Jesse tree window to resemble stained glass and to shine out over your street or garden during the Advent season and on through Christmas. Use overhead projector acetate sheets and either print pictures from the Internet onto them, enlarged to an appropriate size, or draw your symbols on using bold black outlines and then colour in the pictures with permanent ink pens designed for acetate sheets. Arrange these on your window, attaching them with tiny pieces of clear sticky tape. You might then fill in the intervening spaces with coloured cellophane. People cheer up the winter gloom in all sorts of ways over the Advent and Christmas period and this would rival Santa and his reindeer admirably!

Adapt the idea to fit with an appropriate story

The Christmas Mystery by Jostein Gaarder (see the Resources Section) tells the story of a child who finds a magic Advent calendar that reveals a simple history of Christianity through a series of characters who travel back in time and across Europe to the crib at Bethlehem. It is an ingenious book in 24 short chapters that can be read one each night through Advent. It is suitable for children to have read to them from the age of about seven and would make a lovely bedtime story. Older children might read it for themselves, of course, but would also still enjoy listening to it. You could follow the journey told in the story and build your own Journey tree to Bethlehem, starting perhaps at the top and working your way down until you reach the crib (and perhaps Jesse the ancestor) at the foot of the tree.

The Jesse tree in outreach

A Jesse tree 'Advent Calendar'

In its form like a stained-glass window, the Jesse tree

has much of the potential of an Advent calendar and it could be used in this way as a build up (rather than a count down!) to Christmas. If you were to use each of the prophets, with Jesse, David, Solomon, Mary and Joseph and Jesus, (perhaps both as a child and as Christ in Majesty) at the very top, you would have enough scenes to fill most days of Advent.

In a public place

You might look for the possibility of building this in your local library or even in a shop window.

In a school

Or you could offer to help a class in a school do this as part of an RE project. It would also make an excellent collective worship focus for a school through Advent, with an understanding that it could be made to meet RE objectives for the whole school also. It might even be possible to make cross-curricular links with the art curriculum. If you propose working with a school in this way, be sure to make the proposal while the coming year's curriculum is being planned at the end of the summer term. It would not really be fair to make such a proposal just before Advent begins. If it works well the first time, this could even become part of a school's rolling programme of RE and collective worship.

What to do

To prepare this, you might provide the quotations from each of the prophets (see page 65) and give pupils the opportunity to create a prophet figure who reflects or demonstrates his words. Pictures of famous stained-glass windows, available from the Internet and displayed on an interactive whiteboard, might serve as a reference point and an inspiration. A further development of this might be to reflect together on what each of the prophets might say today.

Involving other organizations

If you were to create your Jesse tree as a 'window' or in some other way in a public building such as a library or a shop, you might get in touch with your local family history society to see whether they would like to be associated with the project as a means of promoting their own activities. Family history is a very popular interest at present and it would be good to build on this and create what is a fairly obvious link. There could be an explanation of the Jesse tree beside the window and also details of the local family history society, its activities and perhaps its programme for the coming year. Other possible natural links would be with a bookshop, in association with promoting Christmas art books, an art shop, a picture framing shop or even a supplier of double glazing!

A church web site

You could also make this a feature of a church web site over the Advent period, loading up a new picture each day, or liaise with your local adult education organization to promote their various art classes.

CHRISTMAS

Seasonal introduction

Don't forget the people!

After the abstinences of the Advent season, Christmas is marked with generosity or even extravagance as we celebrate the birth of Christ. We eat rich food and indulge ourselves in all sorts of ways. A whole variety of expectations may surround the way we mark Christmas at home: whether we have turkey, chicken, duck or goose; whether we eat sprouts; what we do with our Christmas pudding; whether we watch the Queen's speech; how and when we give and open our presents. There may even be negotiations about whether we go to church on Christmas Eve or on Christmas Day. And on top of all this, for some, there will be differing expectations about where Christmas will be spent, which might make the season of goodwill to all seem like a bit of an effort. Taking all this into consideration, it may be important for those planning the liturgies for Christmas to ensure that they offer a space for calm and for some peace as well as for joy and celebration.

It would be all too easy to allow the church and the liturgy itself to become over-busy or cluttered. With a Christmas tree, a crib, the Jesse tree, the flower arrangements, it might almost be difficult to find room for the people in a smaller church. Try to focus on what is important, and on decoration that will support and complement the liturgy. Moments of silence are important to allow people space to take in some of the mystery. Perhaps silence could be kept following the readings or keeping silence during the intercessions might also be an appropriate way to create space.

Christmas is a time for enjoying the riches of grace that God lavishes upon us and having fun as a community in the presence of the Lord, as well as for remembering the cost of the Incarnation. In liturgical terms we are encouraged to celebrate the feast with all due solemnity. There may be something countercultural in this, and determining how we achieve it demands great sensitivity. Congregations grow at Christmas and people come to worship because they feel at home with the familiarity of a story and carols that they know. One way in which we can respond is to provide a service that is not simply dominated by sentimentality or a feel-good factor that lasts only until we walk out of the door, but which seeks to provide a genuine encounter with the God who becomes flesh of our flesh in order to restore our fallen humanity. This will always be something of a challenge!

Remember the isolated and sensitive

It is also important to remember that Christmas can be a very lonely time for some people and within the church community we need to be aware that not everyone is surrounded by family and friends; some people may be facing Christmas alone without the company of a partner or loved one who has died. What might the church offer in these circumstances? You could consider whether a meal might be provided in the church for those who would otherwise spend Christmas Day alone or whether invitations might be coordinated so that they can spend Christmas day with someone else. And there are particular issues for the liturgy on Christmas morning, particularly when the service is all age. It is important that the needs of those who come alone are not overshadowed by assumptions that everyone is going home to celebrate their Christmas with other people.

Help to make people feel at home

The presence of visitors, especially people who are unfamiliar with being in church, will add a particular dimension to the preparation of liturgy at Christmas. It may affect the choice of music and carols and you will need to ensure that directions for movement, both routine and extraordinary, are well communicated. It is often a puzzle to know whether this is best done verbally or by printing instructions on service sheets. There isn't an easy answer, but what is important is that you consider your situation and work out the best solution for that.

Light

Joy and celebration are the hallmarks of this season. One of the ways the coming of the Christ-child is represented in the worship space is by the use of light, picking up the scriptural references to the sun of righteousness and to Christ as the light of the world. You might want to consider the positioning of spotlights to create particular focus. The use of yellow filters can assist in creating a warm soft light within the building. You could spotlight or illuminate the crib or have a large star that is lit up. Candles may also be an important contribution to the lighting of a church building at Christmas time. In midwinter, the live flame of a candle seems to have the capacity to light up hearts and minds in a way that is very helpful in this darkest of seasons. Try reducing the church's usual electric lighting and using candles and spotlights to create a different pattern. (You need to bear in mind, however, that, if you are singing or reading unusual words, people will need enough light to read by.)

The senses

Music at Christmas will contrast with that used in Advent. It is worthwhile remembering that the first Christmas carols were words set to dance tunes. The provision of music for Christmas, both original carols and new settings, increases every year. There are now a good many books with carols from across the world so it might be good to explore the celebration of Christmas in a different tradition (see Resources). Congregation members from ethnic minorities would be well placed to provide advice about this.

Floral arrangements also may feature prominently in this season, in appropriate colours and styles. Consider the balance between the position of the Advent wreath in relation to other flowers so that the wreath, which has a liturgical function, is not overshadowed by huge floral displays too close by. When the last, white candle on the wreath is lit, consider an appropriate way of recognizing this representation of the presence of Christ in our midst. Will you do this with silence, or with a sung response to a prayer, perhaps?

If the use of incense is a normal part of the liturgical practice of the church, the variety, and amount, of incense used may be varied. If you do not normally use incense, you might consider using it at Christmas. It highlights the divinity of the child born in the stable in a subtle and non-verbal way, and provides a further sensory stimulation to help people remember the worship, pointing up the change in the mood and impetus of the season. It is not necessary for the incense to be carried and swung in the procession if you do not have the means to do this. You might simply use a bowl of hot charcoal near the crib or the Advent wreath and add grains of incense to the burning coals. Do not use too much on a first occasion but experiment to see how much is appropriate. And if you use this method, be sure that the hot bowl cannot be accessed by anyone, including children, unwittingly and accidentally. Do the dreaded risk assessment!

Gatherings and processions

Particular attention might be given to the Entrance Procession and to the Offertory on Christmas Day. What might be suitable ways for the praises and thanksgivings of God's people to be offered at the Lord's table? Who might be included in the offertory procession and what music might accompany these processions? Would it be good to use extra musical instruments? Would drums and percussion add to the excitement or solemnity? If you have brass players available, how could they be used?

If you do not have musicians available, you might use the procession idea in a different way. You could have people converging at the front of the church from different parts of the building, carrying all that you need for the service and then assembling the holy table or focal place as part of the Preparation. This is a particularly good way in a small congregation to ensure participation by a number of people. It might be good, though, to have had the opportunity to walk and talk it through beforehand. If you have a small congregation, the Preparation section of the service could be observed at the crib.

And at the end

You might consider offering rather more exciting refreshments after a Christmas service: mulled wine is seasonal but non-alcoholic punch will be more appropriate if driving is an issue. Make sure you also provide something suitable for children.

The provision of hospitality at Christmas is particularly significant and helps visitors to feel involved and welcome. Even if your church has no facilities at all, you could consider cutting and sharing a Christmas cake. Draw attention to this during the Dismissal and invite people to stay. Children enjoy serving people and the offer of a piece of cake or a mince pie from a child might just encourage the hesitant as well as demonstrating the value we place on simple, humble, service.

You might also wish to identify a way of encouraging the congregation to take the light and presence of Christ out from the church and into their homes and the rest of the day. The Christingle does this admirably, of course, and some churches offer the members of the congregation a card with a suitable image on it, or a star, as they leave, as a token to remind them that the Christ-child goes with them into the whole of their life.

Stand-alone seasonal material

Christmas Eucharist

Preparatory notes

Crib, Jesse tree or wreath: Which pathway?

If you are using material throughout the Advent, Christmas and Epiphany seasons from one of the three pathways suggested in this book, you will need to decide, in planning this service, how you include the ideas provided for Christmas in each pathway. If you are following the wreath pathway, for example, you will include the Prayers around the Wreath, suggested in the *Practical inclusive ideas* section, at the point of lighting the central white candle, and at the intercessions in this service. If you are following the crib pathway, use the ideas suggested in the crib pathway where it is appropriate. The Jesse tree pathway material is most appropriately used during the Liturgy of the Word with the Old Testament reading or during the sermon.

What needs to be prepared leading up to the service?

CRIB

The crib needs to be prepared and ready before the service begins. The Christ-child should not be in the crib, but should be carried in the opening procession and placed in the crib when it is dedicated.

INCENSE

The service makes provision for incense to be used. Prepare for this before the service. Put some scrunched up tinfoil in a metal bowl, ensuring that there is room for air to circulate below it. Put some charcoal tablets on the foil and light them well before the service starts. They will glow red and then grey. At the appropriate point in the service, sprinkle grains of incense on the hot charcoal to release its fragrance as it burns. Carry the bowl on a piece of wood so the person carrying it is not burnt. If your church has a thurible (a traditional incense burner on chain, which is swung as it is carried in procession), use that.

BREAD AND WINE

The bread and wine that are to be used in Communion may be placed near the crib until they are to be carried to the holy table. There is strong symbolism at Christmas in carrying the bread and wine from the crib, the place of Incarnation, to the holy table, where it is broken.

WREATH

If your church has an Advent wreath, move it so that it is close to the crib for this service. The service provides for the lighting of the wreath's white candle immediately after the crib is dedicated.

CANDLES AT THE ABSOLUTION

The service suggests that you might like to give everyone a candle to light when the Absolution is said. If you plan to do this, you will need a candle for each member of the congregation, to be given out when people arrive.

IMAGES FOR THE PRAYERS OF INTERCESSION

The service provides for various images to be placed beside the crib as the prayers are said. The juxtaposition of these images with the crib serves as a reminder that Christ came for all people at all times. There are images provided on the CD-ROM, though of course you may like to provide your own. If you have a digital projector and screen in the church, you may also like to project the images so that they can be seen by everyone as the prayers are said.

RESPONSE TABLE

The service makes provision for members of the congregation to make a practical response to the service and to receiving the bread and wine, if they choose to do so. Although this might seem a rather way-out idea, when this sort of thing is offered, it has been found that it is often appreciated. No one is obliged to take part, but it is there for those who would like to.

Stations may be available around the church so that people may make non- verbal responses to the gift of the Son of God in bread and wine.

A table with some sort of modelling medium, clay or synthetic clay might be appropriate.

There could also be a table with stars. People might take a star and place it near the crib, either to hang with a decoration hanger on a line, or placed on a dark background. The table might be labelled:

*Great little one, whose all-embracing birth
brings earth to heaven, stoops heaven to earth.*
(Richard Crashaw 1612–49)

*What needs to be made ready immediately
before the service?*
- The crib.
- The Christ-child should be where the procession starts so that it can be carried to the crib.
- The bowl or thurible for the incense should be where the procession starts. You will need a burner with which to light the incense.
- Bread and wine should either be placed near the crib before the service begins or carried there in procession at the start of the service.
- Move the wreath to stand near the crib. Make sure there is a light near it so that the white candle may be lit.
- If you plan to use candles at the Absolution, have them available where the service books are to be distributed.
- Images for the Prayers of Intercession, in whatever medium you plan to use them.
- Response tables with stars and modelling medium, placed where people can approach them after communion.

Questions

As you read through the text of the service it might be helpful to jot down any questions that arise for you as you begin to plan. They may be questions about why this particular suggestion is made, or they may be about how you would execute a particular suggestion in your situation, and whether it needs to be adapted. You are reminded to ask these questions as you work your way through this table.

Structure, movement and flow	Words/text	Multisensory	Participation
Questions	*Where is the crib going to be?* *How will you effect the gathering at the crib?*		
THE GATHERING	*You might consider using different voices for the words said at the Gathering. For example:* *President:* 'Do I not fill heaven and earth?' says the Lord. *Mother:* Now the Word is made flesh and laid in a narrow manger. *Congregation:* From eternity to eternity you are God, *Child:* and now we see you as a newborn child. [T&S 77]	As the congregation gathers, the church is unlit. When the ministers enter, they too move to the crib. The Christ-child is carried in procession and placed in the manger. The way in which the baby is carried should be significant: it could be carried by a minister, in a basket raised up so that everyone can see, or on a cushion, or it might be held close; it could be carried by a child or by an adult. The Christ-child should be placed tenderly in the crib. A bowl of burning charcoal and the bread and wine to be used for the Eucharist may be placed near to the manger. You may consider using ordinary bread and placing the wine is a glass jug so that it is visible while it is beside the crib.	The congregation is invited to gather at the crib. If the congregation is too large for everyone to gather at the crib, or if this is not convenient for some other reason, you might consider the children gathering at the crib.
Greeting	*The Greeting is said by the president* Grace, mercy and peace from God our Father and the Lord Jesus Christ be with you **and also with you.**		

Dedication of the Crib	*The dedication is said by the president:*	As words of dedication are said, incense grains may be added to the burning charcoal beside the crib.	The introduction to the Prayer of Dedication should be said by the President and then the congregation might say the rest of the prayer together. You might consider using the alternative collect instead of the prayer set at the dedication.
	Dear friends, as we meet to celebrate the birth of Christ, let us pray that God will bless this crib, that all who worship his Son, born of the Virgin Mary, may come to share his life in glory.		
	God our Father, on this day your Son Jesus Christ was born of the Virgin Mary for us and for our salvation: bless this crib, which we have prepared to celebrate that holy birth; may all who see it be strengthened in faith and receive the fullness of life he came to bring, who is alive and reigns for ever. **Amen.**	The Gospel book may be placed on a stand near the manger.	The congregation might be invited to sing the song 'Open our eyes, Lord, we want to see Jesus'.
	[T&S 77]		
	This prayer is said as the candle is lit. O Emmanuel: Christ with us; baby born in flesh and frailty; born to bring us back to God; we kneel in worship and adore you, bone of our bone and flesh of our flesh; one with us in the world you have made and born to show us the way of love. Though we were a people lost in darkness, your light has shone upon us; though we lived in a land of sorrow; your grace has rescued us. With a joyful noise, with trumpets, music and singing we join the dance of all creation to shout in praise at your coming. Let the earth cry 'Glory!' **Alleluia! Alleluia! Amen.**	The white candle on the Advent wreath may be lit. All the candles in the church may be lit now.	

Prayers of Penitence	The sun of righteousness has dawned with healing in his wings. Let us come to the light of Christ, confessing our sins in penitence and faith. *cf Malachi 4.2* [NP 79] God our Father, you sent your Son full of grace and truth: forgive our failure to receive him. Lord, have mercy. **Lord, have mercy.** Jesus our Saviour, you were born in poverty and laid in a manger: forgive our greed and rejection of your ways. Christ, have mercy. **Christ, have mercy.** Spirit of love, your servant Mary responded joyfully to your call: forgive the hardness of our hearts. Lord, have mercy. **Lord, have mercy.**	The Prayers of Penitence may be offered by the deacon or an assistant minister, from the crib.	As the prayers are said, or at the end of the words, members of the congregation may take straw to place in the crib, or a piece of paper to place beside the crib as a token of their confession of sin.
Absolution	[T&S 78] May God who loved the world so much that he sent his Son to be our Saviour forgive *us our* sins and make *us* holy to serve him in the world, through Jesus Christ our Lord. **Amen.**	At the Absolution, all the lights in the church may be lit or members of the congregation may light candles.	
Gloria in Excelsis	*A carol ('Angels from the realms of glory' or 'The Sussex Carol' at a night-time service), or a Taizé Gloria or the Peruvian Gloria may be sung instead of the Gloria in Excelsis.*	As the Gloria or appropriate carol is sung, those who have gathered at the crib move to their places in the church.	

Collect	Let us pray in the peace of this Christmas celebration that our joy in the birth of Christ will last for ever. *Silence is kept.* Lord Jesus Christ, your birth at Bethlehem draws us to kneel in wonder at heaven touching earth: accept our heartfelt praise as we worship you, our Saviour and our eternal God. **Amen.** [T&S 79]		
Questions	*What are your questions about the Gathering section of the service?*		
THE LITURGY OF THE WORD		The Liturgy of the Word may be celebrated in whatever way is appropriate. A nativity play may replace some of the readings.	
Readings			
Gospel Reading		The Gospel may be read from the crib or it may be appropriate to read it from the customary place. The Gospel book may then be carried in procession from the crib to the reading place.	
Sermon			

The Creed	*If it is appropriate, the following Affirmation of Faith, based on words from Ephesians 3, may be used:* Let us declare our faith in God. **We believe in God the Father, from whom every family in heaven and on earth is named.** **We believe in God the Son, who lives in our hearts through faith, and fills us with his love.** **We believe in God the Holy Spirit, who strengthens us with power from on high.** **We believe in one God; Father, Son and Holy Spirit. Amen.** [T&S 100]		

Prayers of Intercession	Let us pray to Jesus our Saviour.
	Christ, born in a stable,
	give courage to all who are homeless.
	Jesus, Saviour,
	hear our prayer.
	
	Christ, for whom the angels sang,
	give the song of the kingdom to all
	    who weep.
	Jesus, Saviour,
	hear our prayer.
	
	Christ, worshipped by the shepherds,
	give peace on earth to all who are
	    oppressed.
	Jesus, Saviour,
	hear our prayer.
	
	Christ, before whom the wise men
	    knelt,
	give humility and wisdom to all who
	    govern.
	Jesus, Saviour,
	hear our prayer.
		Prayers may be led from the crib.
		
		An image of a homeless person is placed in the crib.
		
		An image of a weeping person is placed in the crib.
		
		An image of oppression is placed in the crib.
		
		An image of the national flags may be placed in the crib.	

	Christ, whose radiance filled a lowly manger, give the glory of your resurrection to all who rest in you. Jesus, Saviour, **hear our prayer.** **Jesus, Saviour, child of Mary,** **you know us and love us,** **you share our lives** **and hear our prayer.** **Glory to you for ever. Amen.** [T&S 67]	An image of resurrection may be placed in the crib.	
THE LITURGY OF THE SACRAMENT			
The Peace	Mercy and truth are met together, righteousness and peace have kissed each other; *from Psalm 85* [CW 693] The peace of the Lord be always with you **and also with you.**		The Peace is shared.
Question	*On this occasion, would the Peace be more appropriate at the Gathering?*		
Preparation of the Table Taking of the bread and wine	With this bread that we bring **we shall remember Jesus.** With this wine that we bring **we shall remember Jesus.** Bread for his body, wine for his blood, gifts from God to his table we bring. **We shall remember Jesus.** [CW 292] Word made flesh, life of the world, in your incarnation you embraced our poverty: by your Spirit may we share in your riches. **Amen.** [T&S 83]	The bread and wine should be carried in procession from the crib to the holy table.	It may be appropriate to invite the whole congregation to gather around the holy table, or the children may be invited to do so. It may be necessary to move any rails.

The Eucharistic Prayer	*Eucharistic Prayer A may be used with the following preface and a congregational response.* All glory and honour be yours always and everywhere, mighty creator, ever-living God. We give you thanks and praise for your Son, our Saviour Jesus Christ, who for love of our fallen race humbled himself, and *[on this night]* was born of the Virgin Mary by the power of your Spirit, and lived as one of us. In this mystery of the Word made flesh you have caused his light to shine in our hearts, to give knowledge of your glory in the face of Jesus Christ. In him we see our God made visible and so are caught up in the love of the God we cannot see. Therefore with all the angels of heaven we lift our voices to proclaim the glory of your name and sing our joyful hymn of praise. [T&S 73, adapted]	The lighting in the church could be lowered so that the holy table and the crib only are lit, to help people to focus on these two places in particular.	
The Lord's Prayer	*The Lord's Prayer is said.*		
Breaking of the Bread	We break the bread of life, and that life is the light of the world. **God here among us,** **light in the midst of us,** **bring us to light and life.** [T&S 167]		
Invitation to communion	*The president says this or another invitation to communion.* Christ is the true bread which has come down from heaven. **Lord, give us this bread always.** [T&S 85]		

Giving of Communion	The bread of heaven in Christ Jesus. The cup of life in Christ Jesus.	Stations may be available around the church so that people may make non- verbal responses to the gift of the Son of God in bread and wine. A table with some sort of modelling medium, clay or synthetic clay might be appropriate. Also a table with stars. People might take a star and place it near the crib, either to hang with a decoration hanger on a line, or placed on a dark background. The table might be labelled: Great little one, whose all-embracing birth brings earth to heaven, stoops heaven to earth. (Richard Crashaw 1612–49)	Members of the congregation are invited to move around the stations to make their non-verbal responses.
Prayer after Communion	Father of all, we give you thanks and praise, that when we were still far off you met us in your Son and brought us home. Dying and living, he declared your love, gave us grace, and opened the gate of glory. **May we who share Christ's body live his risen life;** **we who drink his cup bring life to others;** **we whom the Spirit lights give light to the world.** Keep us firm in the hope you have set before us, so we and all your children shall be free, and the whole earth live to praise your name; through Christ our Lord. **Amen.** [CW 182]		

CONCLUSION	*A hymn may be sung.*		During the hymn, the ministers and the children could move to the crib and the conclusion be led from there.
	This Proclamation of Christ may be used with a loudly shouted response		
	Let us bless the living God:		
	Jesus Christ was born of the Virgin Mary, **revealed in his glory,**		
	worshipped by the angels, **proclaimed among the nations,**		
	believed in throughout the world, **exalted to the highest heavens.**		
	Blessed be God our strength and our salvation, **now and for ever. Amen.**		
	[T&S 75]		
	And the blessing …		
	Go in peace to love and serve the Lord. **In the name of Christ. Amen.**		

A blue Christmas service

Introduction

For some people, the celebrations that accompany Christmas are too joyous for the situation they are in. A blue Christmas service offers the chance to remember and worship, whilst recognizing the pain that can be brought into sharp focus at such times. Because of the emotions that are likely to be around, this service needs to be handled with great sensitivity. Adapt it according to your particular circumstances.

Preparatory notes

What needs to be prepared leading up to the service?

- You will need to have the crib in place for this service.
- You will also need a large branch on which people can tie pieces of blue ribbon or cloth. The branch will need to be held upright in some way. The best way may be to root it firmly in a tub of earth or sand.

- You will need pieces of blue ribbon or strips of blue cloth. There need to be enough for each member of the congregation to have two pieces each, one to hang on the tree and one to take away. Keep them in a basket.

What needs to be made ready immediately before the service?

- As this is likely to be a quiet, intimate, service, consider organizing the furniture so that the chairs are in semicircles. The focus should be a crib scene, with a large unlit candle to one side and a large, bare branch on the other. Place a taper near the candle. The lighting should be subdued.
- Give each person a strip of blue ribbon or cloth as they arrive. Have a basket of extra strips near the bare branch to be given out so that people may take them away.
- The leader should be seated as people arrive.
- Have quiet music playing as people gather.

Structure, movement and flow	Words/text	Multisensory	Participation
			Give each person a strip of blue ribbon or cloth as they arrive.
The Gathering	We meet in the presence of God **who knows our needs, hears our cries, feels our pain, and heals our wounds.**		
	The leader says something like: The season of Christmas can bring grief as well as joy, despair as well as hope. We have gathered together from many places, with burdens and emotions that seem to conflict with the joy of Christ's birth. Yet we are not alone. It was into a world of pain and hurt and confusion that Christ was born. And Christ is with us still.	The large candle is lit.	

Carol	*'O come, O come, Emmanuel'*		
The Word	Reading: Isaiah 4.3-5		
	Leader: Come to us, Incarnate Lord. Meet us in the wilderness of our pain and loss. Help us to recognize signs of hope in our despair, moments of joy in our grief. Bring light into our darkness as we bring ourselves into your presence.		
	Leader: As we prepare to hear the story of Christmas, I invite you to offer your pain and loss to God as you drape or tie cloth to the tree.	Quiet music might be played.	People come forward to drape or tie their cloth or ribbon to the bare branch.
	Reading: Isaiah 9.2b,6,7		
	Reading: Matthew 1.18-21		
Carol	*'O little town of Bethlehem', verses 1 and 2*		
	Reading: Luke 2.1-7		
Carol	*'O little town of Bethlehem',*	*verses 3 and 4*	
Intercessions	Let us pray to the Lord. Lord, come to your people. **In your mercy, set us free.** Unlooked for, Christ comes. To shepherds, watching their sheep through the long, dark night, he comes with the glory of the angels' song and in the humility of the manger. *Silence* Loving God, we pray for our community … In the midst of our everyday lives, surprise us with glimpses of your glorious, humble love, at the heart of existence. Lord, come to your people. **In your mercy, set us free.**		

Searched for,
Christ comes.

To the wise and powerful,
star-led to Bethlehem, seeking a king,
he comes, child of Mary,
crowned with meekness,
worthy of every gift.

Silence

Loving God, we pray for the leaders
    of the world …
Guide them with your light
to seek wisdom, justice and peace.
Lord, come to your people.
In your mercy, set us free.

Longed for,
Christ comes.

To Anna and Simeon,
whose days are lived in faithful
    expectation,
he comes, a new life to the old,
a living prophecy of hope.

Silence

Loving God, we pray for the Church
in all the world …

Unite us by your Spirit,
and make us faithful witnesses to the
    hope we have in you.

Lord, come to your people.
In your mercy, set us free.

Prayed for,
Christ comes.

To men and women crying out in
darkness, pain and loneliness,
he comes, at one with us,
our Saviour, healer and friend.

Silence

Loving God, we pray for those whose
    lives are hard and painful
or whose existence is sorrowful,
    bitter or empty …
In their need, may they know your
    healing touch,
reaching out to comfort, strengthen
    and restore.

Lord, come to your people.
In your mercy, set us free.

	Unlooked for and not searched for, longed for and prayed for, loving God, you come to us now, as you have come to your people in every age. We thank you for all who have reflected the light of Christ. Help us to follow their example and bring us with them to eternal life; through Jesus Christ our Lord. **Amen.**		The leader invites people to take a strip of cloth from the basket during the singing of the last carol as a reminder that God goes with them in their pain, and as a sign of hope for healing.
Carol	*'It came upon the midnight clear'*		

| Dismissal | Restore us, O Lord God of hosts. **Show us the light of your countenance and we shall be saved.** Will you not give us life again **that your people may rejoice in you?** Show us your mercy, O God, **and grant us your salvation.** May God the Father keep you in all your days. May God the Son shield you in all your ways. May God the Spirit bring you healing and peace. May God the Holy Trinity drive all darkness from you and pour upon you blessing and light. **Amen.** Christ, who by his Incarnation gathered into one things earthly and heavenly, fill you with peace and goodwill and make you partakers of the divine nature; and the blessing of God almighty, the Father, the Son, and the Holy Spirit, be among you now and for ever. **Amen.** [T&S 73] | | |
| | | Quiet music plays as people leave. There should not be a sense of 'hurry' to get people out, as some may wish to sit quietly for a while. | |

Ideas for a New Year celebration

Introduction and background

This is an idea for combining some of the prayers and liturgy offered in *Times and Seasons* with a New Year's Eve party, including the Scottish custom of first-footing. This custom suggests that the first person to cross a home's threshold after midnight on New Year's Eve comes bearing gifts: coal, salt, small cakes, and a coin. (Traditionally the gift bearer has been a dark-haired man. This custom may have developed from the time of the Vikings when a fair-haired visitor may well have been a raider.) Various meanings have been attributed to the gifts and these vary slightly from one tradition to another, but for this celebration it is suggested that each is received with a biblical quotation. Quotations are suggested and, if you wished to vary the gifts, you could undoubtedly find relevant references.

In some places, finding a piece of coal will be very difficult and it may be appropriate to substitute something else to represent the idea of fuel, a small log for example, or, if you wish to be more realistic, an electric plug or a small cylinder of gas or even a light bulb. A lit candle might also be appropriate – but don't try wrapping it up! You will need to decide whether to explain the connection with the old symbol of a piece of coal and the connection of all this with the Bible text.

Where to hold your celebration

The celebration suggested here could easily take place in a home. Where the turning of the year is marked in church, then a fuller service would probably be more appropriate, but the suggestions here will provide ideas for linking a less formal act of worship with home celebrations.

At a New Year's Eve party, this celebration might be used sitting around a meal table or at the fireside or at a doorway. If you are going to mark the turning of the year with fireworks and it is a dry evening (or you are very tough and have warm coats), you could even use it outside, under the stars.

You will need

- The words of the service for everyone;
- A tray with a piece of coal, pot of salt, a few small cakes (or perhaps a piece of Christmas cake) and a coin, together with a Bible reference for each of the gifts. These are provided below.
- Something to share around at the end to mark celebration and community. You could open a bottle of sparkling wine, share mince pies or cut a Christmas cake. You might have a few fireworks, or inside, particularly if there are children present, you could use party poppers.

Bible verses for the gifts

Fuel: Isaiah 44.13-16

The carpenter … cuts down cedars or chooses a holm tree or an oak and lets it grow strong among the trees of the forest. He plants a cedar and the rain nourishes it. Then it can be used as fuel. Part of it he takes and warms himself; he kindles a fire and bakes bread … Half of it he burns in the fire; over this half he roasts meat, eats it, and is satisfied. He also warms himself and says, 'Ah, I am warm, I can feel the fire!'

Salt: Mark 9.49

For everyone will be salted with fire. Salt is good; but if salt has lost its saltiness, how can you season it? Have salt in yourselves, and be at peace with one another.

Small cakes: 1 Kings 17.8-16

Then the word of the Lord came to Elijah, saying, 'Go now to Zarephath, which belongs to Sidon, and live there; for I have commanded a widow there to feed you.' So he set out and went to Zarephath. When he came to the gate of the town, a widow was there gathering sticks; he called to her and said, 'Bring me a little water in a vessel, so that I may drink.' As she was going to bring it, he called to her and said, 'Bring me a morsel of bread in your hand.' But she said, 'As the Lord your God lives, I have nothing baked, only a handful of meal in a jar, and a little oil in a jug; I am now gathering a couple of sticks, so that I may go home and prepare it for myself and my son, that we may eat it, and die.' Elijah said to her, 'Do not be afraid; go and do as you have said; but first make me a little cake of it and bring it to me, and afterwards make something for yourself and your son. For thus says the Lord the God of Israel: The jar of meal will not be emptied and the jug of oil will not fail until the day that the Lord sends rain on the earth.' She went and did as Elijah said, so that she as well as he and her household ate for many days. The jar of meal was not emptied, neither did the jug of oil fail, according to the word of the Lord that he spoke by Elijah.

Coins: Luke 15.8-10

What woman having ten silver coins, if she loses one of them, does not light a lamp, sweep the house, and search carefully until she finds it? When she has found it, she calls together her friends and neighbours, saying, 'Rejoice with me, for I have found the coin that I had lost.' Just so, I tell you, there is joy in the presence of the angels of God over one sinner who repents.

The celebration

Begin this celebration at 11.45 p.m. or a little before so that it will end just on midnight.

Introduction

(This is based on the Invitation to Confession below. Do not use both. If you are going to use the Confession section, don't use this.)

As we come to the start of a new year, 20 ..., let us pray that God will be with us through the coming year; and let us seek God's grace to number our days and turn our hearts to wisdom.

Confession section (optional)

INVITATION TO CONFESSION

As we come to the Lord at the start of this New Year, let us seek his grace to number our days that we may apply our hearts to wisdom as we confess our sins in penitence and faith.

KYRIE CONFESSION

Lord Jesus, you are mighty God and Prince of Peace:
Lord, have mercy.
Lord, have mercy.

Lord Jesus, you are Son of God and Son of Mary:
Christ, have mercy.
Christ, have mercy.

Lord Jesus, you are Word made flesh
and splendour of the Father:
Lord, have mercy.
Lord, have mercy.

[T&S 105]

Collect

Eternal Lord God,
we give you thanks for bringing us through the
    changes of time
to the beginning of another year.
Forgive us the wrong we have done in the year that
    is past,
and help us to spend the rest of our days
to your honour and glory;
through Jesus Christ our Lord.
Amen.

[T&S 106]

Gospel Acclamation

Alleluia, alleluia.
I am the Alpha and Omega, the first and the last,
the beginning and the end.
Alleluia.

[T&S 106]

A reading from the Gospel according to Mark,

Mark 13.32-37: The necessity for watchfulness

But about that day or hour no one knows, neither the angels in heaven, nor the Son, but only the Father. Beware, keep alert; for you do not know when the time will come. It is like a man going on a journey, when he leaves home and puts his slaves in charge, each with his work, and commands the doorkeeper to be on the watch. Therefore, keep awake – for you do not know when the master of the house will come, in the evening, or at midnight, or at cockcrow, or at dawn, or else he may find you asleep when he comes suddenly. And what I say to you I say to all: Keep awake.

Intercessions

In a world of change and hope,
faithful God
glorify your name.

In our seeking and our finding
faithful God,
glorify your name.

In prosperity and need,
faithful God
glorify your name.

In words and action,
faithful God
glorify your name.

Among our friends
and in our homes,
faithful God
glorify your name.

In our times of joy and sorrow,
faithful God
glorify your name.

In our strengths and triumphs,
in our weakness and at our death,
faithful God
glorify your name.

In your saints in glory
and on the day of Christ's coming,
faithful God
glorify your name.

[T&S 107, adapted]

As midnight sounds, the door is opened, the wine bottle is opened or a firework is let off outside and, if you are in a church and it has bells, the bells are rung. The first-footer enters with a tray or a bag containing the gifts. The bearer of the gifts presents them to different people, who each read the biblical text accompanying the gift they have received.

When all the gifts have been distributed, you could join hands and say together this prayer, which originates from the Methodist Covenant Service:

I am no longer my own but yours.
Put me to what you will,
rank me with whom you will;
put me to doing,
   put me to suffering;
let me be employed for you
  or laid aside for you,
exalted for you
   or brought low for you;
let me be full,
   let me be empty,
let me have all things,
   let me have nothing;
I freely and wholeheartedly yield all things
to your pleasure and disposal.
And now, glorious and blessed God,
Father, Son and Holy Spirit,
you are mine and I am yours.
So be it.
And the covenant now made on earth,
let it be ratified in heaven.
Amen.

[T&S 110]

Or you could join hands and say The Grace together.

Then share the drinks and food or enjoy the rest of the fireworks!

Christmas:
The wreath pathway

Practical inclusive ideas

Using the wreath through the Christmas season

With the arrival of Christmas, other decoration may be inserted into the wreath. In readiness for Christmas Eve, add white flowers, red berries and white/gold ribbons, which may descend to the floor from the points where the candles are. You may even wish to add tinsel and coloured balls.

The wreath can form a suitable focus for prayer throughout the Christmas season and on into Epiphany, with prayers that centre on the Christ candle and its associations with the coming of Christ and the light of Christ for the salvation of the world.

If there is a crib in the church and you are using a wreath on a movable stand, you might move this to a place near the crib. Alternatively, if you are using four floor-standing candles, four people might take a light from these candles and walk to the crib, where they light a single candle positioned by the crib as the prayer is said. Much will depend on the particular spatial arrangements of your church and where the crib itself is placed. The wreath will need to be reconfigured for Christmas and Epiphany and candle holders placed according to the number of Sundays.

Wreath prayers through Christmas

For use at a crib service

Where the angels dance
and the star swings low:
Come, Lord Jesus!

Where a mother cries
and a child is born:
Come, Lord Jesus!

When the good news is shown
to a world amazed
Come, Lord Jesus!

To earth's darkest place
where all seems lost:
Come, Lord Jesus!

To our hearts and lives
and our hopes for the world:
Come, Lord Jesus!

Come to bring hope;
come to bring peace.
Today and for ever.
Amen.

Christmas Day

O Emmanuel: Christ with us;
baby born in flesh and frailty, born to bring us back
*   to God;*
we kneel in worship and adore you, bone of our
*   bone and flesh of our flesh;*
one with us in the world you have made and born to
*   show us the way of love.*
Though we were a people lost in darkness, your light
*   has shone upon us;*
though we lived in a land of sorrow; your grace has
*   rescued us.*
With a joyful noise, with trumpets, music and
*   singing,*
we join the dance of all creation to shout in praise at
*   your coming.*
Let the earth cry 'Glory!'
Alleluia! Alleluia!
Amen.

The maker of all,
high king of heaven
in mercy and grace
is born for our redemption.
Sing a new song.
Love has come down to meet us!

A star in the sky
and a bright angel host;
the light of the world –
a surprising glory.
Sing a new song.

CHRISTMAS

Love has come down to meet us!

In judgement and joy,
with favour and blessing;
Christ makes all things new
and restores what was lost.
Sing a new song.
Love has come down to meet us!

In the company of God's people,
in the joy of all creation,
present in silence and in shouts of praise,
and with us in bread and wine.
Sing a new song.
Love has come down to meet us!
Today and for ever,
Amen.

The First Sunday of Christmas

O Emmanuel: Christ for us,
glory of God to earth come low;
in your love and pity you have redeemed us by your
*   presence;*
lifting us from the dust to be your people
and clothing us with garments of salvation.
Beneath the dance of the angels and the song of
*   peace on earth,*
be for us a sign of the way and a light to defeat the
*   dark;*
that, though we know our own weakness,
we may find our strength in you,
and become a crown of beauty in your hands.
Let the earth cry: 'Glory!'
Alleluia! Alleluia!
Amen.

Our God is the King over all.
Sing to the Lord a new song!

Light dawns for the righteous.
Sing to the Lord a new song!

The heavens tell of his glory.
Sing to the Lord a new song!

He delights in his people.
Sing to the Lord a new song!

Praise his name with dancing.
Sing to the Lord a new song!

He has become our salvation.
Sing to the Lord a new song!
Alleluia! Alleluia!
Amen.

The Second Sunday of Christmas

O Emmanuel: Christ among us;
a baby sheltered in a mother's arms – soon to grow
*   as child and man,*
living and loving in the world of your making;
you restore what has been broken and lift up the lost
and will in the fullness of time gather all things to
*   yourself.*
Eternal Word, present in creation and light of life to
*   all who believe,*
shine in our hearts and lives
that we who have set our hope on you
may live for ever to your glory and praise.
Let the earth cry: 'Glory!'
Alleluia! Alleluia!
Amen.

To those in darkness, and those in the light,
Christ has come.
Let the earth sing praise!

To his faithful people, and all who are lost,
Christ has come.
Let the earth sing praise!

To those in sorrow, and those in joy,
Christ has come.
Let the earth sing praise!

To both least and great, to first and last,
Christ has come.
Let the earth sing praise!

To speak his peace and to call us to follow,
Christ has come.
Let the earth sing praise!

Today and for ever, and at the end,
Christ has come.
Let the earth sing praise!
Amen!

The wreath in groups

Adults

The following meditations can be used in small groups or as part of a larger gathering for worship or prayer. In a small group, you might want to end the meditation by lighting the candles on the Christmas wreath. Create a focal point by covering a small table with cloth in the appropriate liturgical colours (white and gold). The icon of the nativity by Rublev could be placed in front of the table and a small candle in front of it from which light can be taken to light the wreath candles. You will need to read through the meditations several times in order to become completely familiar with the words. Pauses are suggested but you will need to judge the length of the period of silence according to the group. Spend a few moments in the group to allow people to centre their thoughts and to get comfortable before you start.

Meditation 1

In the beginning was the Word;
the Word was with God
and the Word was God.
Before all things were made
the Word already was.
From the darkness and chaos,
the word drew out the light;
shaped seas below and heavens above;
brought forth the dry land;
called out the multitudes of living things
and sang whole worlds into being.
This word, that was before all, in all, through all,
called man and woman from the dust of earth.

Still calling, still creating,
the word of God
spoke from the burning bush
and was written for the life of the people
on tablets of stone for all time.

This voice,
whispered across the desert night,
was in the cloud and the pillar,
spoke in signs and wonders,
and in the still small voice:
'I am.'

'I am,'
here and now … and present for all eternity
'I am.'

The word of God
burned in the mouths of the prophets
'Turn to me with all your heart!'
The word of God spoke of old in the place of death:
'Shall these bones live?'
'Only you know, O Lord.'
In the valley of dry bones,
your word is water and breath;
in the valley of dry bones,
your word is life itself

for the parched soul.
In the words of the angel to a frightened girl;
in the calling of the disciples;
in the cry of desolation on the cross;
in the words of restoration in a dawn garden;
and in the calling of my own name,
God's voice breathes life.

Into the longings of the human heart;
in the urban desert and suburban emptiness;
the word of God still speaks its 'I am' –
to those who are attentive,
and to those who have yet to hear …
'I am.'
In the midst of life's distress
and in the centre of life's joys,
as the source and end of faith's journey
'I am.'

In the silence I invite you to call to mind the word of
God as breath of life in a dead place …
as fire that burns and cleanses …
and as water in a dry land.

(Keep silence)

Hold these images in your mind, asking that God
would be again for you breath, fire, and water – the
source of life and strength for ministry.

(Keep silence)

And in the silence let us ask God that we might hear
again God's voice calling us by our own name …

(Keep silence)

Teach us, O God,
to hear your word with open hearts.
Teach us, O God,
to respond to your voice with open lives;
and in all our searching and struggling
to know the presence of Christ
and to make known his ways and his works
wherever we are called to be his witnesses.
Amen.

Light the appropriate candles on the wreath, using
the words of the following wreath prayer.

THE FIRST SUNDAY OF CHRISTMAS

O Emmanuel: Christ for us;
glory of God to earth come low;
in your love and pity you have redeemed us by your
    presence;
lifting us from the dust to be your people

and clothing us with garments of salvation.
Beneath the dance of the angels and the song of
*   peace on earth,*
be for us a sign of the way and a light to defeat the
*   dark;*
that, though we know our own weakness,
we may find our strength in you;
and become a crown of beauty in your hands.
Let the earth cry: 'Glory!'
Alleluia! Alleluia!
Amen.

Meditation 2

For the following meditation you will need a CD
containing 'Seven o'clock news/Silent night' by
Simon and Garfunkel. This can be found on the
album *The Definitive Simon and Garfunkel* (Sony
Music Inc. 1991) and other compilation albums. This
is an old recording now but the interplay of the well
known carol 'Silent night' and the voices reading the
news of the day is still thought provoking and
reminds us that it is into the harsh realities of life that
Christ came and still comes today.

The Word became flesh
and dwelt among us;
not God who remains aloof,
distant from the pains and mess of everyday living;
not a God somehow 'above all that',
but a God who steps down
to become one of us.
In a small, enemy-occupied city,
to the least of all peoples,
in the muck of the stable floor …
God is.
In the adulation of the crowds;
in the press and crush of desperate need,
God is.
In healing and hope
and in loss and weeping,
God is –
for the Word became flesh
and dwelt among us.
Where the hungry are fed
and the oppressed go free
God is.
Where children are blessed
and the outcast is welcomed home,
God is.

In death, in life
on the road that lies between,
God is –
for the Word became flesh
and dwelt among us.

In healings and miracles;
in the touch that saves a person from despair,
God is.
In the anguish of the Garden, the torment of the cross
and the power that raised Christ from the dead,
God is.

Not to save us from life's troubles
but to lead us through.
Not to magic pain away
but to whisper the hope of life restored.

And today,
wherever his people call upon his name
and worship in spirit and in truth,
God is.
In the cry for justice
and the turning away of disgrace,
God is –
for the Word becomes flesh today,
and dwells among us.

In the silence I invite you to call to mind the word of
God revealed in Scripture
and today's world in all its beauty and terror.

Hold both in your heart, asking that God would
speak again into the world's distress and breathe new
life through all creation … (pause)

asking that God would meet us again in Scripture
and in the world, enlivening both by his presence.

(Keep silence)

('Seven o'clock news/Silent night' is played.)

(Keep silence)

Teach us, O God,
to speak your word with boldness.
Teach us, O God,
to speak your words of comfort and peace
and in all our teaching and preaching
to make Christ known in the world,
calling women, men and children home to God
in the power of the Spirit.
Amen.

Light the appropriate candles on the wreath, using
the words of the following wreath prayer.

THE SECOND SUNDAY OF CHRISTMAS

O Emmanuel: Christ among us;
a baby sheltered in a mother's arms – soon to grow
   as child and man,
living and loving in the world of your making.
You restore what has been broken and lift up the lost
and will in the fullness of time gather all things to
   yourself.
Eternal Word, present in creation and light of life to
   all who believe;
shine in our hearts and lives
that we who have set our hope on you
may live for ever to your glory and praise.
Let the earth cry: 'Glory!'
Alleluia! Alleluia!
Amen.

The wreath at home

The wreath will need to be reconfigured for this time.
Add white flowers and gold ribbons.

Lighting the candles together

The candles can be lit at the agreed time each day
and one of the following prayers said:

The First Sunday of Christmas

O Emmanuel: Christ for us;
glory of God to earth come low;
in your love and pity you have redeemed us by your
   presence;
lifting us from the dust to be your people
and clothing us with garments of salvation.
Beneath the dance of the angels and the song of
   peace on earth;
be for us a sign of the way and a light to defeat the
   dark;
that, though we know our own weakness,
we may find our strength in you;
and become a crown of beauty in your hands.
Let the earth cry: 'Glory!'
Alleluia! Alleluia!
Amen.

Our God is the king over all.
Sing to the Lord a new song!

Light dawns for the righteous.
Sing to the Lord a new song!

The heavens tell of his glory.
Sing to the Lord a new song!

He delights in his people.
Sing to the Lord a new song!

Praise his name with dancing!
Sing to the Lord a new song!

He has become our salvation.
Sing to the Lord a new song!
Alleluia! Alleluia!
Amen.

The Second Sunday of Christmas

O Emmanuel: Christ among us;
a baby sheltered in a mother's arms – soon to grow
   as child and man,
living and loving in the world of your making;
you restore what has been broken and lift up the lost
and will in the fullness of time gather all things to
   yourself.
Eternal Word, present in creation and light of life to
   all who believe;
shine in our hearts and lives,
that we who have set our hope on you
may live for ever to your glory and praise.
Let the earth cry: 'Glory!'
Alleluia! Alleluia!
Amen.

To those in darkness; and those in the light,
Christ has come.
Let the earth sing praise!

To his faithful people, and all who are lost,
Christ has come.
Let the earth sing praise!

To those in sorrow, and those in joy,
Christ has come.
Let the earth sing praise!

To both least and great, to first and last,
Christ has come.
Let the earth sing praise!

To speak his peace and to call us to follow,
Christ has come.
Let the earth sing praise!

Today and for ever, and at the end,
Christ has come.
Let the earth sing praise!
Amen!

The Twelve Days of Christmas

'The Twelve Days of Christmas' is a well-known Christmas song. It seems entirely secular, has something of the folk song about it and perhaps reflects the fun of Christmas traditions from several centuries ago. However, there are those who suggest that it was actually a secret catechetical song, used for teaching aspects of Christianity at a time when a particular religious group was forbidden to practise its faith, possibly during the time of the English Civil War or the Commonwealth. It appears there is no evidence to bear out this theory but the song is still fun to sing and could still be used to teach the bits of information in a way that is great fun. It often features on Christmas cards so finding pictures for each verse should not be too difficult.

The possible hidden meanings

1.	A partridge in a pear tree	Jesus, the only Son of God
2.	Two turtle doves	Testaments in the Bible, Old and New
3.	French hens	Virtues: faith, hope and love (sometimes called charity) (1 Corinthians 13.13)
4.	Calling birds	Gospels: Matthew, Mark, Luke and John
5.	Gold rings	Books of the Law (the first five books of the Old Testament: Genesis, Exodus, Leviticus, Numbers and Deuteronomy)
6.	Geese a-laying	Days of creation (Genesis 1)
7.	Swans a-swimming	Gifts of the Spirit (Romans 12.6-8; see also 1 Corinthians 12.8-11)
8.	Maids a-milking	Beatitudes (Blessed are the poor, etc. Matthew 5.3-10)
9.	Ladies dancing	Fruits of the Spirit (Galatians 5.22-23a)
10.	Lords a-leaping	Commandments (Exodus 20.1-17)
11.	Pipers piping	Faithful apostles (those called by Jesus originally, without Judas Iscariot, who betrayed him) (Luke 6.14-16)
12.	Drummers drumming	Points of doctrine in the Apostles' Creed

Make Twelve Days of Christmas boxes

Find twelve tiny boxes: the kind in which jewellers supply earrings would be ideal but you can often find tiny boxes elsewhere. Put inside each one an account from the table above of one of the Christian ideas it could represent, together with the relevant Bible passage if you like. You could also add a tiny present. Wrap up each tiny box in coloured paper. Stick on to it a picture of the relevant verse of the 'Twelve Days of Christmas' song and put them around the wreath (or into it if it is large enough). Unpack one box each day when you light the candles. For children, just reading out the explanation will be enough. You could pin the explanations up on a family noticeboard for a while. Adults might be interested in doing a bit more research about some of the less obvious ideas.

Add a star to the wreath each day to express your thanks.

The wreath in outreach

Christmas is most often thought of as a time for families and friends. Thus those people who find themselves alone at Christmas are acutely aware of those who are absent, whether through death, separation, divorce or living abroad. As this is the Feast of the Incarnation, God with us, it is appropriate to reflect on the ways we might make the presence of God's love real where we live and work, in our homes and families, with our friends and in our communities.

Some thoughts

In preparation for Christmas you might consider, as a church, where the homeless, the stranger, the widow and the orphan are to be found in your neighbourhood. Plan to take a little wreath with its five candles, and perhaps a small Christmas cake or a Christmas pudding to people in this situation.

People could be invited to revisit the legend of Good King Wenceslas and the tradition of Boxing Day and make time to visit someone outside the family circle.

Christmas:
The crib pathway

Practical inclusive ideas

Use of the crib through Christmas

The crib needs to be fully prepared on Christmas Eve. If you are intending to install the figures during a service, make sure they are all prepared and ready to add. If the crib is to be already set up, you will need in place the animals, Mary and Joseph, the shepherds and angels. Ensure the Christ-child is ready to be placed in the crib. The child can be placed in the crib at a service on Christmas Eve, or at midnight, or even on Christmas Day.

Liturgical use

Continue to use the meditation space beside the crib created in Advent, with the bowl and the sentences from the Scripture readings to be written on slips of paper. Roll these up and place them in the bowl beside the crib and tie them with gold ribbon for Christmas. Invite people to take a sentence and use it as an aid for prayer, thought or meditation during the week.

Here are some suggestions for these Scripture sentences:

Christmas Eve

Year A

By the tender mercy of our God, the dawn from on high will break upon us, to give light to those who sit in darkness and in the shadow of death, to guide our feet into the way of peace.

Luke 1.78-79

Year B

I will make him the firstborn, the highest of the kings of the earth.

Psalm 89.27

Year C

Blessed be the Lord God of Israel, for he has looked favourably on his people and redeemed them.

Luke 1.68

Christmas Day

Year A

When they saw this, they made known what had been told them about the child; and all who heard it were amazed at what the shepherds told them. But Mary treasured all these words and pondered them in her heart.

Luke 2.17-19

Year B

Do not be afraid; for see – I am bringing you good news of great joy for all the people: to you is born this day in the city of David a Saviour, who is the Messiah, the Lord.

Luke 2.10-11

Year C

The shepherds returned, glorifying and praising God for all they had heard and seen, as it had been told them.

Luke 2.20

The First Sunday of Christmas

Year A

Get up, take the child and his mother, and flee to Egypt, and remain there until I tell you; for Herod is about to search for the child, to destroy him.

Matthew 2.13

Year B

God sent his Son, born of a woman, born under the law, in order to redeem those who were under the law … And because you are children, God has sent the Spirit of his Son into our hearts, crying 'Abba! Father!'

Galatians 4.4-6

Year C

Jesus increased in wisdom and in years, and in divine and human favour.

Luke 2.52

The Second Sunday of Christmas

Year A

And the Word became flesh and lived among us, and we have seen his glory, the glory as of a father's only son, full of grace and truth.

John 1.14

Year B

He was in the world, and the world came into being through him; yet the world did not know him. He came to what was his own, and his own people did not accept him. But to all who received him, who believed in his name, he gave power to become children of God.

John 1.10-12

Year C

The true light, which enlightens everyone, was coming into the world.

John 1.9

Intercessions at the crib

A. On Christmas Eve or Christmas Day for prayers led by children. The prayer should be very simple, if possible drawing from the children the subjects for intercession.

Jesus, whose mother was Mary:
we pray for ... [families].
Lord Jesus,
hear our prayer.

Jesus, cradled in a manger:
we pray for ... [homeless, refugees].
Lord Jesus,
hear our prayer.

Jesus, sharing the stable with the animals:
we pray for ... [the creation].
Lord Jesus,
hear our prayer.

Jesus, worshipped by shepherds and kings:
we pray for ... [nations, races, peoples].
Lord Jesus,
hear our prayer.

Jesus, our Emmanuel:
we pray for ... [those in particular need].
Lord Jesus,
hear our prayer.

[T&S 71]

B. Prayers to be used at the crib

The congregation could gather at the crib for these prayers.

Let us pray to Jesus our Saviour.

Christ, born in a stable,
give courage to all who are homeless.
Jesus, Saviour,
hear our prayer.

Christ, for whom the angels sang,
give the song of the kingdom to all who weep.
Jesus, Saviour,
hear our prayer.

Christ, worshipped by the shepherds,
give peace on earth to all who are oppressed.
Jesus, Saviour,
hear our prayer.

Christ, before whom the wise men knelt,
give humility and wisdom to all who govern.
Jesus, Saviour,
hear our prayer.

Christ, whose radiance filled a lowly manger,
give the glory of your resurrection to all who rest in
*   you.*
Jesus, Saviour,
hear our prayer.

Jesus, Saviour, child of Mary,
you know us and love us,
you share our lives
and hear our prayer.
Glory to you for ever.
Amen.

[T&S 67]

Crib service – for a smaller congregation

Introduction

A crib service provides an opportunity for families to hear the nativity story together in the midst of all the commercial build up to Christmas. As it often attracts young children, think carefully about the best time to hold it – maybe late afternoon on the fourth Sunday of Advent, or as darkness falls on Christmas Eve. This outline service takes everyone on a journey around the building, collecting the crib characters on the way as the story is told. It ends at the stable, with the characters being placed ready for the birth of Jesus.

Preparatory notes

ARRANGING THE SETTING

Move as much furniture out of the church as is possible so that people can move around freely. Identify where the crib scene will be located. Ideally this is where it will remain throughout the Christmas season. Decide on a route that will take the congregation from the initial gathering place towards it. You will need to have six stopping points – five from which the characters will be collected, and one where the wise men will start their journey towards Epiphany. Place the crib characters at the appropriate stopping points.

If you wish to light the Christmas candle at the end of the service, make sure that it is located close to the crib scene.

LIGHTING

Create a subdued atmosphere with dimmed lighting. If possible, rig a spotlight that can be shone on the stable scene when the Christ-child is placed in the manger. If you can light a star over the place, so much the better.

PARTICIPATION

Fix a large silver star on a stick or pole to be carried by a child or adult. The star holder will need to be chosen in advance and walked through the route you are going to take as he or she will lead the procession to Bethlehem.

Choose an adult or child to carry the Christ-child on the journey. He or she will need to be given the Christ-child before the service begins.

You might provide either candles with drip guards or a night light in a jar with a carrying handle for family groups to light their way on the journey.

Provide enough silver and gold stars for each person to be given one on arrival.

MUSIC

Have quiet music playing as people arrive to help create an expectant atmosphere. If you don't have a suitable musician, use recorded music.

Although suggestions are given for carols (see below), you may prefer to use others. It may be appropriate to include songs the children have been singing in the local school or in their Sunday groups. You do not need to sing all the verses of each carol – be selective, if necessary, to tell the story.

WORDS

Consider how you will provide the words for people to say the responses and sing the carols. You might provide printed sheets with the words large enough to be read in subdued lighting. If you are using a data projector, make sure it is situated so that people can see the words at every point of the journey. If you can borrow enough overhead projectors, you could position one at each stopping point and project the words on to the wall or an improvised screen.

The leader should tell the story rather than read it. It does not need to be learnt by heart – rather, the narrative indicates how the story might be told.

Structure, movement and flow	Words/text	Multisensory	Participation
The Gathering		Use quiet music and dimmed lights to set the atmosphere.	People gather either in the church entrance or church hall. Give each person a star and (if you are using them) each family group a candle.

CHRISTMAS

	The leader says something like: Tonight we are going on a journey. We journey back over two thousand years to a little town in the hill country of Judea. The town is Bethlehem – and Bethlehem is crowded! The Roman Emperor has called for everyone to go back to the place where they were born to be counted. It's a busy night for Bethlehem – but it is also a special night – for God has promised that in Bethlehem the Messiah will be born. And now is the time. Come, let us journey. The star will show us the way. Jesus Christ is the light of the world. **Jesus is our Way.** With Jesus even dark places are light. **Jesus is the Truth.** In Jesus we shall live for ever. **Jesus is our Life.**		The star-bearer holds the star high and the bearer of the Christ-child holds the baby high.
Procession **Carol**	*A carol to set the scene – for example 'O little town of Bethlehem'.*		Led by the star, the congregation sings as people move to the first stopping point.
	The leader says something like: Here are Mary and Joseph. Joseph was born in Bethlehem so they have to travel there to be counted. But it's a hard journey because Mary is expecting a baby. She's tired and wants to find somewhere to stay. We will journey with them.		Give Mary and Joseph to a child to carry. Sing as you journey towards the second stopping place where the wise men are.
	A travelling carol, for example 'Little donkey'		
	The leader says something like: These people are not from Bethlehem! They are from far away to the east of the country. They are wise men, magi, maybe even kings. They study the stars – and when they saw this bright star appear they knew that God had done something special. They just knew that they had to follow the star to see what God had done. They will join us on our journey.	Shallow bowls with frankincense and myrrh could be placed here to recall two of the gifts the Magi brought.	Give the wise men to children to be carried. Sing whilst journeying towards the third stopping place.

Carol	*A carol about the kings, for example 'We three kings of Orient are'.*		
	The wise men had to journey so far that they did not reach Bethlehem with everyone else. We will leave them here – but don't worry, they will arrive to see what God has done. They will arrive at Epiphany. They will not be disappointed.		Leave the wise men at this point. Continue the journey to the place where the shepherds are.
	Outside Bethlehem there are hills and fields where people graze their sheep. These shepherds have been busy all day looking after their flocks – and now that it is nearly night, they are getting ready to sleep. But they are going to hear amazing news!		Give the shepherds to children to be carried. Sing as you journey towards the fourth stopping place.
Carol	*A carol about shepherds, for example 'While shepherds watched their flocks'.*		
	What are these? Angels! Messengers from God. No one in Bethlehem expected angels that night! But, as the shepherds watched over their flocks, they saw the brightness in the sky. They were terrified until they heard the angel saying, 'Don't be afraid! I have brought you good news. Hurry to Bethlehem and you will find God's promised Messiah – a baby in a stable. Go – hurry!' The shepherds were so amazed that they left their sheep in the field and ran towards the town.	Create an angelic light effect using a small disco ball. There could also be a collection of angel ornaments and decorations, perhaps hung from a small Christmas tree. Angel chimes on top of an overhead projector would produce an interesting projected image.	
Carol	*A carol about angels, for example 'Angels from the realms of glory' (omit the verses about Magi and the Temple).*		The angels did not go to the stable, so you may want to leave them in this place. Otherwise, give them to a child to carry as you journey towards the place where the innkeeper is.
	This man is happy! He is an innkeeper – and tonight his inn is full of people! But he will have two strangers knocking at his door asking for somewhere to stay. It will be Mary and Joseph. The baby is about to be born and they need somewhere warm and comfortable. But the only room left is where the animals eat! Maybe they will stay there.		Give the innkeeper to a child to carry. Sing as you journey to the stable and have everyone gather around – maybe sitting on the floor.

Carol	A carol that brings the story together for example 'See amid the winter's snow' or 'It came upon the midnight clear'.		
	We have arrived! And there is still time. We are not too late. This is where the star stops. This is where the baby is to be born. *(Place the innkeeper beside the stable.)* The stable is the only room left in Bethlehem. *(Place Mary and Joseph in the stable.)* Mary and Joseph are grateful that there is somewhere safe for the baby to be born. *(Place the shepherds close to the stable.)* The shepherds have hurried. They want to see God's promised Messiah. Everything is ready for the baby to be born – God's promised Messiah, Jesus.		
Carol	A carol, for example, 'The Virgin Mary had a baby boy' or 'Born in the night, Mary's child'.	If you have a spotlight trained on the stable, switch it on now.	As the carol is sung, the Christ-child is placed in the manger.
	Every year we remember the birth of this baby. Every year we get ready to celebrate his coming. Lord God, in the birth of Jesus, you show us how much you love the world. Help us to be ready to welcome him into our lives. Forgive our sins, make us holy and let us worship as the shepherds did on that first Christmas morning. **Amen.**		

Carol	Let us place our stars near the stable as a sign that we welcome Jesus. *A lullaby type of carol, for example 'Away in a manger' or 'Silent night'.*	Sing the carol as the stars are placed in the stable. If you wish, encourage people to touch the Christ-child with gentleness. Continue the music until people have finished coming forward.	People come forward with stars to place in the stable.
	Jesus Christ is the light of the world. **Jesus is our Way.** With Jesus even dark places are light. **Jesus is the Truth.** In Jesus we shall live for ever: **Jesus is our Life.** [T&S 94]	Light the Christmas candle as these words are said.	
	God has come into the world. Let us creep away and return on Christmas morning to celebrate again the birth of Jesus, the Messiah, the Son of God.	Fade out the spotlight. Play quiet music.	Leader quietly moves away from the scene and beckons the congregation to do the same.

Crib service – for a larger congregation

Introduction

A crib service provides an opportunity for families to hear the Nativity story together in the midst of all the commercial build-up to Christmas. As it often attracts young children, think carefully about the best time to hold it – maybe late afternoon on the Fourth Sunday of Advent, or as darkness falls on Christmas Eve. This service is designed for a larger congregation, where movement around the church is not possible.

Preparation

ARRANGING THE SETTING

Identify where the crib scene will be located. Ideally this is where it will remain throughout the Christmas season. Move the furniture so that it is possible for the children to sit comfortably in front of the crib scene.

Decide where the Magi are to be placed – possibly near the back of the church – so that their journey can continue towards the stable until they arrive at Epiphany. Make sure that those who are given the Magi to carry know where this is!

If you wish to light the Christmas candle at the end of the service, make sure that it is located close to the crib scene.

LIGHTING

Create a subdued atmosphere with dimmed lighting. If possible, rig a spotlight that can be shone on the stable scene when the Christ-child is placed in the manger.

PARTICIPATION

Provide enough silver and gold stars (possibly cut from card) so that each person can be given one on arrival.

MUSIC

Have a CD or tape of quiet music playing as people arrive to help create an expectant atmosphere.

Although suggestions are given for carols, you may prefer to use others. It may be appropriate to include songs that children have been singing in the local school or in their Sunday groups. You do not need to sing all the verses of each carol – be selective, if necessary, to tell the story.

Consider how you will provide the words for people to say the responses and sing the carols. You might provide printed sheets with the words large enough to be read in subdued lighting. If you are using an overhead or data projector, make sure it is situated so that people can see the words clearly without obscuring or being distracted from the crib scene.

The leader should tell the story rather than read it. It does not need to be learnt by heart – rather, the narrative indicates how the story might be told.

Structure, movement and flow	Words/text	Multisensory	Participation
The Gathering		Quiet music and dimmed lights.	As people arrive, give each one a small star. Distribute the various crib characters with the instruction to bring them forward at the appropriate time.
	The leader says something like: We are going on a journey with Mary and Joseph. We journey back over two thousand years to a little town in the hill country of Judea. The town is Bethlehem – and Bethlehem is crowded! The Roman Emperor has called for everyone to go back to the place where they were born to be counted. It's a busy night for Bethlehem – but it is also a special night – for God has promised that in Bethlehem the Messiah will be born. And now is the time. Come, let us journey. The star will show us the way.		
	Jesus Christ is the light of the world. **Jesus is our Way.** With Jesus even dark places are light. **Jesus is the Truth.** In Jesus we shall live for ever: **Jesus is our Life.** [T&S 94]		Invite all to hold their star aloft as the opening words are said.
Carol	*A carol to set the scene, for example 'O little town of Bethlehem'.*		
	The leader says something like: There is a happy man in Bethlehem tonight! He is an innkeeper – and tonight his inn is full of people! But two strangers are knocking at his door asking for somewhere to stay. It is Mary and Joseph. They have had a long journey from Nazareth. The baby is about to be born and they need somewhere warm and comfortable. But the only room left is where the animals eat! Maybe they will stay there.		The innkeeper, Mary and Joseph are brought forward and placed by the stable.

Carol	*A travelling carol, for example 'Little donkey'.*		
	Far away from Bethlehem, to the east of the country, are wise men, magi, maybe even kings. They study the stars – and tonight they have seen a new star appear. The star tells of something special that has happened, something special God has done. They just know that they have to follow the star to see what it is. They are from so far away that they will not arrive tonight. But they won't be disappointed. They will arrive at Epiphany and see what has happened.		As the carol is sung, those carrying the Magi take them to their journey's starting place.
Carol	*A suitable carol at this point would be 'The First Nowell' – use selected verses.*		
	Outside Bethlehem there are hills and fields where people graze their sheep. The shepherds have been busy all day looking after their flocks – and now that it is nearly night, they are getting ready to sleep. But they won't sleep tonight! Instead they are going to hear amazing news!		Children who have shepherds hold them up – but do not bring them to the stable just yet.
Carol	*A carol about shepherds, for example 'While shepherds watched their flocks'.*		
	What are these? Angels! Messengers from God. No one in Bethlehem expected angels that night! But, as the shepherds watched over their flocks, they saw the brightness in the sky. They were terrified until they heard the angel saying, 'Don't be afraid! I have brought you good news. Hurry to Bethlehem and you will find God's promised Messiah – a baby in a stable. Go – hurry!' The shepherds were so amazed that they left their sheep in the field and ran towards the town.		The angels are held up and then they and the shepherds are brought to the stable.
Carol	*A carol about angels, for example 'Angels from the realms of glory' (do not use the verses about the Magi and the Temple).*		

	Everything is ready. And there is still time! We are not too late. This is where the star stops. This is where the baby is to be born. The stable is the only room left in Bethlehem. Mary and Joseph are grateful that there is somewhere safe for the baby to be born. The shepherds have hurried. They want to see God's promised Messiah. Everything is ready for the baby to be born – God's promised Messiah, Jesus.	If you have a spotlight trained on the stable, switch it on now.	
Carol	*A lullaby type of carol, for example 'Away in a manger' or 'Silent night'.*		As the carol is sung, the Christ-child is placed in the manger.
	Every year we remember the birth of this baby. Every year we get ready to celebrate his coming. Let us pray that we will be ready this year: Lord God, in the birth of Jesus, you show us how much you love the world. Help us to be ready to welcome him into our lives. Forgive our sins, make us holy and let us worship as the shepherds did on that first Christmas morning. **Amen.**		
	Let us place our stars near the stable as a sign that we welcome Jesus.	Play quiet music as the stars are placed in the stable. If you wish, encourage people to touch the Christ-child with gentleness.	People come forward with stars to place in the stable.
	Jesus Christ is the light of the world. **Jesus is our Way.** With Jesus even dark places are light. **Jesus is the Truth.** In Jesus we shall live for ever: **Jesus is our Life.** [T&S 94]	Light the Christmas candle as these words are said.	
	Everything is ready for God to come into the world. Let us creep away and return on Christmas morning to celebrate again the birth of Jesus, the Messiah, the Son of God.	Fade out the spotlight. Play quiet music.	Leader quietly moves away from the scene and beckons the congregation to do the same.

The Lectionary and the crib

Intercessions at the crib

At Christmas itself, continue to build up the crib scene you began during Advent. As the figures are added, the following prayers could be used as a focus for intercession:

CHRISTMAS DAY: THE CHRIST-CHILD

When the Christ-child was born, the Word became flesh and dwelt among us.

The Light of the World has come to us: Glory to God in the highest!

And peace to God's people on earth.

THE SUNDAYS AFTER CHRISTMAS

Most crib sets will not have extra characters to add on the Sundays after Christmas but, if you are to maintain the pattern begun in Advent throughout this Christmas season, it would be good to have something to bring to the crib to act as a focus for the prayers of intercession. One idea is to follow the Spanish tradition and add other characters, which may need to be made specially. Another possibility might be to ask each member of the congregation, or each family that plans to be present on the Sunday or Sundays after Christmas, to bring an ornament from home, or even a character from their own crib set to place beside the church crib for the duration of the service. This will reflect and remind us of the diversity of the humanity to whom Jesus came.

Each person or family comes and places a figure around the crib and then joins the crowd around the crib, where the following prayer is said:

*When the Christ-child was born, the Word became flesh and dwelt among us
and the glory of the Lord was revealed.*

*We give thanks for the diversity of humanity:
we pray for those who add to the richness of our lives by sharing their culture, their food and their differences with us;
we pray for those with whom we share apparently problematic differences;
we pray for reconciliation in communities torn apart by division;*

*Lord God, in this season of goodwill,
help us to greet one another kindly,
love one another tenderly,*

*and share with one another generously:
Lord in your mercy:*
hear our prayer.

(or)

People of God, in this season of goodwill, will you greet one another kindly, love one another tenderly, and share with one another generously:
With the help of God, we will.

The crib at home

After Joseph and Mary have made their way to Bethlehem, they arrive at the stable on Christmas Eve. Move the ox and ass aside, and make the manger ready in the middle of the stable.

Jesus' birth was announced to the shepherds by night, so you might put Jesus in the crib at any suitable time after dark. Though there could be merit in having Jesus there when children get up in the morning – if they wait that long!

An important element is the star, to announce the birth of Jesus and to signal to the wise men. At the crib you could then sing 'Away in a manger'.

If you have figures of angels, they need to come first to the shepherds. If your crib set has no angels, don't worry – you can be the angels bringing them the good news, and telling them to go to Bethlehem. You go to the shepherds and sing 'While shepherds watched their flocks by night' before bringing the shepherds to the manger. Someone may have their angel costume from a nativity play, or just want a halo of tinsel for singing 'All glory be to God on high'.

It is good to keep the momentum of the Christmas season going for the twelve days of Christmas. If the wise men start their journey on Boxing Day, they can stop at twelve different locations before arriving at Bethlehem on the Feast of the Epiphany. You may wish to sing the first verse and chorus of 'We three kings' as they move each day. Remembering the line 'field and fountain, moor and mountain', the journey could be quite long. They might even spend a night or two, suitably protected, out in the garden!

January 1 is the Feast of the Naming of Jesus. Celebrate the New Year with a favourite hymn that uses the name of Jesus. It may be time to start moving the holy family out of the stable and into a house – see the Epiphany section.

Stained-glass window

If you have another prominent window, add a scene with the wise men on their journey carrying gifts.

The crib in outreach

An all-around-the-village nativity play

The village of Grantchester, just outside Cambridge, performed a nativity play that travelled around various locations and involved a cast of over 50. The play took a year to plan and, whilst many children were involved, it was most definitely designed to give a message to adults as well as children. Their own summary describes the action.

Summary of the plot

The story moves seamlessly between history and the present day. The biblical characters are caught up in a world they do not understand but, by the end of the play, it is the modern world that is challenged to understand them. Biblical characters wear biblical costumes.

List of characters

Mary

Joseph

Gabriel

The Christ-child (use a real baby if you can, otherwise a doll)

Roman dignitary (Chair of council or similar person)

Soldiers (who act as stewards to the audience)

Innkeepers (possibly three, but that would depend on the number of inns you have. Try to use the pub landlords)

Shepherds – any number

Angels – any number

Three Magi

Magi's attendants

Herod

Herod's courtiers – any number

Village girls

Simeon

Anna.

The characters were all played by local people.

Other details

The play was staged twice, on the Saturday and Sunday before Christmas. It involved closing the village to traffic, for which the help of the local police was sought, and use was made of this in the army occupation of the village in the opening scenes. The registering of the audience for their identity cards enabled stewards to guide groups, wearing distinctive coloured badges, around the village from one location to another.

The weather could have posed a problem, but the scenes were short, walking between their locations kept people warm, and an interlude in the village hall, where hot drinks were provided, helped to warm people also. It was standing room only in the church at the end, with plenty of bodies to keep each other from freezing.

The script

The play was written by a professional script writer, who worked with three local people. Though the script might be made available, it would be best to tailor the idea to your own locations.[1]

Planning and recruitment

Planning started a year in advance. An open meeting to invite participants produced little response, and invitations to cheese and wine parties proved more successful as events for doing the casting. A huge amount of administration was needed to keep everything moving forward.

Costs and marketing

The major expenses were the tiered seating for one of the locations, and radio microphones linked to speakers in all the locations. This was very costly, and the group producing the play applied for lottery funding and a grant from the district council to assist. Tickets were £7.50 with some concessions. Each day 250 people saw the play. Marketing was helped by some publicity involving well-known local figures.

Tickets were sold in advance, and included a set of instructions about car parking, road closures, the need to wrap up warmly, and advice on standing, sitting, and disabled access. All the scenes were short, no more than eight minutes, apart from the one for which seating was supplied. The whole production took two hours, including the time required to move from place to place.

Reflections

The producers came to see the event as holding up a mirror to the community, giving village life a special significance, including that the Christ-child appeared as a refugee but was in fact a real baby born to a new family in the village and was blessed by long-term, elderly residents, as Simeon and Anna. All who participated would like to share in something similar again, wondering if this is something to be staged every ten years, like Oberammergau's Passion Play.

SCENE 1: IN GARDEN

Gabriel appears to Mary in the garden and Mary and Joseph are betrothed. The chairman of the Parish Council, under the direction of the army, tells the audience to register for their identity cards. Joseph and Mary, now expecting her baby, go off to be counted. Stewards conduct the audience out of the garden across the road to the car park of a local pub, and musicians sing and play 'Gaudete' (see Resources)[2] as the play moves around the village.

SCENE 2: IN A PUB CAR PARK

The audience queues at tables to register with officials. In vain Mary and Joseph ask the landlord of the pub for a room.

SCENE 3: OUTSIDE ANOTHER LOCAL PUB (where tiered seating is installed)

A messenger tries unsuccessfully to book a room at another pub next door and then Mary and Joseph, now with their pony, ask for room at yet another pub but are sent across the road.

Shepherds, having lost their sheep, run in to report strange signs (fireworks) and follow Mary and Joseph. Three wise men, their minister and child attendants drive up in a stretch limo and are met by an angry and envious Herod. They set off to follow the star but go in the wrong direction. The audience crosses the main street to the Village Hall.

INTERLUDE

The audience goes to the Village Hall for a hot drink and to watch a 'news' video (produced by a local sixth-form college) of other events around the time of Jesus' birth (the slaughter of the innocents, for example). In Grantchester, this featured 'guest appearances' by local television news presenters, and you may have local media personalities who would be willing to give their time to the project.

SCENE 4: A FIELD

The audience is led up a muddy lane into a field. Village girls discover Mary and Joseph and their baby, Jesus, attended by angels.

SCENE 5: A FIELD

The three wise men appear with their minister and offer their gifts. They go to a place to sleep, where they are visited by Gabriel, who tells them not to return to Herod.

Joseph dreams that Gabriel tells them to escape to Egypt – but first they must go to present their child in the Temple. The audience is led out of the garden to the church

SCENE 6: THE CHURCH

In the temple, Simeon and Anna greet the infant Jesus.

The narrators reveal their identities and interpret the meaning of the Christmas story for today. The play ends with Simeon's prayer, 'Lord, now lettest thou thy servant depart in peace' sung, with an organ and trumpet accompaniment, to the setting by Geoffrey Burgon (see Resources).[3]

Christmas:
The Jesse tree pathway

Practical inclusive ideas

Using the Jesse tree for the Main Service Lectionary

Follow the pattern you used during Advent to add figures and decorations to the tree.

Years A and C

CHRISTMAS EVE

On Christmas Eve you may like to add a nativity scene to the tree. It is now quite easy to buy a small stable to hang on a Christmas tree (some fair trade catalogues include them). You may want to add the nativity scene without Jesus, saving the child for Christmas Day. If the tree is large enough, you may like to invite each member of the congregation to come and add a star, or a shepherd or a sheep, during the singing of a carol. If it is not large enough for this, people could perhaps light candles around it, or you may create your crib scene beside it.

CHRISTMAS DAY

Add the Christ-child at the very top of the tree. Or, if you are adding the Christ-child to sit on the knee of the Virgin (or if you have already done so), you might like to add the figure of Christ in Majesty, as a king.

You can still add to the tree on the Sundays after Christmas.

Year A

THE FIRST SUNDAY OF CHRISTMAS

One possibility is to create a frieze of all the fruits of creation mentioned in Psalm 148, which could be placed around the base of the tree, instead of the mountain scene, and thus create a link between God the Creator and God the Son. Or you could simply add a symbol of the flight into Egypt, with Joseph leading Mary and the child on a donkey.

THE SECOND SUNDAY OF CHRISTMAS

You might add a sign of the compass, symbolizing the gathering in of the peoples, mentioned in verse 8 of the reading from Jeremiah, or you might add another frieze of the young women dancing and men and the old being merry! Wine, corn and oil could also be added.

Year C

THE FIRST SUNDAY OF CHRISTMAS

One possibility is to create a frieze of all the fruits of creation mentioned in Psalm 148, which could be placed around the base of the tree instead of the mountain scene, and thus create a link between God the Creator and God the Son. Or you might wish to add an image of Jerusalem or even a picture of Christ and the doctors of the law in the Temple as a reminder of the Gospel reading.

THE SECOND SUNDAY OF CHRISTMAS

You might add a sign of the compass symbolizing the gathering in of the peoples, mentioned in verse 8 of the reading from Jeremiah 31, or you might add another frieze of the young women dancing and men and the old being merry! Wine, corn and oil could also be added.

You may want to add a light and a small globe to reflect the words of the Gospel reading from the opening of John's Gospel.

The Jesse tree at home

At Christmas you will want to add Jesus, the Christ-child, to your tree. It will remain then as one of your Christmas decorations and as a focus throughout the twelve days of Christmas. Enjoy having it there and telling your Christmas visitors all about it. You might even have a basket of stars available and invite each person who visits you over Christmas to add a star to your tree so that its sparkle grows through the season.

The Jesse tree in outreach

The Jesse tree you made during Advent can remain over the Christmas period but you should remember to make arrangements before 6 January to take it down. One of the important things, having collaborated with another organization, is to ensure that you undertake clearing up as well as setting up. Perpetuating the Jesse tree beyond Christmas in a public place – a shop window, a school, a library or wherever – will almost certainly be unsuccessful. So even if this is something that is done at church or at home, it is not really appropriate in this situation. The perpetuation of Christmas in public spaces after Twelfth Night is not a normal pattern and would probably be rather puzzling. However, it might be profitable to spend some time after dismantling the tree discussing with the hosts whether there might be opportunities for further cooperation through Lent and leading up to Easter, and whether you might use their hospitality for further events and even to advertise other events and occasions the Christian community is planning.

Even so, it might be good to have a card made, with the Jesse tree on it, that could be given away with an explanation and directions for people to make their own simple tree during Advent and Christmas the following year.

Photograph your Jesse tree with a digital camera and print the pictures on the outside of the card. Inside the card print a short history of the Jesse tree. (You could use the one provided below):

The image of the tree of Jesse has its origins in the first two verses of chapter 11 of the Book of the prophet Isaiah:

A shoot shall come out from the stock of Jesse,
and a branch shall grow out of his roots.
The spirit of the Lord shall rest on him,
the spirit of wisdom and understanding,
the spirit of counsel and might,
the spirit of knowledge and the fear of the Lord.

During the Middle Ages this theme was developed in a variety of ways and became widely used in art. You find Jesse trees in stained-glass windows, illuminated manuscripts and wood and stone carvings. One of the most famous is in the west window of Chartres cathedral in France. They often show a short family tree of Jesus and the prophets who spoke of his coming. The Jesse tree on the front of this card was made by …

You can make your own Jesse tree as a Christmas decoration. Use a dead branch and spray it gold. Add little figures of Jesse (at the bottom) King, King David (harp) and King Solomon (crown) above and then a figure of Mary and Jesus. Write the words of the prophets on ribbons, twirl these using scissors and then hang them on the ends of the twigs.

Isaiah:	A shoot shall come out from the stock of Jesse.
Jeremiah:	I will raise up for David a righteous Branch.
Joel:	For in Mount Zion and in Jerusalem there shall be those who escape.
Obadiah:	The kingdom shall be the Lord's.
Jonah:	Deliverance belongs to the Lord!
Nahum:	Look! On the mountains the feet of one who brings good tidings.
Habakkuk:	The earth will be filled with the knowledge of the glory of the Lord, as the waters cover the sea.
Haggai:	The treasure of all nations shall come.
Zechariah:	I am going to bring my servant the Branch.
Daniel:	To him was given dominion and glory and kingship.
Zephaniah:	The Lord, your God, is in your midst.
Ezekiel:	This gate shall remain shut; it shall not be opened, and no one shall enter by it; for the Lord, the God of Israel, has entered by it.
Hosea:	Out of Egypt I called my son.
Micah:	For lo, the Lord is coming out of his place.
Malachi:	The Lord whom you seek will suddenly come to his temple.
Amos:	How can Jacob stand? He is so small.

EPIPHANY

Seasonal introduction

Key themes and Scriptures

The carol 'We three kings of Orient are' encapsulates the key themes of this season. The gifts the Magi offer: gold for kingship, frankincense for divinity and myrrh for suffering, tell us a great deal about the kind of king that has come among us and the kind of kingdom he will establish. The readings for the Sundays of Epiphany explore the identity of Jesus – from his baptism and the voice of affirmation, 'This is my beloved Son', to the wedding at Cana, and the Scriptures concerning the fulfilment of the prophecies of the Messiah and, finally, to Candlemas and the recognition of the child who has come to save the world. On each occasion we are asked to reflect on our own responses to God incarnate and to consider again the cost of following this God. And so we arrive at Candlemas, a pivotal time, when the liturgy bids us to turn and face the cross, still at some way distant from us, but present, nevertheless in the images and Scriptures of this feast.

The theme of journey runs through this season too. The Magi leave homes and their security to follow the star that leads them to the Christ-child. The disciples, similarly, are called from their old way of life to follow Christ. We are called to live out our baptism and to renew our commitment to take the life of Christ out of the Church and into the world. The Incarnation is not just a private business: it is God's risky adventure of self-giving in a world that loves darkness rather than light. Epiphany turns the Church outwards again after the more reflective period of Advent and the celebrations of Christmas.

Some of the themes of the Epiphany season are less familiar to people than those of Christmas and consideration should therefore be given to ways of educating the congregation. Transforming the wreath to use throughout the Epiphany season is also an unfamiliar practice and it might be a good idea to provide some helpful pointers for understanding the symbolism. White and gold are the colours of the season. These colours should feature in floral decorations as well as in vestments and frontals for the holy table.

Light

The feast of the Epiphany has a keynote of light. It is important to pick this up by considering how to increase the lights in the worship space. Candles at points around the church are one possibility or giving lights to the congregation at the reading of the Gospel is another. Lights could form part of the offertory procession or be placed around the holy table. Uplighters or spotlights could be used to give extra focus to the wreath and, on the first Sunday of Epiphany when we celebrate the Baptism of Christ, to the font.

Beginnings and thresholds

Since there is much in this season about beginnings – the start of the new year, the new beginning for the Magi, the beginning of Christ's ministry, the call of the disciples and their new adventure into faith, the new beginning that baptism represents for us – you might want to think about thresholds and doorways as representative of these ideas of beginnings, both secular and religious. Prayers could be offered in the places of welcome and beginning in the church building, and a simple act of blessing the doorway of the home could be a reminder of the welcome we may extend in the name of Christ to all those who come and go at the threshold of our homes.

Turning outwards

Now is the time to consider our giving and to evaluate what we have to offer in service both to God and to our neighbour. The emphasis of the intercessions might shift accordingly to give particular focus to mission and to the world into which the Christ-child came.

Epiphany carol services may be opportunities for hospitality and for inviting members of the community into the church. Celebration of baptism services are also mission opportunities in the context of hospitality.

In the context of an Epiphany supper, another possibility might be to organize a storytelling evening based on legends, poetry and traditional tales about seeking and finding and the journey of the Magi. Encourage members of the congregation to take candles into their homes to light as they pray for the needs of the world – perhaps a prayer bulletin could be issued to give people prompts for prayer.

Stand-alone seasonal material

A Eucharist for the Feast of the Epiphany: The Arrival of the Magi

Preparatory notes

If you have been following one of the three pathways – crib, wreath or Jesse tree – through Advent and Christmas, you will need to decide how to include the pathway ideas in this service as you do your planning.

The crib may be transformed for the season of Epiphany, so that the stable becomes a 'house'. The account of the Magi's visit in Matthew's Gospel describes them entering a house to offer their gifts. You may wish to change the location also, but whether you do this will probably depend on the nature of your building, and whether there is space to gather around the 'house'.

If you are following the wreath or Jesse tree pathways, you could use the place where the wreath or tree stands as the place of gathering at the start of the service, but this will depend on the availability of space in your building. Another possibility would be to move the figures of the Magi to stand beside the wreath or the tree after the service and for some time during Epiphany.

What needs to be prepared leading up to the service?

As suggested above, you may wish to change the 'stable' of your crib into a 'house'. You will need to identify three figures to be the Magi: most crib sets come with these figures. You will also need to decide how to represent the three gifts: gold, frankincense and myrrh. For gold you might use a piece of jewellery, a gilded chalice (if your church happens to have one), or something completely artificial but highly visible, such as gold coloured chips obtainable from decoration shops or florists. Incense can be bought from ecclesiastical suppliers and you will need charcoal tablets on which to burn it. You will also need a suitable vessel in which to burn it: if

your church does not have a thurible (the traditional church incense vessel) then you could use a heatproof bowl: put crinkled aluminium foil in the bottom and place the charcoal tablets on this. You will need a heatproof tray of some kind to carry the bowl. For the myrrh you might use perfumed oil: for example the oil for anointing the sick, which is blessed on Maundy Thursday, would be appropriate. It is also often possible to obtain myrrh oil or grains either from aromatherapy shops or herb shops.

What needs to happen before the service?

It would be helpful to have a rehearsal. The service suggests that, instead of carrying candles in the procession for this service, the figures of the Magi might be carried. You will need to ask three people to do this, rather than the more usual two candle carriers. You may also need three other people to carry the three gifts. If you are planning to have people from the congregation leading the affirmation of faith and the prayers, these people will also need to be identified and recruited.

What needs to be made ready immediately before the service?

The bowl or thurible with the charcoal and incense needs to be prepared just before the service and the charcoal lit. Make sure all those carrying Magi and gifts are present and that they each have their gift or figure.

Questions

As you read through the text of the service it might be helpful to jot down questions that arise for you as you begin to plan. They may be questions about why this particular suggestion is made, or they may be about how you would execute a particular suggestion in your situation, and whether it needs to be adopted. You are reminded to ask these questions as you work your way through this table.

Structure, movement and flow	Words/text	Multisensory	Participation
THE GATHERING	Blessed are you, Lord our God, King of the universe. **From the rising of the sun to its setting** **your name is proclaimed in all the world.** [T&S 159]		
Processional hymn	*Possibly a traditional Epiphany hymn such as:* *'As with gladness men of old',* *'Bethlehem of noblest cities',* *'O worship the Lord in the beauty of holiness'.*		Any procession could be led by a star (rather than a cross) followed by the 'kings' (rather than candles), which are placed on the holy table.
Greeting	The Lord of glory be with you. **The Lord bless you.** (*or*) The Lord be with you **and also with you.** [T&S 159] *The president may introduce the service.*		
Praise and prayer	Blessed are you, Lord our God, King of the universe. **To you be glory and praise for ever.** From the rising of the sun to its setting, your name is proclaimed in all the world. **To you be glory and praise for ever.** When the time had fully come, you sent the Sun of Righteousness. In him the fullness of your glory dwells. **To you be glory and praise for ever.** *This collect is said:* **Creator of the heavens,** **who led the Magi by a star** **to worship the Christ-child:** **guide and sustain us,** **that we may find our journey's end** **in Jesus Christ our Lord.** **Amen.** [T&S 161]		This prayer may be said by all.

Questions	What are your questions about the gathering section?		
LITURGY OF THE WORD			
Hymn/song	*Choose a fairly long hymn for this or a song that can be repeated until the procession has been made.*		During which the star and the 'kings' lead a procession of everyone. All gather round the crib/nativity house. Alternatively, people turn to face the crib/nativity house. The figures of the kings are placed directly into the crib/nativity house.
Gospel Reading	Alleluia! Alleluia! Arise shine, for your light has come. The glory of the Lord is risen upon you! **Alleluia!** Hear the Gospel of our Lord Jesus Christ according to Matthew. **Glory to you, O Lord.** *Matthew 2.1-12* This is the Gospel of the Lord. **Praise to you, O Christ.**		The acclamation could be announced by a member of the congregation. The Gospel is read from the crib/nativity house. This could be read dramatically.
Offering the Gifts			

As the star is brought in	*We sing* **We three Kings of orient are, bearing gifts we traverse afar, field and fountain, moor and mountain, following yonder star.** ***O star of wonder, star of night, star with royal beauty bright, westward leading, still proceeding, guide us to thy perfect light.***	If it has not been placed there before the service, a star is brought to the crib/nativity house.	
Comment	*The president, or another minister, provides a* brief comment *linking following the star to our journey of faith.*		

The Affirmation of Faith	*If this is a principal service of the day, the following authorized Affirmation of Faith may be inserted here.*
	
	A member of the congregation says
	Let us declare our faith in God.
	
	A child says
	We believe in God the Father,
	**from whom every family
	in heaven and on earth is named.**
	
	A man says
	We believe in God the Son,
	**who lives in our hearts through
	    faith,
	and fills us with his love.**
	
	A woman says
	We believe in God the Holy Spirit,
	**who strengthens us
	with power from on high.**
	
	The leader says
	We believe in one God;
	**Father, Son and Holy Spirit.
	Amen.**
	                  cf Ephesians 3
	
	[CW 148]
			Each section of the Affirmation of Faith is introduced by a different person.

| At the offering of gold | *We sing*
Born a King on Bethlehem's plain, gold I bring to crown him again, King for ever, ceasing never over us all to reign.

O star of wonder, star of night, star with royal beauty bright, westward leading, still proceeding, guide us to thy perfect light.

This prayer may be said:
Blessed are you, Lord our God,
   King of the universe:
to you be praise and glory for ever.
As gold in the furnace is tried
and purified seven times in the fire,
so purify our hearts and minds
that we may be a royal priesthood
acceptable in the service of your
   kingdom.
Blessed be God for ever.

[T&S 163] | The gold is brought in and placed in the crib/nativity house. | This prayer could be said by the person offering the gift or by one of the ministers or it could be omitted. |
| Collection | *The president, or another minister, provides a* brief comment *linking the offering of gold to the collection, which will follow.*

If there is to be a Collection, it is done here in silence. | When the Collection is taken, it is brought forward and placed in the crib/nativity house. If there is a collection as people arrive, those offerings are placed in the crib/nativity house at this point. | |

At the offering of incense	We sing **Frankincense to offer have I,** **incense owns a deity nigh.** **Prayer and praising, all men raising,** **worship him, God most high.** *O star of wonder, star of night,* *star with royal beauty bright,* *westward leading, still proceeding,* *guide us to thy perfect light.*	A bowl of lit charcoal and incense is placed near the crib/nativity house.	

	This prayer may be said:
	Blessed are you, Lord our God, King of
	    the universe:
	to you be praise and glory for ever.
	As our prayer rises up before you as
	    incense,
	so may we be presented before you
	with penitent hearts and uplifted hands
	to offer ourselves in your priestly service.
	Blessed be God for ever.
	
	[T&S 163]
			This prayer could be said by the person offering the gift or by one of the ministers or it could be omitted.

Comment	*The president, or another minister, provides a brief comment linking the offering of incense with the prayers of penitence that follow.*		
Prayers of Penitence	Christ the light of the world has come to dispel the darkness of our hearts. In his light let us examine ourselves and confess our sins. *Silence is kept.* Lord of grace and truth, we confess our unworthiness to stand in your presence as your children. We have sinned: **forgive and heal us.** The Virgin Mary accepted your call to be the mother of Jesus. Forgive our disobedience to your will. We have sinned: **forgive and heal us.** The wise men followed the star to find Jesus the King. Forgive our reluctance to seek you. We have sinned: **forgive and heal us.** [T&S 65, 66 adapted]		The introduction and each of the three sentences may be led from the congregation.
	The president pronounces the Absolution. **Amen.**	As the president says the Absolution, more incense is placed on the charcoal.	

At the offering of myrrh	*We sing* **Myrrh is mine, its bitter perfume breathes a life of gathering gloom; sorrowing, sighing, bleeding, dying, sealed in the stone cold tomb.** ***O star of wonder, star of night, star with royal beauty bright, westward leading, still proceeding, guide us to thy perfect light.***	A bottle of perfumed oil is placed in the crib/nativity house.	
	This prayer may be said: Blessed are you, Lord our God, King of the universe: to you be praise and glory for ever. As you give medicine to heal our sickness and the leaves of the tree of life for the healing of the nations, so anoint us with your healing power that we may be the first-fruits of your new creation. **Blessed be God for ever.** [T&S 163]		This prayer could be said by the person offering the gift or by one of the ministers or it could be omitted.
Comment	*The president or another minister may offer a brief comment linking the offering of myrrh with the intercessions that follow.*		
Prayers of Intercession	Today the wise men knelt before our Saviour. Let us also kneel to worship him with great joy, and to make our prayer to his heavenly Father. Father, the wise men came from the east to worship your Son: grant to Christians everywhere a true spirit of adoration. Lord, in your mercy **hear our prayer.** Father, your Son is the King of kings and Lord of lords: grant an abundance of peace to your world. Lord, in your mercy **hear our prayer.** Father, the Holy Family shared the life of the people of Nazareth: protect in your mercy our neighbours and families, together with the whole community of which we are part. Lord, in your mercy **hear our prayer.**		If the oil used is the Oil of Healing, it may be used as part of the prayers that follow to anoint the sick.

	Father, your Son was rich, yet for our sakes he became poor: show your love for the poor and powerless, and strengthen [… *and all*] those who suffer. Lord, in your mercy **hear our prayer.** Father, the wise men presented to your Son gold, incense and myrrh: accept the gifts we bring, and the offering of our hearts at the beginning of this new year. Lord, in your mercy **hear our prayer.** Father, you are the King of heaven, the hope of all who trust in you: give to [… *and all*] the faithful departed the wonders of your salvation. Lord, in your mercy **hear our prayer.** Rejoicing in the fellowship of wise men, shepherds, and angels, and of the Blessed Virgin Mary and Saint Joseph, we commend ourselves and all Christian people to your unfailing love. Merciful Father, **accept these prayers** **for the sake of your Son,** **our Saviour Jesus Christ. Amen.** [T&S 164] *We sing* **Glorious now behold him arise,** **King and God and sacrifice;** **Heaven sings 'Alleluia!'** **'Alleluia!' the earth replies.** ***O star of wonder, star of night,*** ***star with royal beauty bright,*** ***westward leading, still proceeding,*** ***guide us to thy perfect light.*** [John Henry Hopkins 1820–91]		Members of the congregation return to their places.
Questions	*What are your questions about the Liturgy of the Word?*		

THE LITURGY OF THE SACRAMENT			
The Peace	Our Saviour Christ is the Prince of Peace. Of the increase of his government and of peace there shall be no end. The peace of the Lord be always with you **and also with you.** *All share the Peace.* [T&S 165]		
Hymn/song		During which the holy table is prepared.	
Eucharistic Prayer	*An authorized Eucharistic Prayer is used. Material for the Eucharist on the Feast of the Epiphany can be found on pages 159–69 of* Times and Seasons.		
After Communion	Lord God, the bright splendour whom the nations seek: may we who with the wise men have been drawn by your light discern the glory of your presence in your Son, the Word made flesh, Jesus Christ our Lord. **Amen.** [T&S 167]		
Hymn	*The hymn may be introduced by these words:* Having been warned in a dream not to return to Herod, they left for their own country by another road. Let us prepare to leave this place ready to walk with the wise men a new path of life.		During the hymn, the star and the figures of the 'kings' lead a procession to the church door. This may include everyone or the congregation may be asked to face the procession.

CONCLUSION			
Blessing and Dismissal	Let us bless the living God: He was born of the Virgin Mary, **revealed in his glory,** worshipped by the angels, **proclaimed among the nations,** believed in throughout the world, **exalted to the highest heavens.** Blessed be God, our strength and our salvation, **now and for ever. Amen.** [T&S 75] And the blessing … Christ is in the midst of his people. Go in peace to love and serve the Lord. **In the name of Christ. Amen.**		The first part of the blessing could be led from the congregation.
Questions	*What are your questions about the conclusion of the service?*		

Epiphany procession

Preparatory notes

Background and introduction

On the First Sunday of Epiphany we celebrate the Baptism of Christ. The whole Epiphany season, from Christmas to Candlemas, focuses on the manifestation of Jesus, the Son of God, the Messiah, to the world, and on three early events that accomplish this: the visit of the Magi, the wise men, with their gifts, the baptism of Jesus and the miracle at the wedding feast in Cana, when Jesus made water into wine. Although separate events, described in different passages in the Gospels, the three cling together as if parts of a whole, and so on this day, when we celebrate particularly Christ's baptism, the other two events are also remembered. In some eastern churches, Epiphany, or the Theophany, particularly commemorates Jesus' baptism, with the visit of the Magi linked to Christmas. In some churches the day we call Epiphany, 6 January, is celebrated as Christmas, with Epiphany/Theophany occurring on January 19. These celebrations overflow with symbols and there is a danger of being overburdened with ideas. Perhaps we should remind ourselves that what we are out to do is catch glimpses of the divinity of Christ. St John calls the wedding at Cana 'the first sign' that Jesus gave. For the wise men, the star was a sign, but so were their gifts signs – signs of the one who was both human and divine. And the baptism is full of signs too: the overwhelming and washing of the waters, the voice declaring that 'this is my Son', the opening of the heavens and the descent of the dove, a sign of the Spirit, and the testimony of John himself. The apparent presence of three persons of the Trinity on this occasion even led St Augustine of Hippo to declare, 'Let us go to the Jordan and see the Trinity.'

The baptism of Christ has inspired artists throughout the ages. One of the earliest known representations comes from a mosaic in the ceiling of a sixth-century baptistery in Ravenna. People here were baptized in a huge round pool within a round building, and looking up would have seen this image of the baptism of Christ himself above them. Many of the significant medieval and Renaissance artists produced pictures of this scene and it is not difficult to find paintings of it produced even today. Many, many of the paintings are now available to view on the Internet, so studying them and comparing the insights of the different artists would be a worthwhile method of preparing for this celebration.

The diversity and richness of the images and symbols associated with this occasion may be almost overwhelming, but the need to make them truly visible does give scope for the involvement of a good number of people within the liturgy, making this ideal for an intergenerational service. And lest it be thought that this is mere mechanistic involvement, let us remember that it is through engagement and involvement that we often develop insight. If what we are about is catching glimpses, for some people, especially those who are younger, and for whom the bigger picture will certainly be overwhelming, then perhaps their small involvement will be the source of their first glimpse of what this festival has to say to us about the manifestation of Christ.

What needs to be prepared leading up to the service?

Use symbols to reinforce the connection between the stations of the procession and the three Gospel narratives:

- The crib might be enhanced by adding a large star above it, reminding us of the star followed by the Magi.
- The holy table or altar, where the wine will be placed at the story of the wedding at Cana, can be enhanced by the addition of a bouquet of flowers and a bridal veil and champagne glass, or even a wedding ring on a cushion, if it can be carried safely.
- The font can be enhanced with a dove, perhaps a christening robe and a picture of the baptism of Christ. This could be bought from a poster supplier, downloaded from a free Internet site or (if you have time) made in the church using ideas from historic pictures.
- The gifts of the wise men might be a piece of gold jewellery, incense and myrrh. Incense is available from many church suppliers, though you have to buy it in quite large quantities. Myrrh is more difficult to obtain. However, spice and herb shops and aromatherapy outlets often stock both around Christmas time. They need to be burnt to appreciate them and incense is much more powerful than myrrh, so the latter should precede the former in a procession. You might use myrrh oil instead of grains. Churches that use incense regularly will

have a special vessel in which to burn it, on charcoal. If you do not have a thurible, as it is called, both myrrh and incense can be burned over a candle in a scented oil burner, or in a metal sieve over a night light. Unless you have a proper thurible, it is unwise to carry a burning vessel around, so they might be carried in beautiful containers and then burnt beside the crib when the procession has arrived. Another possibility is to place crinkled tinfoil in a large bowl (there needs to be room for air to circulate the foil) with charcoal discs on top of it. Carry it on a block of wood.

- A large quantity of wine should be used. *Times and Seasons* suggests using the wine to be used for communion during the year: this might amount to a crate of bottles, but certainly several bottles might be carried, or, if your church has a large flagon for wine, use that. Another possibility is to fill a large glass water jug.

- The water to be poured out also needs to be abundant. Again, you could carry it in several vessels, thus involving a larger number of people. Remember that carrying large quantities of water is heavy and, unless you have someone who can carry a large water pot on his or her head, as water carriers in poor communities have done from generation to generation, people are likely to hurt their backs, or at the very least look undignified. Using several carriers renders the carrying much safer.

Notes on movement and inclusion

Visual foci need to be large enough for everyone to see and recognize, and to be carried through the congregation so that everyone has a chance to see them. Small children can help in this very effectively, which provides them with a role and includes them, even if they cannot read the words of the service. The degree of concentration they commit to the role of carrying large and interesting things serves as an invitation to the rest of the congregation to concentrate and focus on them also.

One of the excitements of this service is that people are able to move around and focus on an idea at three different points in the church building. This requires thought and planning. Walk through the service beforehand and work out where people will stand. In a very small building it may not be possible for everyone to move throughout the building, so

plan how you might invite different groups to move at different times. Even in a large building that is very full, you may need to do this. However, in a large building that is not full, it should be possible for the whole congregation to move. Make sure that you make provision for those with special needs. Children and people of small stature should be invited to the front of a crowd; make sure you take a route in which a wheelchair user can be included if present, and remember that, for some people, standing for all this time may be difficult, so invite people to sit down at points where appropriate seating can be made available, reminding those still standing about ensuring there are sight lines. This might all sound rather prescriptive, but with a few words of reminder during the welcome, and the odd informal direction as you proceed, it should be perfectly possible.

Crib, Jesse tree or wreath: which pathway?

If you have been using material throughout the Advent, Christmas and Epiphany seasons from one of the three pathways suggested in this book, you will need to decide, in planning this service, how you include the ideas provided in that pathway. If you have followed the crib pathway, this will be quite straightforward, but if you have followed the wreath or Jesse tree pathways, it will be more complicated. One possibility would be to use the wreath or the Jesse tree as the place from which the gifts to be carried in procession to each of the stations begin their journey. The service suggests the back of the church for this, but the wreath or Jesse tree would be equally appropriate.

Ideas for music

When Jesus came to Jordan
Crown him with many crowns
Songs of thankfulness and praise
The sinless one to Jordan came
A special star
Along the road to Bethlehem
Eastern strangers
Jesus went into the river
Why join a large and noisy crowd
Jesus, you're the king.

What needs to happen before the service?

If different voices from the congregation are to be used, the people concerned need to be invited and prepared. It would be helpful if all those talking part in the procession had the opportunity to walk through the route beforehand. Service sheets could be annotated and highlighted for each participant.

What needs to be made ready immediately before the service?

Gifts for the procession: star, gold, incense and myrrh; wine and wedding symbols; water

Each station – for example, uncover the font, remove the holy table cover, make sure the crib is where you want it to be.

Structure, movement and flow	Words/text	Multisensory	Participation
PREPARATION			
The ministers and members of the procession gather at the back of the church (or at the wreath or Jesse tree if this is more appropriate).	*The president says* Three wonders mark this holy day. This day a star leads the wise men to the Christ-child. **Alleluia.** This day water is made wine at the wedding feast. **Alleluia.** This day Jesus is revealed as the Christ in the waters of baptism. **Alleluia. Praise to you, Lord Jesus Christ.** [T&S 186 adapted]	Lights are extinguished, except at the back of the church where the procession will begin. A star is held high and the bearer says: A transparent container of wine is held up and the bearer says: A large container of water or a baptismal ewer is held high and the bearer says:	The congregation turns towards the back of the church, or if the congregation is small, people may gather at the back of the church (or at the wreath or Jesse tree if this is more appropriate).
Hymn	*A hymn such as* *'Songs of thankfulness and praise', verses 1 and 2.*	As the procession of the gifts moves forward, the lights are switched on at the front of the church and switched off at the back.	During the hymn, the star and some incense, the wine and water are brought in procession through the people.

	The president greets the people Grace, mercy and peace from God our Father and the Lord Jesus Christ be with you. **and also with you.** [T&S 186] *Words of welcome or introduction may be said.*		
	Almighty God, in Christ you make all things new: transform the poverty of our nature by the riches of your grace, and in the renewal of our lives make known your heavenly glory; through Jesus Christ your Son our Lord. **Amen.** [CW 384]		
Questions	*What are your questions about the Preparation section?*		
THE KING OF ALL THE WORLD IS REVEALED TO THE MAGI	This day a star leads the wise men to the Christ-child. Arise, shine out, for your light has come; **the glory of the Lord is rising upon you.** The nations will come to your light, **and kings to your dawning brightness.** They shall bring gold and frankincense, **and proclaim the praise of the Lord.** [T&S 186]	The person carrying the star says: A member of the congregation leads this Responsory from his or her place.	
Hymn		As the procession of the gifts moves to the crib, the lights are switched on around it and switched off elsewhere.	The procession, with the gifts, moves to the crib. The congregation may follow.

	Hear the Gospel of our Lord Jesus Christ according to Matthew. **Glory to you, O Lord.** *Matthew 2.1-2,8-11* *At the end* This is the Gospel of the Lord. **Praise to you, O Christ.**		
		The star is placed near the crib and incense is placed on the charcoal in a burner.	
	The president says Blessed are you, Lord our God, King of the universe: you receive our sacrifice of praise and thanksgiving. May our prayer be set forth in your sight as incense, and the lifting up of our hands be an evening sacrifice. **Blessed be God for ever.** [T&S 186]		
		Music or silence.	People are invited to come forward and each place a few grains of incense on the charcoal. This may be done in silence or quiet music may be played.
Questions	*What are your questions about the King section?*		

THE NEW CREATION IS REVEALED IN THE WATER MADE WINE		The person carrying the wine says:	
	This day water is made wine at the wedding feast.	A member of the congregation leads this Responsory from his or her place.	
	Behold, I make all things new: **I am the Alpha and the Omega, the beginning and the end.** To the thirsty I will give water as a gift **from the spring of the water of life.** [T&S 188]		
Hymn		As the procession of the gifts moves to the holy table, the lights are switched on at the holy table and switched off at the crib.	During the hymn, the procession moves to the holy table. The wine is held high in procession. The congregation may follow.
	Hear the Gospel of our Lord Jesus Christ according to John. **Glory to you, O Lord.** *John 2.1-11* *At the end* This is the Gospel of the Lord. **Praise to you, O Christ**.		
	Blessed are you, Lord our God, King of the universe: for the marriage of the Lamb has come. Make your Church ready, and clothe her with the righteous deeds of the saints, to join the praises of your new creation. **Blessed be God for ever.** [T&S 188]		

		As people taste the wine, there may be silence, or quiet music may be played.	People are invited to move forward and to taste the wine. The wine used should be as different as possible from that used for Holy Communion.
Questions	*What are your questions about the Water made Wine section?*		
THE CHRIST IS REVEALED IN THE WATERS OF BAPTISM	This day Jesus is revealed as the Christ in the waters of baptism. I will take you from the nations, **and gather you from all the countries.** I will sprinkle clean water upon you, **and you shall be clean from all your uncleanness.** A new heart I will give you, **and put a new spirit within you.** You shall be my people, **and I will be your God.** [T&S 189]	One of the people carrying the water says: A member of the congregation leads this Responsory from his or her place.	
Hymn		As the procession of the gifts moves forward, the lights are switched on at the font and switched off at the holy table.	During the hymn, people move to the font, the water (or baptismal ewer) held high and leading the procession. The congregation may follow.
	Hear the Gospel of our Lord Jesus Christ according to Mark. **Glory to you, O Lord.** Mark 1.1-11 (or 1.4-5,7-11) This is the Gospel of the Lord. **Praise to you, O Christ.**		

			Water is poured into the font by the bearer.
	The president says Blessed are you, Lord our God, King of the universe: you bring waters out of the stony rock. For with you is the well of life, and in your light shall we see light. **Blessed be God for ever.** [T&S 189]		
		This may be done in silence or quiet music may be played.	People are invited to come forward and use the water in the font in whatever way may be appropriate for them. This might include making the sign of the cross on the forehead or on the hands, pouring water over the head, touching the lips with the water …
	Remember your baptism into Christ Jesus. **Thanks be to God.**	This may be done in silence or quiet music may be played.	Alternatively, the leader(s) may sprinkle water over the congregation saying:

	The leader says this prayer
	 May God the creator, the rock of our
	    salvation,
	 who has given us new birth by water
	    and the Holy Spirit
	 and forgiven all our sins
	 through our Lord Jesus Christ,
	 keep us faithful to our calling, now and
	    for ever.
	 Amen.
	
	 [T&S 192]
	
	 The Lord's Prayer is said.		

Questions	*What are your questions about the baptism section?*		
THE SENDING OUT			

	The president says
	May God, who in Christ gives us a
	    spring of water welling up to eternal
	    life,
	perfect in you the image of his glory;
	and the blessing …
	
	[T&S 193]		

Hymn	*Such as 'Songs of thankfulness and praise', verses 4 and 5.*	As the procession moves to the exit the lights are switched on at the door and switched off at the font.	During which the procession goes to the exit. The congregation may follow. Any remaining water is carried to the door. The water is poured out over the threshold, if possible in such a way that everyone has to walk through it.
	A person pouring the water says Go in peace to love and serve the Lord. **In the name of Christ. Amen**		
Questions	*What are your questions about the Sending Out section of the service?*		

Candlemas service: The Eucharist on the Feast of the Presentation of Christ in the Temple

Preparatory notes

The crib should remain in the church after Christmas until this service takes place. You may have turned it into a 'house' at Epiphany. The shepherds will have left and the three wise men will leave at some point during the Epiphany season. Leave Mary and Joseph and the Christ-child in place. You may also like to leave the animals outside the accommodation.

Identify a place in the church that will represent the Temple in Jerusalem for this service. You could project a picture of the Temple onto the wall in this place or you may like to place symbols there representing the Jewish people and their worship in the Temple: a star of David, burning incense, a copy of the Hebrew Bible or the Ten Commandments, and some angels.

The congregation assembles in a convenient gathering place before the service begins. Each person receives a candle.

The ministers enter without announcement and the service begins with the Greeting.

What needs to be prepared leading up to the service?

You will need to identify people to be Simeon and Anna and Mary and Joseph. You will also need a life-sized representation of the Christ-child: you will probably need to use a doll unless there happens to be a small baby available! If there is a baby, use the baby's parents as Mary and Joseph. Anna and Simeon are also responsible for reading the Gospel, so they will need to be prepared to do this as well as to act. You may need to decide how you are going to 'represent' each of the

characters. Will they wear some sort of costume or can the representation be effected in another way?

What needs to happen before the service?

Make sure you have enough candles available. It helps if the congregation's candles have rings of cardboard to catch drips.

You will also need to have candles for the Prayers: four large ones and twelve smaller ones – but probably larger than those for the congregation.

Identify a place to become the Temple for the purpose of this service. Represent it in the way suggested above. You will need to place the candles there for the Prayers. You will also need to be sure that you have a box or basket in which the crib figures can be removed. Finally, you will need to have a cross to place where the crib has been.

What needs to be made ready immediately before the service begins?

Have candles in place to be given out to the congregation and also in the Temple area for the Prayers.

The lid should be removed from the font.

Questions

As you read through the text of the service it might be helpful to jot down any questions that arise for you as you begin to plan. They may be questions about why this particular suggestion is made, or they may be about how you would execute a particular suggestion in your situation, and whether it needs to be adapted. There are places in the table that follows where you are reminded to ask these questions as you work your way through the planning for the service.

Structure, movement and flow	Words/text	Multisensory	Participation
THE GATHERING	*A hymn may be sung.* *'Angels from the realms of glory' is a particularly suitable hymn for the beginning of this service. The verses about the angels, shepherds and sages take us back to Christmas, while the last two verses place us in the Temple. It links the two events perfectly.*		The congregation assembles in a convenient place and candles are distributed. The ministers join the people.
Greeting	In the name of the Father, and of the Son, and of the Holy Spirit. **Amen.** The Lord of glory be with you. **The Lord bless you.** [T&S 195]		
The Welcome and Introduction	*The president welcomes the people* Dear friends, forty days ago we celebrated the birth of our Lord Jesus Christ. Now we recall the day on which he was presented in the Temple, when he was offered to the Father and shown to his people. As a sign of his coming among us, his mother was purified, as we now come to him for cleansing. In their old age Simeon and Anna recognized him as their Lord, as we today sing of his glory. In this eucharist, we celebrate both the joy of his coming and his searching judgement, looking back to the day of his birth and forward to the coming days of his passion. [T&S 195]		

Acclamation	*A hymn or chant may be sung at the lighting of the candles.* The Taizé chant 'The Lord is my light' note needed would be appropriate or, if there are children or very elderly people present, 'Jesus bids us shine' might be appreciated. *The president says* Blessed are you, Lord our God, King of the universe! **Blessed be God for ever.** You gave us Jesus to be the light of the world; he makes our darkness to be light. **Blessed be God for ever.** As we bear your light, may our lips never cease to sing your praise. **Blessed be God for ever.** [T&S 205]	The candles are lit.	Two older people dressed to represent Simeon and Anna lead the procession from the place of gathering to the body of the church. Two people dressed to represent Mary and Joseph, together with the Christ-child, follow at the end of the procession
Gloria in Excelsis	*A version of the Gloria in Excelsis is sung. This may be the* Common Worship *text or it may be another version, for example a Taizé Gloria or the Peruvian Gloria.*	When all have reached their places, the candles are put out.	As the Gloria in Excelsis is sung, the procession moves to the body of the church and people take their places. Mary and Joseph stand near to the crib with the Christ-child. Simeon and Anna go to stand in the place that has been chosen to represent the Temple.
Collect	*The president introduces a period of silent prayer with the words* Let us pray that we may know and share the light of Christ. *Silence is kept.* Lord Jesus Christ, light of the nations and glory of Israel: make your home among us, and present us pure and holy to your heavenly Father, your God, and our God. **Amen** [Common Worship: Additional Collects 9]		

Questions	What are your questions about the preparation section?		
THE LITURGY OF THE WORD			
Readings	*The Old Testament reading.*		The person representing Anna could read the Old Testament reading.
			Before the Gospel reading, Simeon and Anna lead the congregation in procession to the place in the church that represents the Temple. Psalm 24 may be said or sung as people move.
Gospel Reading	*This acclamation may herald the Gospel reading.* Today the Lord is presented in the Temple in substance of our mortal nature. **Alleluia.** Today the Blessed Virgin comes to be purified in accordance with the law. **Alleluia.** Today old Simeon proclaims Christ as the light of the nations and the glory of Israel. **Alleluia. Praise to Christ, the light of the world.** [T&S 197] *When the Gospel is announced, the reader says* Hear the Gospel of our Lord Jesus Christ according to Luke. **Glory to you, O Lord.** *At the end* This is the Gospel of the Lord. **Praise to you, O Christ.**		The Gospel may be read by one reader or it may be read dramatically. In this case, Simeon should read the words of the Nunc Dimittis and Mary and Joseph should enter the 'Temple' at the appropriate point in the narrative. Simeon and Anna should each take the Christ-child in their arms. The people return to their seats in the body of the church. Simeon, Anna, Mary and Joseph remain in the Temple area.

Sermon	During the sermon or address, the preacher explains that on this day we turn from the crib to the cross; that this day marks the end of the Christmas season and marks the beginning of a change of focus, towards Lent and the cross.	The crib and the figures may be put away as part of the action of the sermon. A large cross may be brought to stand where the crib has been.	

The Creed	Let us affirm our faith in Jesus Christ the Son of God:
	
	**Though he was divine,
	he did not cling to equality with God,
	but made himself nothing.
	Taking the form of a slave,
	he was born in human likeness.
	He humbled himself
	and was obedient to death,
	even the death of the cross.
	Therefore God has raised him on high,
	and given him the name that is above
	     every name:
	that at the name of Jesus
	every knee should bow,
	and every voice proclaim that Jesus
	     Christ is Lord,
	to the glory of God the Father.
	Amen.**
	
	[CW 147]		

Questions	*What are your questions about the Liturgy of the Word?*		
Prayers of Intercession	*Subjects for prayer may be given before the prayers of intercession, and the words below are then said without further additions. Different people may lead each section.* Let us pray to the Father through Christ who is our light and Life. Father, your Christ is acclaimed as the glory of Israel: look in mercy on your Church, sharing his light. Lord, have mercy. **Christ, have mercy.** Father, your Christ in his temple brings judgement on the world: look in mercy on the nations, who long for his justice. Lord, have mercy. **Christ, have mercy.**	As each of the sections is said, one of the main characters of the story lights a large candle in the 'Temple' area of the church and carries it out to stand among the people with it. As 'Lord, have mercy' is said, three people from the congregation light smaller candles from the large candle and stand beside it.	

	Father, your Christ, who was rich, for our sakes became poor: look in mercy on the needy, suffering with him. Lord, have mercy. **Christ, have mercy.** Father, your Christ is the one in whom faithful servants find their peace: look in mercy on the departed, that they may see your salvation. Lord, have mercy. **Christ, have mercy.** Father, your Christ is revealed as the one destined to be rejected: look in mercy on us who now turn towards his passion. Lord, have mercy. **Christ, have mercy.** Lord God, you kept faith with Simeon and Anna, and showed them the infant King. Give us grace to put all our trust in your promises, and the patience to wait for their fulfilment; through Jesus Christ our Lord. **Amen.** [T&S 198]		
Prayers of Penitence	Hear the words of our Saviour Jesus Christ: 'I am the light of the world. Whoever follows me shall never walk in darkness but shall have the light of life.' Let us therefore bring our sins into his light and confess them in penitence and faith. [T&S 199] In a dark and disfigured world we have not held out the light of life: Lord, have mercy. **Lord, have mercy.** In a hungry and despairing world we have failed to share our bread: Christ, have mercy. **Christ, have mercy.** In a cold and loveless world we have kept the love of God to ourselves: Lord, have mercy, **Lord, have mercy**. [NP 93] An authorized absolution is used.	The prayer candles are extinguished before the Peace is shared.	

Questions	*What are your questions about the penitential section and the prayers?*		
THE LITURGY OF THE SACRAMENT			
The Peace	In the tender mercy of our God, the dayspring from on high has broken upon us, to give light to those who dwell in darkness and the shadow of death, and to guide our feet into the way of peace. The peace of the Lord be always with you **and also with you.** *These words may be added* Let us offer one another a sign of peace. [T&S 200]		The Peace is shared between those present.
Preparation of the Table	*The gifts of the people may be gathered and presented.* *The table is prepared and bread and wine are placed upon it.*		
Taking of the Bread and Wine	*This prayer may be said* Father, in Christ there has sprung up a light for the righteous; accept the gifts we bring before you and grant that Christ may shine in us to the praise and glory of your name. **Amen.** *The president takes the bread and wine.* [T&S 200]		
The Eucharistic Prayer	*Use one of the Eucharistic Prayers provided in* Common Worship, *with this Preface* And now we give you thanks because, by appearing in the Temple, he comes near to us in judgement; The Word made flesh searches the hearts of all your people, and brings to light the brightness of your splendour. [T&S 201]		
The Lord's Prayer	The Lord's Prayer is said.		

Breaking of the Bread	We break the bread of life, and that life is the light of the world. **God here among us, light in the midst of us, bring us to light and life.** [T&S 202] *The Agnus Dei may be used, as the bread is broken.*		
Giving of Communion	*The president says this or another invitation to communion* God's holy gifts or God's holy people. **Jesus Christ is holy, Jesus Christ is Lord, to the glory of God the Father.** [T&S 202] *The president and people receive communion.* *Authorized words of distribution are used and the communicant replies* **Amen.**		
Hymn		A hymn may be sung as the giving of communion is completed, the remaining bread and wine are consumed and the holy table is cleared. During the singing of the hymn, the individual candles are lit again.	
Prayer after Communion	Lord, you fulfilled the hope of Simeon and Anna, who lived to welcome the Messiah: may we, who have received these gifts beyond words, prepare to meet Christ Jesus when he comes to bring us eternal life; for he is alive and reigns, now and for ever. **Amen.** [CW 386] Let us now follow Simeon and Anna and prepare to proclaim Christ to the world.		

THE CONCLUSION			
		The cross that has been placed where the crib had been may be carried in the procession also and placed beside the font.	Simeon and Anna lead the ministers in moving from the altar to the font.
		The Nunc Dimittis may be sung as the procession is made.	
	Now, Lord, you let your servant go in peace: your word has been fulfilled. My own eyes have seen the salvation which you have prepared in the sight of every people; A light to reveal you to the nations and the glory of your people Israel. Glory to the Father and to the Son and to the Holy Spirit; as it was in the beginning is now and shall be for ever. **Amen.** [CW 86]		The congregation follows the ministers in procession to the font.
Final Responsory	Father, we have sung your praise with shepherds and angels: may Christ be born in our hearts today. **Praise to Christ our light.** We have shared in the joy of Simeon and Anna; help us, like them, to trust your word. **Praise to Christ our light.** We have greeted Jesus, the light of the world; may we be filled with the light of your love. Praise to Christ our light. *All now extinguish their candles.* We stand near the place of new birth. **Let us shine with the light of your love.** We turn from the crib to the cross. **Let us shine with the light of your love.** We go to carry his light. **Let us shine with the light of your love.** **Thanks be to God.** [T&S 205] *The ministers and people depart.*		
Questions	*What are your questions about the Conclusion and Dismissal?*		

Epiphany:
The wreath pathway

Practical inclusive ideas

Using the wreath through Epiphany

A wreath near the crib

During the Sundays of Epiphany, a wreath that stands near the crib may remain in its place. If the four candles in the ring have become very short or difficult to burn, you may like to replace the coloured ones of Advent with white or gold ones, but if they are still usable, you could keep them as a reminder of the progression of this season, which began with Advent.

A suspended Advent crown

If you have created an Advent crown for use in the Advent season, you could perhaps suspend it over the font during the Sundays of Epiphany. Huge swathes of fabric in white and gold could be attached to this arrangement, creating the effect of a canopy. Floor-standing candles would then be used beneath this to be lit when the prayer is said. For a photograph of this type of hanging wreath look at the CD-ROM, file 000. If the wreath is suspended in the crossing of the church, two or four swathes of fabric could also be used running down to pillars and a large star could be hung through the centre of the wreath.

Water images and the wreath

Water images run through this season – water into wine, the waters of the River Jordan, the waters of creation, the water of baptism, the Water Gate, the call beside the Sea of Galilee. You might want to consider using a huge bowl of water on a pedestal into which floating candles are placed or lighting candles on stands around the bowl of water.

The white candle and the Lectionary Gospel images

Alternatively, you might have just one large candle representing the light of Christ standing where the wreath had been, to which you add other symbols – the gifts of the Magi or the offering of our own gifts and talents described on paper and collected in a bowl to be brought and placed beside the candle.

On the Feast of the Epiphany, you could burn incense beside the candle and, on the first Sunday of Epiphany (The Baptism of Christ), a piece of blue cloth can be wound around the candlestick. Other Epiphany themes fall in different Sundays in the three different years of the Lectionary:

- *The Call of the Disciples* (Epiphany 2 and 3 of Year A and 2 of Year B). The focus is on being called by name and the calling of the disciples, so names written on paper and gathered up in baskets might be brought to be placed by the candle.
- *The Wedding at Cana* (Epiphany 4 in Year A, Epiphany 3 in Year B and Epiphany 2 in Year C). Add the largest jug or container you can find filled with water to the brim.
- *Jesus the Teacher* (Epiphany 4 of Year B). An icon of Christ the Teacher.
- *Jesus in the Synagogue at Nazareth* (Epiphany 3 of Year C). A Bible or scroll could be added.
- *The Feast of The Presentation of Christ in the Temple* (Epiphany 4 of Year C). A cross may be added and myrrh burnt on charcoal.

Epiphany and baptism

Epiphany is a good time for members of the congregation to reflect on their own baptism and on what it means to be a community of the baptized. It is also appropriate in this season to consider vocation, time and talents, giving or mission. These themes may be picked up in the intercessions or in the kind of educational and reflective opportunities provided in the church and in the focus of notices and displays on the walls. It is important to consider how the themes of giving, of time and talents and of vocation, are dealt with in children's groups and youth groups if these things are not to be seen as adult matters. One way of encouraging a world focus in terms of congregational prayer might be to put a map of the world on the noticeboard, perhaps surrounded by newspaper stories, and invite people to put their prayers for parts of the world on sticky notes that can then be stuck on the map, or to take away photocopies of the news articles to provide an impetus for prayer during the week. It is a time not only for reflecting on one's own calling but also for considering how that calling is worked out in the world so community outreach projects might be a way of working with this.

Prayers around the wreath in Epiphany and at Candlemas

At the Candlemas service, the congregational candles may be lit from the wreath's central candle. At the end of the service, the prayer for Candlemas (among the 'Prayers at the wreath' below) may be used as a reminder of the world for which Christ came and our responsibility to be bearers of the Christ-light into that world. Here the wreath lights may be extinguished as we take up the call to go out and shine as lights in the world – living out our baptism.

THE EPIPHANY

Pilgrim God: way of truth,
the Magi followed the shining star
leaving behind the life they knew to go in search of you.
God who speaks to us through the gifts of the stranger
and in the unknown and unexpected places,
you have come to seek and to save – not with the might of armies –
but through the child born to die for the world's redemption.
Open our ears to hear you and our eyes to see you
that we may recognize you speaking beyond the confines of the familiar
and know you as the God beyond our limitations,
whose glory fills the earth.
The light of Christ reveals the path to God.
We travel in the way by the Spirit's grace.
Amen.

Deliver us when we call upon you,
O God of our salvation.

Be for us the lifter of our heads
and protect us from violent hands.
Deliver us when we call upon you,
O God of our salvation.

May the earth bring forth goodness
and the peoples of earth flourish.
Deliver us when we call upon you,
O God of our salvation.

Be for us the wellspring of life
that we will be thirsty no more.
Deliver us when we call upon you,
O God of our salvation.

Save us from darkness
and let your glory rise upon us.
Deliver us when we call upon you,
O God of our salvation,
now and for ever
Amen.

THE BAPTISM OF CHRIST – THE FIRST SUNDAY OF EPIPHANY

Liberating God,
glorious in strength;
your voice swept over the mighty deep, bringing life from chaos;
you brought your people to freedom through the waters of death,
calling them by a new name and making them your own.
Walk with us, O God, through all that threatens to overwhelm;
deliver all held captive by sin and living under the shadow of destruction,
that we might hear again your voice calling us and taking away our fear,
and rising to new life in Christ;
and rejoice again in your power to save.
The light of Christ reveals the path to God,
we travel in the way by the Spirit's grace.
Amen.

Heaven and earth bless the name of the Lord,
the God who is strong to save!
Heaven and earth bow down to the Lord
for he is King for ever!
All God's people cry 'Glory!'

God's name is mighty in all the earth,
his word upholds the heavens.
All God's people cry 'Glory!'

God's voice sweeps over the waters
and flashes with flames of fire.
All God's people cry 'Glory!'

God brings us through the flood
and rescues us from death.
All God's people cry 'Glory!'

Made, known and loved by God,
redeemed and called by name.
All God's people cry 'Glory!'

Be the strength of your people, O God,
and give us the blessing of peace.
All God's people cry 'Glory!'
Amen.

THE SECOND SUNDAY OF EPIPHANY

Steadfast God, your love is unending.
You have searched us and known us,
in tenderness you called us from before we were
born –
seeking us out and making us your own.
When we strayed from your ways, you heard our cry,
lifted us from trouble and made our steps secure.
Give us listening hearts that we may hear you
speaking our name
and grace to follow where you lead us,
that we shall be known as the redeemed of the Lord
and beautiful in his sight.
The light of Christ reveals the path to God.
We travel in the way by the Spirit's grace.
Amen.

God, you have searched me and known me.
Nothing is hidden from you.
How precious is your love, O God.
All peoples find refuge in you.

You will feed your people
and gather your lambs in your arms.
How precious is your love O God.
All peoples find refuge in you.

You search us out and call us by name,
giving us drink from the river of delights.
How precious is your love, O God.
All peoples find refuge in you.

Your faithfulness is beyond all telling.
Your deliverance is our song of praise.
How precious is your love, O God.
All peoples find refuge in you –
today and for ever.
Amen.

THE THIRD SUNDAY OF EPIPHANY

God our salvation,
the heavens proclaim your glory and tell of your
wonderful works to the ends of the earth!
You bring to light what is hidden in darkness and
raise your people from the gloom,
transforming the ordinary into a sign of your glory.
Teach us to walk in the light of your truth,
following your commandments and turning away
from sin.
Lift up our heads, O God, that we may see your face
and your goodness may shine on us all our days.
The light of Christ reveals the path to God.
We travel in the way by the Spirit's grace.
Amen.

The Lord is the light and salvation
of all who seek his face.

If all who love me turn away,
God will preserve my life.
The Lord is my light and salvation.

He hears me when I call on his name
and sets my feet upon the rock.
The Lord is my light and salvation.

He will teach me his ways
and lead me on straight paths.
The Lord is my light and salvation.

I will not be afraid
though evil surrounds me.
The Lord is my light and salvation.

The Lord is the light and salvation
of all who seek his face.
Amen.

THE FOURTH SUNDAY OF EPIPHANY

God our redeemer,
your name reaches to the ends of the earth and your
arm is strong to save!
You have sent redemption to your people according
to your promise,
welcoming us to feast at your table and to drink of
the water of life.
May we who have received your blessings
open our hands to a hungry world
that, living in the light of your gospel
and breaking our bread with strangers,
we may bring others to taste and see your goodness.
The light of Christ reveals the path to God.
We travel in the way by the Spirit's grace.
Amen.

Give thanks to the Lord all people.
His praise endures for ever!
God's ways are faithful and just.
Great are the works of the Lord!

God has sent redemption.
Great are the works of the Lord!

God's love is steadfast and sure.
Great are the works of the Lord!

God shows us the path to life.
Great are the works of the Lord!

Give thanks to the Lord all people.
His praise endures for ever!
Amen.

CANDLEMAS

Note: There is an important unity to be observed in the lighting of the lights in the wreath and the dismissal when the congregation goes out into the world, bearing the light of Christ. It may be appropriate, therefore, to take the light to be distributed to the congregation from the central light in the wreath. At this point, the four candles in the ring are extinguished, leaving only the Christ-light burning within the ring.

O Saviour of the world: King of glory,
our eyes have seen you revealed in the work of creation.
The whole world belongs to you and is your delight –
sky, sea and rivers, the heavens above, the ground beneath our feet
and all peoples who inhabit the earth
are fearfully and wonderfully made by your hand.
Who is like you, O God, marvellous in holiness?
Who can stand in your presence and worship you?
Keep our hands from doing wrong and our ways pure before you,
that we may shine ever more with your light
until we come into your glory and see you face to face.
The light of Christ reveals the path to God.
We travel in the way by the Spirit's grace.
Amen.

The following prayer may be suitable for dramatic reading.

Lift up your heads, O people!
Your God comes.
Lift up your heads, O gates!
Your God comes in glory.

Who is this king of glory?
He is God, the Lord of all.

Who is this king of glory?
He is God, your maker and redeemer.

Sing aloud to the God of salvation.
Seek his face and praise him for ever.

Keep our hearts faithful to you, O God,
that we may serve you.
Keep our hands from doing wrong,
that we may bless you.

Lift up your heads, O people!
Your God comes.
Lift up your heads, O gates.
Your God comes in glory.

Sing aloud to the God of salvation.
Seek his face and praise him for ever.

Let your face shine upon us, O God,
our strength and our redeemer!
Amen.

The wreath in groups

Children

This season is concerned with marking the presence of Christ as the light of the world and reflecting on the revelation of God to everybody. The colours for this season are gold or white for Epiphany, the baptism of Christ and Candlemas, white for the other weeks. You could change your Advent wreath into an 'Epiphany wreath' by replacing the coloured candles with white or gold ones. Keep the white Christ-light in the centre. You may want to add gold ribbons or some flowers. Make an emphasis on light on your focal table by using candles on each corner. If you can obtain some light sticks, you could invite the children to hold these during the prayer time each week.

Week 1: The visit of the Magi

PREPARATION

We call them the three kings, the three wise men, the Magi. We don't know that there were three of them, though three gifts are mentioned in Matthew's

Gospel, and we know that they came 'from the East'. The well-loved carol 'We three kings of Orient are' explains to us the significance of these gifts in a fairly accessible way. This session provides an opportunity to think about the significance of the visit of the wise men and of their gifts.

YOU WILL NEED

- The focal table prepared with a white or gold cloth and the wreath redecked for Epiphany, and candles at each corner.
- The three gifts: gold, frankincense and myrrh. You can represent the gold in many ways: bits of gold-coloured stones from a flower shop, a wedding ring, some shiny coins and so on. Frankincense and myrrh can be obtained as either grains or oil from aromatherapy stalls or bathroom shops and similar places. The oils can be burnt in an oil burner over a candle; the grains work better on charcoal, but a few grains placed into the flame of a night light will provide scented smoke for a short time. The children will enjoy smelling the grains unlit, and could smell the oil from the bottles too, but be careful that these strong oils do not come directly into contact with the skin of young children.
- Three crowns – make them out of gold card, or take them from your nativity costumes.
- A small sponge cake that can be cut into slices so that everyone present can have one: there must not be any left over. Alternatively, use tiny individual fairy cakes made in sweet papers. Beware of food allergies: gluten, wheat and egg. If you have people with food allergies, discuss with parents whether you can provide something that everyone can eat. Into the sponge cake insert three hard beans or dried peas. Use haricot or butter beans. Do not use red kidney beans, as they are poisonous until cooked. Include the three beans in the mixture if you are making the cake yourself. If using a bought cake, you will have to insert them carefully into the cake from underneath. Put one into just three of the little cakes if you choose this option.
- You will need a knife to cut the cake with. Keep it in a safe place.
- Serviettes or kitchen roll.

THE FOCAL TABLE

- Use a white or gold cloth.
- Have three crowns ready to be worn by three kings.

- Display the three gifts: gold, frankincense and myrrh, together with means of burning the incense.
- Display the cakes.
- More candles to emphasize the light theme.

THE GATHERING

Talk together about what has happened in the past week. If you have not met since Christmas, you may want to share Christmas experiences together. Cut up the cake into the same number of pieces as those who are present and offer everyone a piece of cake. Ask them to eat their cake slowly and carefully and, if they feel something hard, to take it out of their mouth. Make sure everyone has a serviette! Hopefully, three people will come across the three beans or peas. Those who find the beans or peas can wear the crowns and be kings for the session. Explain that this is an old French tradition: the people who find the beans are kings for the day on the Feast of the Epiphany.

TELL THE STORY

Tell the story of the journey of the wise men, from Matthew's Gospel. You may wish to use a children's Bible or a picture book, or you could tell it in your own words. But beware: there are a good many retellings of this story that add in all sorts of details. This is not the occasion for that sort of retelling: stick to the bald Gospel version on this occasion. (The version to be found in *The Children's Illustrated Bible*[1] would be suitable.)

TALK TOGETHER AGAIN

What would the three visitors have had to do to prepare for their journey?

What dangers might they have faced?

What do you think they might have hoped to find?

How might they have felt when they reached Herod's palace and found the baby was not there?

Do you think you might set out on a journey like that? Do you know anyone who might do it?

THINK ABOUT THE GIFTS

Warm the incense in whatever way you have chosen and smell its scented smoke. Try the same with the myrrh, though it doesn't smell as strongly. You might simply pass it round instead.

Ask people to think which of the three gifts they might like to have taken – or would they have taken something else? Does anyone know the hidden meaning of the gifts?

Either sing, or listen to a recording of, the carol 'We three kings' and then discuss the meaning of the gifts again.

KEEP SILENCE TOGETHER

Relight the incense and, as the smoke rises, keep a moment or two of silence. Remind people about being still as they were during the Advent sessions.

After a few moments, use this prayer:

God be gracious to us and bless us,
and make your face shine upon us:
Lord, have mercy.
Lord, have mercy.

May your ways be known on the earth,
your saving power among the nations:
Christ, have mercy.
Christ, have mercy.

You, Lord, have made known your salvation,
and reveal your justice in the sight of the nations:
Lord, have mercy.
Lord, have mercy.

[T&S 121]

THE RESPONSE TIME

If there is still time, you might want to think about ways of providing children with time to respond to God in a variety of ways. Provide a variety of materials and give the children time to use these in whatever way they choose, to respond to the space they have created and the prayers they have offered, just as they did during Advent.

Week 2: The Baptism of Jesus

PREPARATION

This week add some blue cloth to the gold and white of Epiphany and the Baptism of Jesus. Add the largest container of water you can obtain, filled to the brim and add also a picture of the baptism of Jesus. If you can find a representation of a dove, add that also. During the session you will share one of the accounts from the Gospels of the baptism of Jesus and

encounter the associated symbols. There is an opportunity to reflect on all this and respond by using water, and praying an ancient prayer used in the eastern Church on the feast of the Baptism of Christ.

YOU WILL NEED

- The focal table you had last week;
- A blue cloth;
- The largest attractive bowl you can find, filled to the brim with water;
- Some bowls for washing hands, soap, towels, hand cream;
- Floating candles (these tend to go in and out of fashion in the shops so look in good time. They are always available on the Internet);
- A model or picture of a dove;
- A picture of the baptism of Christ (again, look on the Internet).

THE GATHERING

As people arrive today, give them the opportunity to wash their hands. Have several bowls of warm water so that a queue does not develop. Provide a choice of attractive soaps, some soft warm towels and some hand cream. Simply invite people to choose what they would like to use, then, having washed their hands, to come and sit down. (Warning: be aware of the need to be vigilant about skin allergies and provide a choice of safe soap and creams if necessary.)

Discuss the week as people gather and you may like to encourage people to compare one another's choice of scented soap and hand cream.

Ask people to listen carefully to the story you are going to tell them. Explain that it is a story that is full of signs and ask them to try to spot these signs as they listen to the story. Tell the story of Jesus' baptism. You may read it from the Bible or a children's Bible or tell it in your own words. Keep the story simple, however, and do not add details. You can find the story in Matthew 3.13-17 or Mark 1.9-11. When the story is over, discuss the signs that people spotted. (There are no right answers or prizes for people who spot the most!)

TALK TOGETHER

Discuss together which of the signs would have impressed people most if they had been there. Look at the picture together and see what you observe in that. Discuss similarities with and differences between the biblical accounts. If you had been there, what might you have said? What signs do we use in baptism?

Invite people to come and put their hands in the water. They might like to wash their faces with the water or just dip in a finger and then draw a cross with the water on the back or the palm of their other hand. They can choose.

Finally, light some floating candles and invite people to come and place them on the water.

When all the candles are lit and floating on the water, use the following set of responses. Older children could be invited to read one of the sentences each and everyone join in with the response. You might like to practise the response first.

The Father's voice bears witness to the Son.
God shows himself to us.

The Son bows his head beneath the Baptist's stream.
God shows himself to us.

The Spirit as a dove descends from heaven.
God shows himself to us.

Submitting to John's baptism, Christ delivers us from bondage.
God shows himself to us.

[T&S 182, adapted]

THE RESPONSE TIME

If there is still time, you might want to think about ways of providing children with time to respond to God in different ways. Provide a variety of materials and give the children time to use these in whatever way they choose, to respond to the story and the water.

Week 3: The call of the disciples

PREPARATION

You are almost never too young to think about vocation. A three-year-old friend told me recently that, when he grows up, he is going to be a superhero. He is going to be a fireman – like Fireman Sam. The Church has often used the term vocation with reference to people who are seeking ordination, but many roles involve a vocation – and indeed, any job can become a vocation. The churches went through a period recently when it seemed to be

understood that vocation was really something for older people 'who had seen a bit of life'. We are now realizing that was a mistake and that young people, even children, do have vocations to Christian service, which we must take seriously. This session looking at the call of the disciples gives an opportunity to raise awareness of this.

There are quite a number of accounts of Jesus calling people to follow him, spread through the four Gospels. This session concentrates on those that describe the calling of the fishermen. There are even several versions of these! You might like to choose the one that features in the lectionary readings for the year currently being observed.

YOU WILL NEED
- The focal table with its white cloth, wreath and candles.
- Add a fishing net (buy netting from a garden centre if you cannot get the real thing) this week.

THE GATHERING

Once you have gathered and talked about the past week, ask if people have any idea what they want to do when they leave school or when they grow up. Responses will no doubt vary, from those who are very clear to those who don't think about it. Do people know what they might need to do to achieve their goal – have they thought about it? Do they think they might really be able to do it? Do they think they might be surprised one day? As the adults present, tell the children briefly about your own experiences in a way that they will be able to appreciate: tell them about any unexpected twists and turns in your own experiences and surprises you may have had. If you don't want to talk about your own experiences, you could describe a well-known person, but personal experiences are more vivid.

TELL THE STORY

Tell the story (whichever you have chosen) of the call of the fishermen by Jesus. Read the verses from the Bible or tell it in your own words but stick pretty closely to the biblical text. Don't add details.

When you have heard the story, ask the children to think about the story for a few moments, then discuss together anything that was surprising about the story. Ask yourself, what would you have done, if you had been one of the fishermen? Suppose they had all said no, what might Jesus have done then? What might their families have said? Which family members might have been affected? Why do you think they might have said yes? Do you think it was exciting?

Very carefully, take the net off the table and spread it out on the floor so that everyone can gather around it. Invite people to hold the net and observe how it holds everyone together. Ask people to be silent for a few moments and, this time, to close their eyes. Suggest that, in holding the net, even though we cannot see, we are aware of one another and how we are held together. Pray that you may each learn to see how to help and serve one another and have the courage to do it.

Finish with this prayer, adapted from *Times and Seasons*:

May the Lord Jesus Christ,
Son of the living God,
teach us to walk in his way more trustfully,
to accept his truth more faithfully,
and to share his life more lovingly;
that by the power of the Holy Spirit
we may come as one family to the kingdom
   of the Father.
Amen.

[T&S 145]

THE RESPONSE TIME

If there is still time, you might want to think about ways of providing children with time to respond to God in different ways. Provide a variety of materials and give the children time to use these in whatever way they choose, to respond to the story and idea of being called.

Week 4: The Wedding at Cana

PREPARATION

There are lots of dimensions to this event.

It's an 'epiphany' story because it describes the first miracle performed by Jesus that shows that he is God's Son. An important part of the story is that Jesus wondered whether he was ready to show himself in this way. When his mother asks him to do something, he says 'My time hasn't come, yet.' But maybe mother knows best. After all, she has been following God's guidance since the message of the angel telling her

that she would be the mother of God's Son. Sometimes other people, parents, friends and so on, can know us better than we know ourselves and can help us at the point where decisions need to be made.

The story is unique, yet in many ways similar to the miracles of the feeding of the 5,000, in which Jesus answers people's greatest need, but the need is to be fed, rather than to be healed. Like the other feeding stories, this miracle seems to foreshadow Holy Communion, in which the bread and wine are transformed by God's gift into the body and blood of Christ.

Like many miracle stories, this stresses the importance of asking God. Jesus acts in response to his mother's request. In Holy Communion we ask God to transform the bread and wine – 'grant that by the power of your Holy Spirit these gifts … may be to us his body and his blood …' [CW 185]

After this event, there's no going back. Up to this point, most of the things Jesus had done were hidden. From now onwards, he will be pursued by crowds. He will be known. He can't hope to be unrecognized, as he was when he came to John the Baptist at the Jordan.

The quantity of wine is enormous. It's not just enough for the party, but it's the best ever, and there are six huge jars, each holding 20 to 30 gallons of wine. It is the enormous generosity of God that makes people realize this is a miracle. We might almost describe God as being 'prodigal' in his generosity.

YOU WILL NEED
- The focal table with its white cloth, wreath and candles.
- Wine for the focal table, (which could be presented later at the holy table to use in Holy Communion).

THE GATHERING

When you have talked about the week that has just gone by, turn to the idea that sometimes we realize we can do new things.

Ask about how we know when we are old enough to do new things. For example, did someone buy you a bike when they thought you were old enough to learn to ride it? How old do you have to be to join Beavers or Rainbows, or Cubs or Brownies? How old do you need to be to be asked to go to a shop on your own? What does it feel like when somebody has confidence in you and believes you will be able to do things, play in a football team, play a musical instrument in a group, balance on a piece of play equipment in a park, dive head first into a swimming pool? How do people give you confidence in yourself? How can you help others to be confident in themselves?

TALK TOGETHER

Tell the story of this event. If it is already likely to be familiar, ask people first to imagine they are one of the characters in it, and think about their thoughts and reactions as the story is told. What is it like to be Mary, Jesus, a disciple, the steward of the feast?

REFLECT TOGETHER

What is your reaction, as people in the story, when you start to realize that there is not just enough wine, which might have been brought in easily, but just so much wine that is so good that it's more than would have existed in the village, and it must be miraculous?

How do you look on Jesus when you realize what has happened?

Jesus tells lots of stories in which the kingdom of God is described as a great celebration at a feast. We remind people of this story at marriage services in church. Jesus wanted the celebration to be a great occasion for the people getting married, and for all their families and friends. We can invite him to share our celebrations and bless them. How might we do that? Could we say a prayer, say grace, ask God's blessing, at our family celebrations?

PRAY TOGETHER

Give everyone a glass of water to hold as you say this prayer:

Almighty God,
whose Son revealed in signs and miracles
the wonder of your saving presence:
renew your people with your heavenly grace,
and in all our weakness
sustain us by your mighty power;
through Jesus Christ your Son our Lord.
Amen.

[CW 385]

THE RESPONSE TIME

Make up prayers together, either to use at a service of Holy Communion, or for a celebration party. Include something to ask for, just as Mary asked; and something to be thankful for, as they must have been for the gift of wine.

Older children might write a prayer to say when the bread and wine are brought to the holy table for Communion. The prayers could be said aloud as the gifts are presented. They may be prayers that refer to bread and wine, or different prayers, for bread, and wine (and water).

If there is still time, you might want to think about ways of providing children with time to respond to God in different ways. Provide a variety of materials and give the children time to use these in whatever way they choose, to respond to the story and idea of being called.

FOCUSING

Prayer for the needs of the world may form an important focus for the group during this time. You might wish to make a focal point in the room where you gather using the seasonal colours of white or gold and simple symbols such as a cross and a Bible. A wreath could be used into which white candles are inserted for the weeks of Epiphany. Otherwise you might like to use candles in appropriate holders, one for each week. You should maintain a central candle to remind the group of the light of Christ.

Adults

Epiphany is a good time to reflect on the meaning of baptism and on living as the community of the baptized. Indeed, baptism provides one thread to weave through the weeks of Epiphany. Mission is an important thread, set alongside the inclusive nature of the gospel and the kingdom.

Exploring baptism
- Share experiences of starting again. What helps us to sustain commitments and fresh starts?
- Consider the baptism of Christ. Find a painting of this occasion to help with this. There are many copies available on the Internet. Type 'baptism of Christ' into a search engine and then choose and print off the picture you think will be most helpful to your group.

- Read an account of the baptism of Christ: Matthew 3.13-17 or Mark 1.4-11.
- What might the ideas of dying and rising to new life have to teach us in this season about the cost of discipleship and the cost of the salvation Christ came to bring?
- How easy are new beginnings? Reflect on some of the meanings of T. S. Eliot's poem 'The Journey of the Magi'.[2]
- Organize a prayer walk around your own church, praying at
  - the door: the point of entry for you and for the visitor and stranger;
  - the porch or narthex: pray for the welcome of Christ to fill your church;
  - the font: the point of entry into the Christian life and for all who have been instrumental in bringing you into faith and sustaining you in your faith journey;
  - the nave: the gathering place – pray for your church as community;
  - place for prayer: pray that this might be a house of prayer and praise;
  - pulpit: pray for all who preach and teach; give thanks for the word of God in Scripture and for the gospel story;
  - holy table: pray that your church may be shaped into eucharistic living.

Exploring our faith journey

Reflect on the interplay of baptism, encounter with God, spiritual experience, community of faith, communion, confirmation in our journey of faith to date and the experiences of our lives. Each member of the group could plot his or her life journey and then faith journey either in images or as a time line. They could then reflect on the following:
1. Where have you felt closest to God?
2. What for you has been the pattern of baptism, encounter with God, spiritual experience, community of faith, communion, confirmation?
3. How important has church been for you in marking and in growing through these experiences?

Exploring our calling: vocation and mission

Look at the calling of the disciples in Matthew 4.12-23.

Other Scriptures might include Isaiah 43.1-7, ('I have called you by name, you are mine'), and Psalm 139.

Reflect together on the meaning of being known and called by God, and, if possible, share stories of your experience of being called by God.

Consider the idea of being made in the image of God and the importance of this for vocation.

To think about:
1. How might we as a church call out the image of God in each other?
2. What do the spaces and places look like where it is possible for us to do this work together? What gets in the way of it?
3. Why is living as a community important in helping us to grow into the image of Christ?
4. How might the church as community be a powerful witness in the world?
5. How can we call out the image of God in the lost, the broken, the dispossessed, the poor and the vulnerable? When is it most difficult to see the image of God in others?

Some session ideas linked to other seasonal and lectionary themes

Session 1: Matthew 2.1-12 – The visit of the Magi

PREPARATION

You will need to provide
- pictures from magazines/newspapers to use in the opening part of this session;
- night lights for the worship.

FOR DISCUSSION

Ask each person to identify just one object that would in some way reflect his or her identity, and tell everyone else about this.

Then ask the group members to choose three pictures from those provided to talk about together.

STUDY THE BIBLE

Read Matthew 2.1-12 out loud. Talk together about why you think Matthew included this story in his account of the birth of Jesus.

Reflect on the symbolism of the gifts. 'Magi' means wise person. The three Magi may have been astrologers who studied the planets and stars. The three gifts given to Jesus are important symbols that tell us three things about him. The words of the carol

'We three kings' explain this for us:

gold for kingship;

frankincense for holiness, divinity;

myrrh for suffering.

The story of the visit of the Magi is therefore telling us that Jesus is no ordinary baby! The story reminds us that God's kingdom is open to everyone – the Magi were outsiders who made a risky journey of faith to find Jesus.

1. What can we learn from their story?
2. How easy is it to make a journey of faith when we can't see the destination?
3. How difficult is it to accept the message of the outsider?

The New Year is a time when people reflect on the year that has gone past and look forward to the year about to begin. As Christians, we may wish to remember what God has done in the past year and to pray about our hopes and concerns for the future.

In pairs, discuss:

1. What are your hopes for the coming year?
2. What things concern you about the future?

Choose one hope and one concern to offer in the time of worship.

WORSHIP

- Light a candle and place it in the centre of the circle.
- Keep silence together.

Leader: We light this light in the name of Christ, who came into the world.
Jesus is the light of the world.
We bring into his light our concerns and our hopes for ourselves our families and friends and our world …

Invite the group to light a candle and to offer their concerns to God and to pray aloud if they wish as they light their candle, saying, for example: I pray for the peace of the world and especially for …
Leader: Jesus is the light of the world.
All: The light shines in the darkness and it will not be overcome. Amen.

FOR THE NEXT SESSION

Ask the members of the group to find some pictures or stories in the news that show how people across the world are caught up in conflicts not of their making.

They might also like to find some information about the work of individuals or organizations that try to help in some way (for example Christian Aid, Save the Children, UNICEF).

They might also want to consider conflicts closer to home and difficulties that cause suffering for children. Ask them to bring pictures and stories from the news to the next meeting.

Session 2: Matthew 2.13-23 – The slaughter of the innocents

This chilling story is a reminder of the vulnerability of Jesus and of the brutality of powerful systems when they feel under threat. The focus for this session is the modern-day massacre of the innocents – the children across the world whose lives are disrupted or destroyed in the wars that rage around them.

PREPARATION

Make sure you have available a world map or a large atlas.

Have literature from a charity concerned with British children in need, for example The Children's Society or NSPCC.

FOR DISCUSSION

In your search for news articles and pictures to bring this week, what have you discovered since the last session about the dangers faced by children in many parts of the world?

SOME MORE FACTS

A child risk measure was developed using figures compiled by UNICEF in 1999. According to the information obtained, the 20 worst places to be a child are: Angola, Sierra Leone, Afghanistan, Somalia, Ethiopia, Guinea-Bissau, Niger, DR Congo, Burundi, Eritrea, Liberia, Rwanda, Guinea, Chad, Mali, Mozambique, Central African Republic, Burkino Faso, Cambodia, and Sudan.[3] Find some of these places on a map or in an atlas.

Do not forget that there are many places in our own country where growing up is hard and children are suffering. Share some stories or concerns from the information you have from British children's charities.

STUDY THE BIBLE

Ask a member of the group to read out Matthew 2.13-23. Then address the following questions:
1. What does this story show us about God?
2. What does this story show us about human beings and about societies?
3. Who do you think are the innocents of today?
4. Why do you think it is important that this story is in the Bible?

WORSHIP

Spread a large map of the world out on the floor.

Use night lights in containers and place them on the map as a sign of prayer and hope for all those whose lives are damaged through no fault of their own, especially for children who are caught up in the wars of adults.

You might like to say:

We pray for the children of … and light this candle as a sign of our prayers.

Keep silence for a few moments and then say The Grace together.

Session 3: Matthew 22.1-14 – The kingdom of God and the parable of the wedding feast

PREPARATION

If you plan to use either of the films suggested (see the 'Study the Bible' section) you will need to make sure you have a copy and are sufficiently familiar with it to select appropriate clips to watch and discuss.

Make sure you have a white cloth, glass of wine, a silver tray, plate or tinfoil and a bottle of children's bubbles to be blown.

FOR DISCUSSION

Talk about parties and the invitation issue!

STUDY THE BIBLE

Ask a member of the group to read out Matthew 22.1-14.
1. Who is 'in' and who is 'out' in God's kingdom?
2. What surprises do we find?
3. What might this reveal to us about the gospel and the kingdom that Christ came to bring?
4. Why does Jesus so often use images of feasts, parties and banquets to teach people about the nature of God and the kind of kingdom he was speaking of?
5. Talk about hospitality – share experiences and stories.
6. Watch *Chocolat* or *Babette's Feast* (see Resources)[4] or clips from them and explore the issues of inclusion and exclusion as revealed in these films.
7. How good are we in the church at being communities of welcome, joy and abundance?

WORSHIP AND PRAYER

Place the wreath or candles on a white cloth overlaid with a piece of silver. Place a glass of wine on the table.

Blow bubbles as a way of providing both boundary and space for reflective prayer. Invite individuals in turn to take the bubbles and to pray using words something like:

'I pray for the joy that Christ came to bring to touch the life/lives of (name individual or community or group)' and then to blow the bubbles.

Keep silence for a few moments and then say The Grace together.

Session 4: Matthew 4.12-23 – The call of the disciples

PREPARATION
- You will need a large net. A gardening shop will probably supply netting, either from a roll or in a packet.
- Pieces of coloured ribbon long enough for people to tie into the net.

- What do you normally take with you on a journey?
- If someone arrived on your doorstep and asked you to leave home immediately, would you be able to go without taking anything with you?
- Would you be prepared to leave everything behind in order to follow Christ?

STUDY THE BIBLE

Read aloud Matthew 4.12-23.

Is a call to follow Christ always a welcome thing?

Consider the stories of costly commitment to God's call that run through the Advent, Christmas and Epiphany narratives. Ask all members of the group to imagine that they are one of the people who feature in these accounts: the Virgin Mary, Joseph, Elizabeth, John the Baptist, a shepherd, one of the Magi, and now, also, one of the disciples who feature in this reading. Talk about how it felt to be making the decision to respond to the call of God.

> How does the idea of vocation link to the meaning of our baptism?
>
> What do you think it means to live out our baptismal promises and commitments in daily life?
>
> How important is the church community in this?

WORSHIP AND PRAYER

Place the wreath on a large piece of netting so that the netting extends a long way around the wreath. You will need to find netting with large enough holes to slot pieces of ribbon through. Give members of the group pieces of ribbon and invite them to tie the ribbons on to the netting as a sign of their prayers. Pray aloud for people who may at this time be considering a particular call.

Keep silence for a few moments and then say The Grace together.

The wreath at home

You will need to reconfigure your wreath for the season of Epiphany. You might like to insert stars and ribbons by the candles on the wreath you made for Advent and, depending on the number of Sundays after the Feast of Epiphany, you may need to change the arrangement of the candles and candle holders. However, you might like to redevelop the wreath completely by using candlesticks of different heights and arranging them in an increasing spiral around a globe to reflect the revelation of Christ to the world theme of Epiphany. Floor-standing candle holders would also work well in a similar arrangement. This employs the same principles as reconfiguring the wreath in church. At Candlemas, these candles could be moved to indicate the points of a cross (or make a cross from pieces of wood and place the candles at four points or five points depending on the number of Sundays) and a bowl of incense or frankincense oil on an oil burner could be used alongside.

Stars could be added to the wreath during the time for prayer around the wreath, as symbols of our hopes for the world or you could use bigger ones and write or draw something to be offered as prayer for the world.

Stories can be shared around themes of journey, seeking and finding, for example the story of Baboushka or the Fourth Wise Man. (There are several published versions of each of these stories.) At Candlemas, you might like to share the story of *The Three Trees* before the lighting of the candles. Details of these publications can be found in the Resources section.

You might like to light the candles at dusk on the Sundays of Epiphany and use one of the wreath prayers on pages 149–51. By doing this you will notice that the days are beginning to lengthen. Note the time that you lit the candles each succeeding Sunday. If you notice some spring flowers emerging (possibly snowdrops or viburnum blossom) pick one or two if you can, and put them in a tiny vase beside the wreath.

The wreath in outreach

Themes

Epiphany turns our attention first to the world into which Christ came as light and as Saviour; second, our attention is drawn to questions concerning the nature of Christ and of the kingdom into which he calls us. Candlemas brings these questions into sharp focus as we turn from the crib to the cross and go out into the world bearing the light into the dark corners and difficult places, and knowing that we are called to take up the cross and to model our lives on Christ's self-giving love, for the sake of the world.

This is, then, a natural time to consider issues of mission and vocation. The baptism of Christ reminds us of our identity as children of God and as the community of the baptized. This focus on baptism also provides us with an impetus to reconsider our faith journey and the people, places and experiences that have played important parts in that journey. Within the congregation it is perhaps a good time to reflect on what God's call is today – as individuals and as a community. The call of the disciples reminds us that we are set in communities full of people very unlike ourselves, and for good reason. It reminds us that we are to work out our salvation within community, with all its joys and its irritations, and that we are to seek the image of God in each other – calling it out in one another just as God himself continues to call it out in us.

Things you could do

- Consider holding a Celebration of Baptism for the children who have been baptized in the church in the past year, together with their parents or carers, siblings, godparents and friends. Provide a short service and a celebration afterwards. You can find suggestions for a service of this kind in *Baptism Matters* by Nick and Hazel Whitehead.[5]
- The church community might wish to extend hospitality to couples who have been married in the church in the past year. You could invite them to a service based on the story of the wedding at Cana.
- Hold a 'Hospitality Sunday' when members of the church extend hospitality to others in the congregation that they don't know, or organize a lunch or tea for newcomers.
- Create a prayer space in the church containing materials and images to focus attention on issues in the news: bring specific local, national and international matters before God in prayer. In this space you might want to have a world map on display with some cards that outline prayer needs in different parts of the world or simply display a world map on the wall and provide night lights and a stand or tray in front of this on which the candles can be placed.
- You might want to organize a prayer gathering for particular world issues and concerns according to the news at the time.
- Hold an Epiphany carol service and invite neighbours and friends.
- Since Candlemas marks a turning point in seasonal terms, it might be an appropriate time to hold a day of workshops and learning together and to consider ways of including some of this work in a Candlemas service.

Epiphany:
The crib pathway

Introduction

People would probably expect to dismantle the crib after the Feast of Epiphany. If you follow the suggestions in this crib pathway, however, you will adapt it. You may like to turn the stable into a house for the Feast of the Epiphany, reflecting the account in St Matthew's Gospel that the wise men from the East entered a house and presented their gifts. The suggestion is to keep the house for the whole of Epiphany, though the wise men will leave, and then, on the Feast of Candlemas, create a representation of the Temple, either in a place in the church or, if you still have your crib at home, you replace the house with something to represent the Temple, just for the day. At the end of Candlemas, the crib figures are put away until next year.

Practical inclusive ideas

Liturgy

On the Feast of the Epiphany, or in the week in which you celebrate the arrival of the Magi, the following prayers could be used as a focus for intercession:

Epiphany

THE MAGI

When the Christ-child was born, wise men journeyed from the East following the light of his star. When they found the child, they offered gifts of gold, frankincense and myrrh as they worshipped him. We pray for all who are seeking to follow the light of Christ.

Lord God, as we journey through Christmastide, lead us by the light of your Son, and accept our gifts of hearts and voices raised in praise.
Lord, in your mercy
hear our prayer.

(or)

People of God, will you strive to follow the light of God's Son, bringing gifts of hearts and voices raised in praise to the Christ-child?
With the help of God, we will.

After this you may move the crib to a less significant place, or replace it with Mary, Joseph and the Christ-child in a house. At Candlemas, you may wish to represent the Temple in some way in the place where the crib had been before. To change the stable into the Temple you will need to remove the Magi, the stable building, the manger and the animals. In church you could move the figures of the Holy Family to another place in the building, which will 'become' the Temple for the act of worship, and add Simeon and Anna. Add some symbols that remind people of the Temple, a Hebrew Bible or Old Testament, and some burning incense. Try to choose a place that can be a focal point for the liturgy and which is spacious enough to give an impression of size while still making it possible to see the figures. At home you may like to use bricks or even cardboard boxes to build high walls on either side of the figures, giving an impression of their smallness in the vast building. Add Mary, Joseph and the Christ-child and figures to represent Simeon and Anna, if you can find a way of doing this. Otherwise, use two candles. Use the following prayers.

Candlemas

SIMEON AND ANNA

When the Christ-child was born, Simeon and Anna saw in him the coming of God's promised Messiah – a light to lighten the Gentiles and to be the glory of God's people, Israel. In him is found the salvation of the world.

Lord God, as we journey beyond Christmas and turn towards the cross, help us to walk by the light of your Son and so share in your salvation.
Lord, in your mercy
hear our prayer.

(or)

164

*People of God, will you walk beyond Christmas
taking the light of Christ into your hearts, your homes
and your lives?*
With the help of God, we will.

Other intercessions for use during Epiphany

*We pray for the coming of God's kingdom.
Father, by your Spirit*
bring in your kingdom.

*You sent your Son to bring good news to the poor,
sight to the blind,
freedom to the captives
and salvation to your people:
anoint us with your Spirit;
rouse us to work in his name.
Father, by your Spirit*
bring in your kingdom.

*Send us to bring help to the poor
and freedom to the oppressed.
Father, by your Spirit*
bring in your kingdom.

*Send us to tell the world
the good news of your healing love.
Father, by your Spirit*
bring in your kingdom.

*Send us to those who mourn,
to bring joy and gladness instead of grief.
Father, by your Spirit*
bring in your kingdom.

*Send us to proclaim that the time is here
for you to save your people.
Father, by your Spirit*
bring in your kingdom.

*Father, use us, unworthy as we are,
to bring in your kingdom of mercy, justice, love and
    peace.
Empower us by your Spirit and unite us in your Son,
that all our joy and delight may be to serve you,
now and for ever.*
Amen.

[T&S 126]

*In the power of the Spirit and in union with Christ,
let us pray to the Father.*

All or some of these petitions may be used

*God of our salvation,
hope of all the ends of the earth,
we pray:*
Your kingdom come.

*That the world may know Jesus Christ
as the Prince of Peace,
we pray:*
Your kingdom come.

*That we may be bold to speak the word of God
while you stretch out your hand to save,
we pray:*
Your kingdom come.

*That the Church may welcome and support
all whom God calls to faith,
we pray:*
Your kingdom come.

*That all who suffer for the gospel
may know the comfort and glory of Christ,
we pray:*
Your kingdom come.

*That the day may come when every knee shall bow
and every tongue confess that Jesus Christ is Lord,
we pray:*
Your kingdom come.

*Almighty God,
by your Holy Spirit you have made us one
with your saints in heaven and on earth:
grant that in our earthly pilgrimage
we may ever be supported by this fellowship of love
    and prayer,
and know ourselves surrounded by their witness
to your power and mercy;
through Jesus Christ our Lord.*
Amen.

[T&S 152–3]

The crib and the lectionary

Continue to use the meditation space beside the crib
created in Advent, with the bowl, and the sentences
from the Scripture readings to be written on slips of
paper. Roll these up and place them in the bowl beside
the crib and tie them with gold ribbon for Christmas.
Invite people to take a sentence and use it as an aid for
prayer, thought or meditation during the week. Here
are some suggestions for these Scripture sentences:

The Epiphany

*When they saw that the star had stopped, they were
overwhelmed with joy.*

Matthew 2.10

165

The Baptism of Christ – The First Sunday of Epiphany

This is my Son, the Beloved, with whom I am well pleased.

Mathew 3.17

The Second Sunday of Epiphany

YEAR A

When Jesus turned and saw them following, he said to them, 'What are you looking for?' They said to him, 'Rabbi' (which translated means Teacher), 'where are you staying?' He said to them, 'Come and see.'

John 1.38-39

YEAR B

Nathanael replied, 'Rabbi, you are the Son of God! You are the King of Israel!' Jesus answered, 'Do you believe because I told you that I saw you under the fig tree? You will see greater things than these.' And he said to him, 'Very truly, I tell you, you will see heaven opened and the angels of God ascending and descending upon the Son of man.'

John 1.49-51

YEAR C

When the steward tasted the water that had become wine, and did not know where it came from … the steward called the bridegroom and said to him, 'Everyone serves the good wine first, and then the inferior wine after the guests have become drunk. But you have kept the good wine until now.' Jesus did this, the first of his signs, in Cana of Galilee, and revealed his glory; and his disciples believed in him.

John 2.9-11

The Third Sunday of Epiphany

YEAR A

As he walked by the Sea of Galilee, [Jesus] saw two brothers, Simon, who is called Peter, and Andrew his brother, casting a net into the lake – for they were fishermen. And he said to them, 'Follow me, and I will make you fish for people.' Immediately they left their nets and followed him.

Matthew 4.18-20

YEAR B

When the steward tasted the water that had become wine, and did not know where it came from … the steward called the bridegroom and said to him, 'Everyone serves the good wine first, and then the inferior wine after the guests have become drunk. But you have kept the good wine until now.' Jesus did this, the first of his signs, in Cana of Galilee, and revealed his glory; and his disciples believed in him.

John 2.9-11

YEAR C

*The Spirit of the Lord is upon me,
because he has anointed me
to bring good news to the poor.
He has sent me to proclaim release to the captives
and recovery of sight to the blind,
to let the oppressed go free,
to proclaim the year of the Lord's favour.*

Luke 4.18-19

The Fourth Sunday of Epiphany

YEAR A

When the steward tasted the water that had become wine, and did not know where it came from … the steward called the bridegroom and said to him, 'Everyone serves the good wine first, and then the inferior wine after the guests have become drunk. But you have kept the good wine until now.' Jesus did this, the first of his signs, in Cana of Galilee, and revealed his glory; and his disciples believed in him.

John 2.9-11

YEAR B

They were all amazed, and they kept on asking one another, 'What is this? A new teaching – with authority! He commands even the unclean spirits, and they obey him.' At once his fame began to spread throughout the surrounding region of Galilee.

Mark 1.27-28

YEAR C

The child grew and became strong, filled with wisdom; and the favour of God was upon him.

Luke 2.40

The Presentation of Christ in the Temple

'This child is destined for the falling and the rising of many in Israel, and to be a sign that will be opposed so that the inner thoughts of many will be revealed – and a sword will pierce your own soul too.'

Luke 2.34-35

The crib in groups

Children

If children have spent Advent making their own crib sets, it would be a pity to dismantle them and put them away in less than a couple of weeks. The Christmas season is deemed to last until Candlemas, so it is quite legitimate to leave a homemade crib in place until 2 February. If its constructor takes the opportunity to play with it from time to time during the first month of the year, so much the better. One way of keeping it fresh and relevant would be to look for the first flowers of the new year and pick some to put beside the crib each week as January progresses. You may find Christmas roses, then snowdrops and yellow aconites and some shrubs will produce blossom during this time: there will be winter jasmine, various viburnums and witch hazel, which comes into bloom in January.

If you spent time in Advent making an extensive crib scene, you could also make Simeon and Anna and two turtle doves during the weeks of Epiphany, so that you are ready for Candlemas. You might also spend some time researching what the Temple in Jerusalem might have been like.

There is a Godly Play lesson 'The Ark and the Temple'[6] that teaches about the Temple. Wikipedia, the online encyclopaedia on the Internet, has an extensive article about the history of Jerusalem's temples, including a very clear drawing of the Temple built by Herod, (as it might have been in the time of Jesus). Several good children's Bibles also have information about the Temple in them. This research might fit well with the Old Testament reading for the second Sunday of Epiphany in Year B, which is the story of Samuel's call (1 Samuel 3.1-10).

You might also like to prepare for Candlemas by making lanterns to reflect the words of Simeon in the Temple: 'a light for revelation to the Gentiles and for glory to your people Israel' (Luke 2.32).

 Do-it-yourself Candlemas lanterns

This is an activity for older children who have well developed coordination. It is not suitable for preschool or Key Stage 1 children.

YOU WILL NEED

- A clean, safe food can for each child.
- A thick felt pen for each person.
- A large fat nail with a head for each child.
- A small hammer for each child.
- A night light for each can.

WHAT TO DO

Use clean food cans, safely opened with a good tin opener so that there are no sharp edges. It might be easier for one adult to collect these and check that they are safe and clean, rather than asking children to bring their own. Remove the paper label from each can.

Ask the children to draw a simple design on their can, through which the light will shine. Use the thick felt pen to mark the design on the can. A cross is easiest but there may be people who wish to be more adventurous and that is fine.

When the design has been made, prick it out lightly in dots with the nail. Then use the hammer on the nail to knock small holes through the can following the shape of the design.

When this has been done, put a night light or small candle into the can ready for Candlemas.

At a Candlemas service, replace the crib with the lanterns, with the candles inside them, lit so that the light shines out in various patterns, in the place where the crib had been.

After the service, let the cans cool down and then people can take them home.

The candles will need to be lit with a taper and this might be more safely undertaken by an adult than a child.

Adults

In the *Common Worship* Lectionary, the four Sundays of the Epiphany focus on the beginning of Jesus' ministry. The first Sunday of the Epiphany always commemorates the baptism of Jesus and one or two of the other Sundays focus on the call of the disciples. The wedding at Cana also features, and there is a healing story. Over the three different years the pattern varies slightly, according to the focus of the particular Gospel.

These are all vivid stories featuring a number of characters and it would be very worthwhile for each to be the subject of a Bible study in the days before it is read in the church. Following the way in which you may have used the crib, you could use figures and a few other items on a table or other focus area to help people imagine the scene as it unfolds. Use a white or gold cloth as a reminder of the season and some items to indicate the story – for example a bowl of water for the baptism of Christ, a glass of water and a glass of wine for the Cana story and so on. Read the story aloud together and then, to break it open together, you could simply use the questions developed by Jerome Berryman for the sacred stories told in Godly Play.[7]

> I wonder what you liked best about this story?
>
> I wonder what was most important about the story?
>
> I wonder where you are in the story?
>
> I wonder if there is any part of the story we can take away and still have all the story we need?

After you have explored the story as far as you can, you might use some of the following biddings on the theme of mission as a focus for prayer and then say together the collect for the approaching Sunday, followed by the Lord's Prayer and the Grace:

In the power of the Spirit and in union with Christ, let us pray to the Father.

All or some of these petitions may be used

God of our salvation,
hope of all the ends of the earth,
we pray:
Your kingdom come.

That the world may know Jesus Christ
as the Prince of Peace,
we pray:
Your kingdom come.

That all who are estranged and without hope
may be brought near in the blood of Christ,
we pray:
Your kingdom come.

That the Church may be one in serving
and proclaiming the gospel,
we pray:
Your kingdom come.

That we may be bold to speak the word of God
while you stretch out your hand to save,
we pray:
Your kingdom come.

That the Church may be generous in giving,
faithful in serving, bold in proclaiming,
we pray:
Your kingdom come.

That the Church may welcome and support
all whom God calls to faith,
we pray:
Your kingdom come.

That all who serve the gospel may be kept in safety
while your word accomplishes its purpose,
we pray:
Your kingdom come.

That all who suffer for the gospel
may know the comfort and glory of Christ,
we pray:
Your kingdom come.

That the day may come when every knee shall bow
and every tongue confess that Jesus Christ is Lord,
we pray:
Your kingdom come.

Almighty God,
by your Holy Spirit you have made us one
with your saints in heaven and on earth:
grant that in our earthly pilgrimage
we may ever be supported by this fellowship of love
*   and prayer,*
and know ourselves surrounded by their witness
to your power and mercy;
through Jesus Christ our Lord.
Amen.

[T&S 152–3]

The fourth wise man

Another possibility during these extended weeks of Epiphany is to explore the story of the so-called fourth wise man.

Henry van Dyke popularized a legend when he wrote his very beautiful and evocative story of the fourth wise man. You can still find the original van Dyke story in various publications but it has also been widely rewritten with a number of similar titles in a variety of picture books (see the Resources list). It has also been turned into drama and musical and you can find examples of these on the Internet. Working to perform one of these, say, at Candlemas or on the first Sunday of Lent might be a good activity for a group who would like a change from sedentary activities.

St Matthew's Gospel tells us that wise men came from the East, bringing gifts of gold, frankincense and myrrh. The Gospel provides no further details of the individuals themselves, other than that they followed a star and went to the wrong place first of all! All other details – that there were three, they were men, that they had names, where they came from (other than the East) – are simply surmise, legend, tradition, call it what you will.

Van Dyke's story tells us of another man. He is named Artaban and lives in Persia. He planned to join the other three and his gifts were to be a glittering sapphire, a magnificent ruby and a pearl of great price.

On his way to the place where he was to meet the other Magi and begin the journey, Artaban encountered a sick traveller, whom he stayed to help, thereby missing his rendezvous with the other wise men. Faced with making the journey alone, he sold the sapphire to buy the camels he needed to cross the desert but he was sad that the newborn king would not receive this gem. Artaban finally reached Bethlehem to discover soldiers everywhere following Herod's command to slay all baby boys.

Artaban used the ruby to bribe the captain and save some of the children but, of course, now it would not be presented to the newborn king.

But Artaban continued his search until, 33 years later, he found his way into Jerusalem on the very day that crucifixions were to take place outside the city. Somehow he knew that the king he had been searching for all his life was among those to be crucified so he hastened to Calvary intending to use his pearl to bribe Jesus' executioners. But, on the way, he encountered a young woman who was being dragged to the slave market and gave his last jewel – the pearl of great price – for her ransom.

Finally, he reached the place where the crucifixions were to take place, and quickly realized there was nothing he could do to help his King of kings. He was broken-hearted. It was then that the dying Jesus looked down from the cross and explained that Artaban had, after all, given him the three gifts for 'I was hungry and you gave me food … I was stranger and you welcomed me … I was sick you took care of me.' And so the story ends, with a quotation from Matthew 25.

USING THE STORY IN A GROUP

Find a copy of van Dyke's original story, or one of the more recent rewritings, and divide it into sections focusing on the three different jewels. If you have four weeks, you could use the first week to set the scene and research information about the world from which Artaban is said to have come: a Zoroastrian community in the ancient Persian empire. It is worthwhile remembering that this was one of the empires that overwhelmed ancient Israel and took the people into exile. There is a good deal written about the Persian empire in the Old Testament book of Daniel and this would provide a good opportunity to explore some biblical background and gain an insight into the multifaith, cosmopolitan, world into which Christ was born.

In each of the other weeks, prepare a focus table with a crib, some food for the journey (dates, figs, flat bread, water, wine, etc.) and, each week, a representation of the jewel that is to be the focus of the story.

The crib at home

Matthew's Gospel refers to the place where the wise men find Jesus as a 'house'. A different building is needed from the stable – something more substantial, with the ox, ass and manger removed. If you have a large doll's house, that would be ideal, provided the owner didn't object to having the lodgers. The days approaching Epiphany might be used to provide some proper furniture and a cot rather than the manger for Jesus, as Mary and Joseph set up home. The star has to remain in place until the wise men appear on 6 January. The wise men will have spent the twelve days of Christmas travelling to the place where the holy family now find themselves. They need to arrive on 6 January. If you are past the time when your home contains a doll's house, you might simply move the holy family to another place.

Traditions about what happens after Epiphany vary. Some people take all decorations down. Some leave one item until Candlemas, observing 40 days from the birth of Jesus. Following the Christmas story could be helpful. The wise men stayed a night, and were warned in a dream to return by another way. The holy family began their flight into Egypt. If the decorations, the Christmas cards and the crib are all removed, keep a picture of the flight into Egypt on display. You may have been sent a suitable card. You may wish to convert the place that was the stable and then became a house into a representation of journey with the wise men going one way (to the east) and the holy family another (west to Egypt). You could represent the journey with sand or stones or plants.

At Candlemas you will finally mark the end of the Christmas period. You may wish to have one final ceremony and replace the figures of the Christ-child, Mary and Joseph with three candles that burn for the evening. Perhaps before you go to bed tonight, you could say the Nunc Dimittis, the words of Simeon in the Temple. They are ideal words for an evening prayer any night. Perhaps this could be the first night of many.

The crib in outreach

If children spend time making models during Advent and through Epiphany, make sure you keep a good photographic record, with a digital camera. If people knitted nativity figures during Advent also, keep a photographic record of these too. If you are able to add pictures of a crib festival, that would be good. In the period after Christmas, gather together your photographs and write an article about what has been done.

If you manage to achieve this shortly after Christmas, send some photographs to the local paper with the article.

Make the pictures and the article into a little leaflet about what you did. Keep it until the late summer then contact local schools and preschools and offer to run a crib festival with them in the run-up to next Christmas. Send the leaflet to them by post but follow this up with a phone call and an offer for someone to work with RE coordinators to fit this into a scheme of work around Christmas time.

Epiphany:
The Jesse tree pathway

Practical inclusive ideas

Using the Jesse tree with the Main Service Lectionary

Years A and C

EPIPHANY

Carry the gifts of the Magi through the congregation to add them to the tree.

Remember the symbolism of the gifts: gold for a king, incense for God, myrrh foreshadowing the death on the cross.

A gold crown could be added to the top of the tree.

The incense can be burnt on charcoal in an incense burner beside the tree.

The myrrh could be ground and added to some oil (or you can buy myrrh as liquid already) in which you soak a cloth to hang behind the child, overshadowing and foreshadowing the sorrow to come. (If you use oil, be careful that it does not drip on anything that will be spoilt by it.)

You may leave the tree in place now for the rest of the Epiphany season and dismantle it at Candlemas, the Feast of the Presentation in the Temple. If you leave the tree in place until Candlemas, the following symbols might be added to the tree to reflect the subject of the Gospel readings. At the same time, you might start to remove the prophets so that the tree changes to have a more New Testament appearance.

Year A

- **The Baptism of Christ – *The First Sunday of Epiphany*.** Add a dove, a reminder of the baptism of Jesus.
- **The Second Sunday of Epiphany.** Add a lamb, reflecting John's declaration about Jesus.
- **The Third Sunday of Epiphany.** Add fishing nets as reminders of Peter and Andrew, James and John.
- **The Fourth Sunday of Epiphany.** Add jars or bottles, reminders of Jesus turning water into wine at the wedding in Cana.

Year C

- **The Baptism of Christ – *The First Sunday of Epiphany*.** Add a dove, a reminder of the baptism of Jesus.
- **The Second Sunday of Epiphany.** Add jars or bottles, reminders of Jesus turning water into wine at the wedding in Cana.
- **The Third Sunday of Epiphany.** Add a scroll, reminding us of Jesus reading in the synagogue.
- **The Fourth Sunday of Epiphany.** Add a pair of doves in a cage, a reminder of the presentation in the Temple.

The Jesse tree in groups

Children

If you would like to continue building your graffiti board throughout the Epiphany season, you could use it to respond to each of the Gospel stories set in the Lectionary for these weeks. Choose the main statements from the Gospel reading each week and have them written out to add to the board: perhaps the words could be written into speech bubbles.

The texts – Year A

THE BAPTISM OF CHRIST – THE FIRST SUNDAY OF EPIPHANY

This is my Son, the Beloved, with whom I am well pleased.

Matthew 3.17

THE SECOND SUNDAY OF EPIPHANY

Here is the Lamb of God who takes away the sins of the world!
What are you looking for?

John 1.29,38

THE THIRD SUNDAY OF EPIPHANY

Repent, for the kingdom of heaven has come near. Follow me, and I will make you fish for people.

Matthew 4.17,19

THE FOURTH SUNDAY OF EPIPHANY

Woman, what concern is that to you and to me? My hour has not yet come.
Fill the jars with water.

John 2.4,7

The texts – Year C

THE BAPTISM OF CHRIST – *THE FIRST SUNDAY OF EPIPHANY*

I baptize you with water; but one who is more powerful than I is coming; I am not worthy to untie the thong of his sandals. He will baptize you with Holy Spirit and fire.
You are my Son, the Beloved; with you I am well pleased.

Luke 3.16,22

THE SECOND SUNDAY OF EPIPHANY

Woman, what concern is that to you and to me? My hour has not yet come.
Fill the jars with water.

John 2.4,7

THE THIRD SUNDAY OF EPIPHANY

The Spirit of the Lord is upon me, because he has anointed me to bring good news to the poor.
He has sent me to proclaim release to the captives, and recovery of sight to the blind, to let the oppressed go free, to proclaim the year of the Lord's favour.
Today, this scripture has been fulfilled in your hearing.

Luke 4.18-19,21

THE FOURTH SUNDAY OF EPIPHANY

Master, now you are dismissing your servant in peace, according to your word; for my eyes have seen your salvation, which you have prepared in the presence of all peoples, a light for revelation to the Gentiles and for glory to your people Israel.

Luke 2.29-32

These Gospel readings for the weeks of Epiphany each reflect an aspect of Jesus' early ministry: his baptism, acclaim by John the Baptist, the turning of water into wine at the wedding at Cana, the call of the first disciples. A not altogether well-fitting addition in Year C is the story of the Presentation in the Temple, with Simeon's words we now know as the Nunc Dimittis. This reading is prescribed for a

Sunday once in the three-year cycle to ensure that it is regularly heard.

What to do
Hear the Gospel story each week. It can be read from the Bible or you could tell it from a children's Bible or in your own words. Sit around your graffiti board while the story is told and have the words from the story on which you are going to focus displayed also.

After the telling of the story, decide together what you might add to the graffiti board to reflect the story and how and where you will add the words that are in your speech bubbles.

This will involve a fair amount of discussion: remember that the discussion is just as important as the additions to the board that might emerge from it. The process is important; the product is just that, a product. Devote the remaining time to creating any illustrations you have decided to add to the board.

Adults

Having used the period of Advent to explore details about the prophets, you could use this time to discover something about the characters who feature in the early ministry of Jesus as described in the Gospel readings for these weeks of Epiphany. John the Baptist features on several occasions in both Year A and Year C. There are also Peter and Andrew, and James and John. At Cana in Galilee is Mary, Jesus' mother, and, on the fourth Sunday of Epiphany in Year C, are Simeon and Anna.

Again you might borrow books from your minister. The Internet will also be a valuable source and will enable you to follow a wide variety of links. For example, Wikipedia, the free online and constantly edited encyclopaedia, enables you to read about the ways in which Orthodox Christians, as well as the western traditions, celebrate John the Baptist. It also has information on the significance of John the Baptist for Muslims, for whom he is also a prophet. Following the link to Wikimedia Commons provides access to the work of very many artists who painted scenes of the Baptist's life, any of which could be printed, or studied on screen.

There are those who will warn, wisely, that information on the Internet is in no way censored and so you may find material that is challenging, strange, and even absolute rubbish. This is indeed the case.

One of the values of studying together information obtained from the Internet is to decide together, pooling the knowledge and abilities of all members of the group, whether or not the information is useful and valid and how it might be used.

Open your group's time together with one of the Epiphany Kyrie confessions from *Times and Seasons,* as you did in Advent, and close with one of the Intercessions (*Times and Seasons* pages 113–14 and 116–00).

The Jesse tree at home

It is customary to take down the Christmas decorations on twelfth night, but leave just something until Candlemas, the Presentation of Christ in the Temple on 2 February. Perhaps the Jesse tree might be the thing you maintain throughout these weeks of Epiphany.

Perhaps you could add symbols to represent the Gospel readings for the weeks of Epiphany, while removing the prophets a few at a time, so that the tree is gradually transformed.

Symbols for the Gospel readings

Year A

- **The Baptism of Christ – *The First Sunday of Epiphany*.** Add a dove, a reminder of the baptism of Jesus.
- **The Second Sunday of Epiphany.** Add a lamb, reflecting John's declaration about Jesus.
- **The Third Sunday of Epiphany.** Add fishing nets as reminders of Peter and Andrew, James and John.
- **The Fourth Sunday of Epiphany.** Add jars or bottles, reminders of Jesus turning water into wine at the wedding in Cana.

Year C

- **The Baptism of Christ – *The First Sunday of Epiphany*.** Add a dove, a reminder of the baptism of Jesus.
- **The Second Sunday of Epiphany.** Add jars or bottles, reminders of Jesus turning water into wine at the wedding in Cana.
- **The Third Sunday of Epiphany.** Add a scroll, reminding us of Jesus reading in the synagogue.
- **The Fourth Sunday of Epiphany.** Add a pair of doves in a cage, a reminder of the presentation in the Temple.

The Jesse tree in outreach – Epiphany

Photograph the pictures from your Jesse tree calendar with a digital camera, (or reproduce the images in some other way) and, using a colour printer, turn them into cards, notelets, bookmarks and other similar small printed items that members of the church can use throughout the year. Make sure you note below the pictures their source and what they represent. For example: 'The message of Ezekiel' made by Joe and Jennifer Bloggs, from the Jesse tree created in Littletown Library by the people of St Mark's Church, Littletown.

Notes

How to use this book

1. *New Patterns for Worship*, Church House Publishing, 2002.
2. *Sunday by Sunday* is published quarterly by RSCM for its members. For more details, see www.rscm.com; email: musicdirect@rscm.com.
3. Alan Luff, Alan Dunstan, Paul Ferguson, Christopher Idle and Charles Stewart, *Sing God's Glory: Hymns for Sundays and Holy Days, Years A, B and C*, Canterbury Press, 2001.
4. *Common Worship: Additional Collects*, Church House Publishing, 2004.

Living liturgy

1. For more information on when the lectionary readings are mandatory see *New Patterns For Worship*, Church House Publishing, 2004, p. 104.
2. *New Patterns for Worship*, Church House Publishing, 2002.
3. Quoted on p. 75 in *The Celtic Vision*, Esther de Waal (ed.), Darton, Longman & Todd, 1992.

Another way of knowing

1. 'Ritual as Strategic Practice' in Pete Ward (ed.), *The Rite Stuff: Ritual in Contemporary Christian Worship and Mission*, Bible Reading Fellowship, 2004.
2. Anne Dawtry and Christopher Irvine, *Art and Worship*, SPCK, 2002.
3. *Art and Worship*, 2002.
4. Gertrud Mueller Nelson, *To Dance with God*, Paulist Press, 1986.
5. Jerome W. Berryman, *The Complete Guide to Godly Play, Volume 1: How to Lead Godly Play Lessons*, Living the Good News, 2002.
6. Peter Craig-Wild, *Tools for Transformation: Making Worship Work*, Darton, Longman & Todd, 2002, p. 80.
7. *Tools for Transformation*, p. 35.
8. *Tools for Transformation*, p. 88.
9. in Diane Apostolis-Cappadona, *The Sacred Play of Children*, The Seabury Press, 1983.
10. in *The Sacred Play of Children*, p. 59.

Advent, Christmas and Epiphany: mapping the journey

1. *The Promise of His Glory: Services and Prayers for the Season from All Saints to Candlemas*, Church House Publishing, 1991.
2. T. S. Eliot, 'The Journey of the Magi', first published 1927.

Advent

1. The full text of the Christingle Service of the Church in Wales has been published as a card by Church in Wales Publications, 39 Cathedral Road, Cardiff CF11 9XF.
2. Sandy Eisenberg Sasso, *In God's Name*, Jewish Lights Publishing, 1994.
3. Jerome W. Berryman, *The Complete Guide to Godly Play, Volume 3: 20 Presentations for Winter*, Living the Good News, 2002.
4. *Good News Bible: Today's English Version*, The Bible Societies/Collins/Fontana, 1976.

Christmas

1. The script writer was Nick Warburton. See www.davidhigham.co.uk/html/Clients/Nick_Warburton.
2. 'Gaudete, Christus natus est' in Jeremy Summerly (ed.), *Gaudete: Medieval Carols for Upper Voices*, Faber Music, 1998.
3. Published by Chester Music, 1979.

Epiphany

1. Selina Hastings, *The Children's Illustrated Bible*, Dorling Kindersley, 1994.
2. This poem is found extensively in collections of poetry. You will find it in Mary Batchelor, *The Christian Poetry Collection*, Lion, 1995, p. 292.
3. The *Guardian*, 4 May 2002: www.guardian.co.uk/savethechildren/story/0,11965,707165,00.html.
4. *Chocolat*, Buena Vista, 2000; *Babette's Feast*, World Films, 1988.
5. Nick and Hazel Whitehead, *Baptism Matters*, National Society/Church House Publishing, 1998.
6. Lesson 8 in Jerome W. Berryman, *The Complete Guide to Godly Play, Volume 2: 14 Presentations for Fall*, Living the Good News, 2002.
7. See *The Complete Guide to Godly Play, Volume 2*, 2002. For more about Godly Play see www.godlyplay.org and www.godlyplay.org.uk.

Resources

Liturgical resources

Common Worship: Services and Prayers for the Church of England, Church House Publishing, 2000

Common Worship: Times and Seasons, Church House Publishing, 2006

Common Worship: Additional Collects, Church House Publishing, 2004

New Patterns for Worship, Church House Publishing, 2002

Children's Bibles

Where the text suggests reading the story from a children's Bible, you might like to use *The Children's Illustrated Bible,* Stories retold by Selina Hastings, Dorling Kindersley, 1994

General resources

Diane Apostolis-Cappadona, *The Sacred Play of Children,* The Seabury Press, 1983

Jerome W. Berryman, *The Complete Guide to Godly Play* (5 volumes), Living the Good News, 2002

Peter Craig-Wild, *Tools for Transformation: Making worship work,* Darton, Longman & Todd, 2002

Anne Dawtry and Christopher Irvine, *Art and Worship,* SPCK, 2002

Gertrud Mueller Nelson, *To Dance with God,* Paulist Press, 1986

Sandy Eisenburg Sasso, *In God's Name,* Jewish Lights Publishing, 1994

Ester de Waal (ed.), *The Celtic Vision,* Darton, Longman & Todd, 1992

Pete Ward (ed.), *The Rite Stuff: Ritual in contemporary Christian worship and mission,* BRF, 2004

Nick and Hazel Whitehead, *Baptism Matters,* National Society/Church House Publishing, 1998

Complete Poems and Plays of T. S. Eliot, Faber & Faber, 2004. Contains 'The Journey of the Magi'

The Christ We Share: See Jesus through the eyes of Christian artists from Africa, Asia and Latin America (includes free CD-ROM.) CMS, USPG and The Methodist Church

Born Among Us: An all-age Christmas resource inspired by the world Church, USPG and The Methodist Church

Posada, www.churcharmy.co.uk

A Christingle Pack, The Church in Wales, 2006

Small group resources

Hilary Brand, *Christ and the Chocolaterie,* Darton, Longman & Todd, 2002

Hilary Brand, *The Power of Small Choices,* Darton, Longman & Todd, 2004

Jesse tree books

Raymond Anderson and Georgene Anderson, *Jesse Tree,* Fortress, 1966

Marilyn S. Breckenridge, *Jesse Tree Devotions,* Augsburg Fortress

Geraldine McCaughrean, *The Jesse Tree,* Lion, 2003

Dean Meader Lambert, *The Advent Jesse Tree: Devotions for children and adults to prepare for the coming of the christchild at Christmas,* Abingdon Press,1988

Anne E. Neuberger, *Advent Stories and Activities: Meeting Jesus through the Jesse tree,* Twenty-Third Publications Inc.

Marion Richards, *A Shoot from the Stem of Jesse,* Church in Wales Publications

Christmas stories

Jean de Brebeuf, *The Huron Carol,* Eerdman Books for Young Readers, 2003

Angela Elwell Hunt, *The Singing Shepherd,* Lion, 1994

Angela Elwell Hunt, *The Three Trees,* Lion Hudson, 2002

Jostein Gaarder, *The Christmas Mystery,* Orion, 2003

Bob Hartman, *A Night the Stars Danced for Joy,* Lion, 1998

Heather Hemmings and Alison Atkins, *God Sent a Baby King,* Barnabas, 2005

Mary Hoffman, *Three Wise Women,* Frances Lincoln Ltd, 2002

Mig Holder, *Papa Panov's Special Day,* Lion Hudson, 2003

Vickie Howie, *Knock, Knock! Who's there?,*

Barnabas, 2005

Stephanie Jeffs, *The Story of Christmas*, Barnabas, 2005

Elizabeth Laird, *The Road to Bethlehem*, Collins, 1987

Alan MacDonald, *The Not-So-Wise Man*, Lion, 2001

Jan Pienkowski, *Christmas*, Puffin, 1987

Jane Ray, *The Story of Christmas*, Orchard Books, 1994

Arthur Scholey, *Baboushka*, Lion Hudson, 2002

Sparkling Stories, Scripture Union, 2005

Susan Summers, *The Fourth Wise Man*, Dial Books, 1998

Julie Vivas, *The Nativity*, Gulliver Books, 2005

The story of the Fourth Wise Man

Marilyn D. Anderson, et al., *The Fourth Wise Man*, Dramatic Pub., 1998

Wadecha Atiyeh, *The Fourth Wise Man*, Robert Speller & Sons, paperback, 1985

Elizabeth Hale, *The Fourth Wise Man (Plays Over Ten Minutes Long)*, Christian Education Publications (CEP), September 1988

Mig Holder, *The Legend of the Fourth Wise Man*, Candle Books, 1993

Ronald H. Lloyd, Victor Ambrus (Illustrator), *The Legend of the Fourth Wise Man*, Continuum International Publishing Rag Book, 1984

Carol Marshall, *Artoban: The Fourth Wise Man*, New Playwright's Network, 1988

Ted Sieger (Illustrator), *The Fourth King: The story of the other wise man*, Candlewick Press (MA), 2006

Susan Summers, *The Fourth Wise Man*, Dial Books, 1998

Henry Van Dyke, *Story of the Fourth Wise Man, The*, Bridge Logos Publishers, 2000

Music resources

Sing God's Glory: Hymns for Sundays and Holy Days, Canterbury Press, 2001

Songs and Prayers from Taizé, Continuum, 2002

The International Book of Christmas Carols, Stephen Greene Press, 1985

The 'Nunc Dimittis' which is mentioned in the All-around-the-village nativity play, is found in Geoffrey Burgon, *Magnificat and Nunc Dimittis*, Chester Music Ltd, 1979

'Gaudete Christus est natus', which is mentioned in the All-around-the-village nativity play, is found in *Gaudete, Medieval Songs and Carols for Upper Voices* edited by Jeremy Summerly, Faber Music, 1998

'Christ be our Light' is by Bernadette Farrell and can be found in *Christ be our Light: Songbook*, copyright © 1993, OCP publications, available through Calamus

Films

Chocolat, Buena Vista 2000

Babette's Feast, World Films 1988

Web sites

www.domestic-church.com
An excellent source of many religious symbols and ideas for their use in activities at home
http://biblia.com/mary
Source of pictures of St Mary the Virgin
www.godlyplay.org and www.godlyplay.org.uk
Further information on Godly Play

Using the CD-ROM

Running the CD-ROM

Windows PC users:

The CD-ROM should start automatically. If you need to start the application manually, click on Start and select Run, then type d:\tfas.exe (where d is the letter of your CD-ROM drive) and click on OK.

The menu that appears gives you access to all the resources on the CD. No software is installed on to your computer.

Mac users:

The CD-ROM should start automatically. If you need to start the application manually, click on the CD icon on your desktop.

Viruses

We have checked the CD-ROM for viruses throughout its creation. However, you are advised to run your own virus-checking software over the CD-ROM before using it. Church House Publishing and The Archbishops' Council accepts no responsibility for damage or loss of data on your systems, however caused.

Copyright

The material on the CD-ROM is copyright © The Archbishops' Council 2006, unless otherwise specified. All industry trademarks are acknowledged. You are free to use this material within your own church or group, but the material must not be further distributed in any form without written permission from Church House Publishing. When using images or resources from the CD-ROM please include the appropriate copyright notice.

Outline services

The written resources require Adobe Acrobat Reader for display and printing. If Acrobat Reader is already installed on your computer, it will be loaded automatically whenever required. If you do not have it, you can install Acrobat Reader by downloading the Reader from www.adobe.com.

Graphics

The cartoons and images can be loaded into your own image editing software for resizing and printing. The files are within a folder called images on the CD. The CD includes both high and low resolution images; the low resolution images will be more suitable for older computer systems.

The hi-res images are in the TIFF format and are suitable for printing, projection and OHP acetates. The low-res images are in the JPEG format and are more suitable for web pages and other applications where high quality definition is not essential.

You can edit the JPEG and TIFF files with most image software. Remember that the image on the CD is 'read only'. If you want to edit the image, you should first copy it to your computer and remove its read-only attribute.

On the CD are two image browsers called IrfanView (for PC users) and Goldberg (for Mac users). These are free for non-commercial use and can be used to view the images and perform basic editing tasks such as resizing. IrfanView runs under most versions of windows (www.irfanview.com). The version of Goldberg supplied is compatible with Mac OSX 10.2 or later. Please note that Church House Publishing accepts no responsibility for the use of third-party software nor can we provide support for its use.

Error messages

You may receive the error message, 'There is no application associated with the given file name extension.' If you are trying to read one of the handouts, you should install the Adobe Acrobat Reader and try again. If you are opening one of the image files, your system does not have any software registered for use with JPEG or TIFF files. PC users should install the free copy of IrfanView and during its installation make sure you associate .TIF and .JPG extensions with IrfanView. For Mac users, the files should open in Preview and for editing functions install Goldberg.

If you do not have PowerPoint, install the free viewer from the same folder.

Links

The links to web sites require an active Internet connection. Please ensure you can browse the web before selecting an external web site.

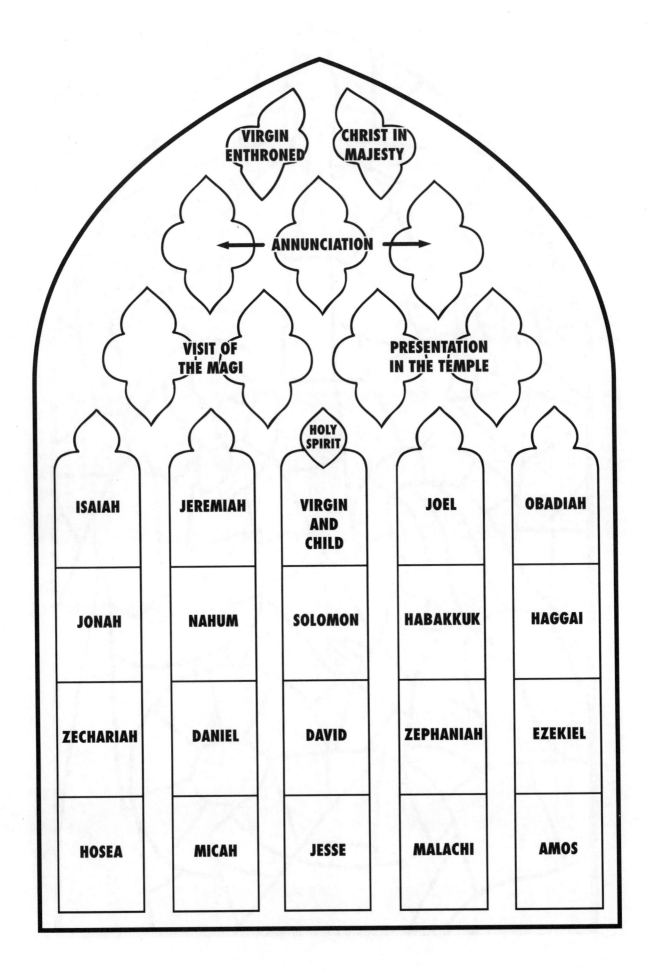